D1299496

# C'EST LA FOLIE

www.booksattransworld.co.uk

# Michael Wright

# C'est La Folie

One man's quest for a more meaningful life

## BANTAM PRESS

LONDON · TORONTO · SYDNEY · AUCKLAND · JOHANNESBURG

TRANSWORLD PUBLISHERS
61–63 Uxbridge Road, London W5 5SA
a division of The Random House Group Ltd

RANDOM HOUSE AUSTRALIA (PTY) LTD
20 Alfred Street, Milsons Point, Sydney,
New South Wales 2061, Australia

RANDOM HOUSE NEW ZEALAND LTD
18 Poland Road, Glenfield, Auckland 10, New Zealand

RANDOM HOUSE SOUTH AFRICA (PTY) LTD
Isle of Houghton, Corner of Boundary Road & Carse O'Gowrie,
Houghton 2198, South Africa

RANDOM HOUSE PUBLISHERS INDIA PRIVATE LIMITED
301 World Trade Tower, Hotel Intercontinental Grand Complex,
Barakhamba Lane, New Delhi 110 001, India

Published 2006 by Bantam Press
a division of Transworld Publishers

Typeset in 11/14pt Sabon by
Falcon Oast Graphic Art Ltd

Printed in Great Britain by Mackays of Chatham plc, Chatham, Kent

3 5 7 9 10 8 6 4 2

Papers used by Transworld Publishers are natural, recyclable products made from wood
grown in sustainable forests. The manufacturing processes conform to the environmental
regulations of the country of origin.

For my parents, Anne and Peter,
who made it all possible

# AUTHOR'S NOTE

Jolibois is the name I have given to the nearest town to La Folie. Though you will not see it on any map, it is not hard to find. And perhaps you will not feel the urge to try. For there are many other little towns, and many other incarnations of Jolibois, waiting to be explored and appreciated, all over France.

# ACKNOWLEDGEMENTS

My deepest thanks are to my school friend and ex-drummer, Jon Stock, for commissioning the *Daily Telegraph* column that was the chicken to the egg of this book, shortly after I moved to La Folie. Or perhaps the column was the egg, and this book is the chicken. Either way, Jon's support has been athletic, and I have lost track of the number of times when his editorial judgements have saved me from myself, and readers from my gothic excesses.

Thanks, too, to those who freely gave their energies and insights to help me to write this book:

Zoë Carnegie, for her sweetness and inspiration

The very special Marisa, and my brother Steven, who both read the manuscript at an early stage and suggested valuable improvements

Guy and Monique, Claire Hajaj, Nick Wright, Fariyal Khatri, Marie-Sylvie Teixier, Jean-François Augrit, Grégory Cheyrou, Guy Dupuigrenet-Desroussilles and all the Benkerts, for encouragement along the way

Patrick Janson-Smith, for championing the book at the start

Simon Taylor, my editor at Transworld, for unremitting enthusiasm and patience beyond the call of duty

Mark Lucas, my agent, for sagacity beyond his years

The many warm-hearted *Telegraph* readers who have taken the trouble to write to me, cheering me on

The cat, for her presence

The mice, for their absence (see above)

And to Alice, for everything else.

*Quand on veut un mouton, c'est la preuve qu'on existe*
When one wants a sheep, it is the proof that one exists

*Le Petit Prince*, Antoine de Saint-Exupéry
© Editions Gallimard

# I

## PRELUDE

I am three years old, and I want to be Queen Victoria's train-driver.

No matter that I have missed the bus by a hundred years. I can daydream for hours about the Royal Queen, gazing at pictures of her carriage in the royal train.

*My* train.

I have regular temper-tantrums, too. Oh, what fun it is, to lie on the floor, screaming and foaming at the mouth. Some people have no respect for the railway timetable.

'He'll be in the loony-bin before he's twenty-one, you mark my words,' predicts Great-Aunt Beryl.

'Oh, don't be ridiculous,' says my mother. Next day, she and my father take their barking three-year-old up to London, to see a child-psychiatrist.

The shrink gives me some coloured blocks, so he can watch me play.

Only I don't want to play with the blocks. I want to tell him about the Royal Queen, and my job as her train-driver. Mum and Dad must be thrilled about this. After all, I could have told him I was Jesus, or Napoleon.

Whereas instead I have plumped for a nineteenth-century railway-worker on a special contract.

Fortunately, the shrink is a switched-on fellow, and an idea occurs to him.

'This child is bored,' he declares, twiddling his chubby thumbs. 'What he wants is books.'

And so I am given all the books I want, even though the only ones I really like are the ones about the Royal Queen. And after a while I decide that I don't want to be the royal train-driver after all.

I want to be a Spitfire pilot in the Battle of Britain.

The advantage of 1940 over 1870 is that I am now only about thirty years too late. I haven't yet twigged that I would need perfect eyesight to be a Spitfire pilot. I'm far too interested in having a pair of tortoiseshell NHS specs like my friend Hancock. So I read nightly under my blanket and stare at my bedside lamp until my retinas ache, in an attempt to strain my eyes. After a while, all I can see on the page is a green-red glow the shape of a lightbulb filament.

Books are good, because they allow me to drive trains and meet the Royal Queen and fly Spitfires in my head. And they provide an excuse for creeping downstairs to the kitchen, where my parents are eating their supper.

'Daddy, what does *naïve* mean?' I ask, peeking round the door of the kitchen to take in the warm smell of garlic and the candle-glow that envelops them.

Some nights they allow me to join them for a few minutes, with a crust of French bread and some watered-down red wine.

'Wine-and-water is what French children drink,' says my mother, topping up my glass with water from the tap, as if it were Ribena. Mum loves France. Her favourite cookbooks are by Elizabeth David, which I think is a funny name, because you don't know if it's a boy or a girl.

For herself and Dad, Mum cooks recipes from *French Provincial Cookery* which look brown and forbidding, but whose rich smells come from another world to the Bird's Eye fish fingers and frozen peas that my brothers and I have for our tea, after *Blue Peter* and *Captain Pugwash*.

My father's culinary gift lies in his appreciation. He venerates my mother's cooking as if she were the Galloping Gourmet, and he always says her latest creation is really first-class.

I like the Galloping Gourmet, but not as much as I like Douglas Bader or Stanford Tuck. I like Achilles and Hector, too, and Don Quixote, Biggles, Mary Plain, Peter Rabbit and all sorts of other animals that can talk. And the more I read, the more clear I become about what I really want to be.

I want to be a hero.

But I don't tell anyone about it this time.

Wanting to be a hero feels like a guilty secret, when you're short and plump and not much good at anything except reading and screaming. So I keep it to myself, and count the days to my twenty-first birthday, hoping that Great-Aunt Beryl made a mistake.

But I'll admit it now: I've wanted to be a hero ever since.

Deep down, perhaps all men do.

The question is, how does one train to be a hero, assuming one is not gifted with all the attributes of an Achilles, a Captain Scott, or a Skywalker? There is no Ladybird book on the subject. And evening classes in Heroism have yet to catch on in the home counties.

I am not talking about the kind of shining hero who rushes in to save children from burning buildings, or flailing women from floods. Nor am I talking about being a public hero, fêted for great deeds. I have in mind a quieter sort of hero. Someone you almost don't notice when you pass them in the street. The kind of person who, through the way he or she lives their life – bravely and simply and openly – can somehow be a force for good.

# 2

## THE END OF THE BEGINNING

My Surrey childhood was as safe and soft as a padded cell in an open prison. The only limitations were the natural restrictions of the Surrey mindset, where doing something wild meant buying a BMW instead of a Cortina, ambition was a well-paid job in the City, and art was the bloke who sang the high bits in 'Bridge Over Troubled Water'.

No childhood rebellion, no fashionable expulsion for me. I had had my tantrums. I was the swotty goody-goody who begged to be allowed to stay at school for extra lessons on a Saturday afternoon, and played Chopin and Schubert instead of football and cricket. I could bash away at our tiny upright piano for hours on end, trying to play pieces that were far too hard for me. My school nicknames were Brain and Ritz Crackers. I was as rugged as a banana.

When I was nine, my parents went to live Abroad, in Bogotà. I was frightened of Abroad. Abroad meant dusty roads and sunburn. It meant women with moustaches and men with too much aftershave. Abroad, people tried to touch our hair, because it was blond. Abroad, people wanted to kidnap our dad, because he was the boss.

I was afraid of Alone, too. Alone meant that my parents had left without me. Alone was screaming in a foreign bathroom, while maids with moustaches muttered outside the door about what to do in a language I didn't understand. Alone meant having no one to distract me from the alarming prospect of being myself.

Boarding school was better than Abroad. Better than Surrey, too. At Windlesham, it felt as if someone had flung open the windows of a stuffy room, allowing fresh air and the sounds and smells of nature to flood in. There were no uniforms, enough Latin, few rules and no bullying. There were girls, too, and you were encouraged to talk to them. At night, Greek myths and Chopin ballades were piped into speakers in all the dormitories, to help us sleep. I thought I had been sent to heaven.

One day our geography teacher took us to visit a real farm, and we drank warm, foaming milk, straight from a cow.

My best friend Toby and I made survival kits: army pouches filled with useful gadgets like pocket tin-openers and fish-hooks and matches dipped in nail-varnish to waterproof them. Toby lived Abroad, too, in the Malaysian jungle with his sister Alice, who was very pretty and always homesick. Toby was forever getting into trouble, and I think he was planning a survival adventure, to take Alice home. But I just liked collecting Useful Gadgets.

It didn't matter that all the other boys – and a lot of the girls – could run faster, stand on their hands for longer, jump out of higher windows than me. There was mist on the sunlit downs. There were thrilling pillow fights. And there were pretty girls in my class, with one of whom – Clara Delaville – I fell desperately in love.

'You can't be in love,' matron told me. 'Children don't understand love. It's just a crush.'

I thought matron was an old bat.

I was convinced that if only I had a Spitfire, I could do a victory roll over the games pitches. And this would make Clara Delaville love me.

One sunny afternoon, another girl in my class led me into the woods. I didn't love Amelia Blunt, even though she let me touch her boobs. They felt soft and smooth and strange. We were both twelve years old. Amelia's mouth tasted of Bluebird Toffee, but I was afraid. So I told her I had carpentry; that I needed to finish making my green cheeseboard. And I ran away.

And then I turn my back for a second, and twenty years have slipped by. The green cheeseboard is finished. But London's friendly red telephone boxes have been uprooted. Train doors no longer slam; they hiss. It's not safe to walk in the park, darling.

For my job, I work as a theatre critic. People act out heroic stories on stage, and I sit in the darkness and criticize them. I have seen *Macbeth* nine times, and haven't enjoyed it once. I think I may be poisoning my mind.

One day, I meet a girl in a black velvet dress at a Christmas party. She is called Marisa and she says she works in publishing.

'What exactly is it that you're looking for?' she asks me, clutching my arm with the insistence of one who has downed one-too-many Moscow Mules. Bright, pretty, curvaceous, determined; tottering on heels too high for her; another child playing at being an adult.

'I'm looking for someone like you,' I tell her, because I have had one-too-many Moscow Mules, too.

After a year or so, Marisa and I move into a little house in East Dulwich together, with stripped wooden floors, a garden, and just enough space for my parents' grand piano, which I have played since I was twelve years old.

We have lively dinner parties and watch mindless television. We drive to the RSPCA rescue centre in Kilburn, and adopt a kitten that has been saved from a laboratory. We don't think we'll get married, and we don't think we'll have children. Marriage and children are for grown-ups, whereas we are only in our thirties.

I join the local tennis club, play in a jazz band, make an easy living as a freelance journalist, criticizing people for money. Life becomes a catalogue of diversions designed to stop us having to think about the fact that, behind the distractions, there might be nothing there at all.

I have the idea that I am going to write a novel, but London keeps getting in the way. Unlike most first novels, this will not be autobiographical. It is going to be about a hopeless young man who sets himself a series of impossible tasks in order to make himself worthy of the woman of his dreams. I know it will be called *The Labours of Jack Larry*, but I can't for the life of me think how to begin. How can I write about someone else's heroic adventures, when I haven't had any of my own?

I finally learn to fly, sweltering in the cockpit of a rented Piper Warrior in Florida. My instructor, Anand, is a small, polite and rather beautiful Indian man who, at twenty-one, already has fifteen hundred hours of flying under his belt. He is reassuringly perfectionistic in his approach, which I appreciate more than the way he shrieks 'Sinking! Sinking! Sinking!' each time I attempt to land us smoothly on Kissimmee's runway zero-three. Yes, Anand, I can see we're sinking. What the hell do you expect me to do about it?

Excited as I am finally to be fulfilling my destiny, sixty years on, I am simply unprepared for how *difficult* learning to fly turns out to be; for how it leaves my brain feeling like warm scrambled egg. I am not a natural Spitfire pilot after all. Flying is a lot more technical, and a lot less romantic, than I imagined.

Nevertheless, by now I have managed to criticize enough *Macbeth*s to buy my own vintage aeroplane: a bright-yellow Luscombe Silvaire built in 1946. Two seats, side by side, squeezed into a tiny leather-lined cockpit, held aloft by a pair of fabric-covered wings and hauled along by a 65-horsepower Continental engine that looks as if it has been recovered from a peat bog. The Luscombe is no Spitfire, but it smells of the 1940s and I think it is perfect. I begin to discover the romance of flight, after all.

In London, the garden goes to seed, and then to weed.

Marisa and I split up. There is no fighting; no flying crockery. Just a sense that the parallel tracks of our lives are ready to diverge. So we hug each other, and wave our handkerchiefs, and steam off on our separate lines.

And then, one blustery January day, I am sent to interview an actor who is about to star in *Macbeth*. I leave black footprints on the sleeted pavement as I trudge to the rehearsal room, a one-time nursery school at the end of an East London street that looks as if it still hasn't recovered from the Blitz. I sit on a child's plastic chair, watching my tenth *Macbeth*, without rapture. And instead of thinking up ways of making yet another insecure actor sound fascinating and important, I decide that I am going to go and live in France with a cat and a piano and an aeroplane.

'So what did you think?' asks the director afterwards, pulling at the neck of his black polo-neck as if to let the steam escape.

'Um . . . interesting,' I mumble.

'It's *such* a great play.'

I nod, desperate to escape his labrador enthusiasm. 'It's made me see my whole life differently,' I add.

'God, really? That's *fantastic*.'

I am not running away. I happen to think that England is a very good place to live, if one happens to like Marmite and hard cheese. But my London life is uncomfortably comfortable, and I need to create some proper problems for myself. I have had enough of living in a hamster's sawdust-lined cage. I want a true adventure, instead of endlessly trying to gallop somewhere – anywhere – on my little plastic wheel.

I want to have sheep and chickens and manly power-tools, and to make friends in a foreign language.

I want to watch the seasons passing, and to learn about things that matter, by looking and watching and digging my hands into the dirt.

I want to become the man I always hoped to be, before life got in the way. Abroad. Alone.

In France, perhaps I shall find myself a dishy French girlfriend. And perhaps I shall at last be able to sit down and write *The Labours of Jack Larry*. I've read enough, absorbed enough, endured enough of the buzzing cacophony of London. In my heart, I am a country person who has lived all his life in towns. And I am tired of being this soft, fearful townie, watching nonsense on the telly, sitting through mediocre plays at the theatre, talking trash with my friends to distract myself from the fact that the meter is ticking and I still have done nothing with my life of which I can feel proud. One day, I would love to be a wise old man. I have been extremely successful at the getting-older part. The getting-wiser part is proving tougher to achieve.

More than anything, I want to be able to look my eighteen-year-old self in the eye when I tell him what I've been up to. I'm tired of his finger-wagging.

'Do you mean to tell me that's all you've done in the last twenty years, after the start I gave you?' he says, as he stands beside my bed with his fresh skin and his blond hair. His face is half in shadow, so I cannot read his expression. But I'd say he isn't angry; just bemused.

# 3

## MARCH: INITIAL VIRILITY TEST

So here I am, driving through rain-tossed rural France, hunting for aerodromes in the dark. Dawn broke an hour ago, and never recovered. The deluge is vicious. It makes me hunch my shoulders and long for hot buttered toast and Horlicks. And I don't even like Horlicks.

My equipment for the heroic quest is slight. My steed, a Korean rental car the colour of a broad bean. My sword, a smattering of rusty A-level French. For guide, all I have is a soggy 1:500,000-scale aeronautical chart to lead me through the murk.

Later, when the sky clears, I may find that the Limousin is a bosky *mélange* of trees and lakes and rolling hills and gap-toothed old men bent double beneath bundles of sticks. But for now, black rain smashes itself upon the windscreen, making a March morning feel like a January dusk. It looks as if someone has blown the entire special-effects budget of a cheap thriller on this one scene.

I have no idea where in France I want to live. I only know that it must be near an aerodrome. If we're drawing Venn diagrams, it should also be far enough south of East

Dulwich for the cat to feel an improvement in the weather, yet still close enough to Blighty for me to sally back and forth from time to time.

As a child, my biggest fear was that my parents might die. As an adult, my biggest fear is that my parents will die. So I want to spend as much time with them as possible, while we're all still breathing.

No one really close to me has ever died, except my grandparents. And even they died at a distance: Pa in hospital, covered in tubes; Nanny in an old people's home, frightened and alone. I wish I had gone to see her, but I was frightened, too. I think I am more frightened of the people close to me dying than I am of dying myself.

So I don't want to be *too* far away. I'd love to pretend that I could simply hop into my Luscombe, yell 'Chocks away, Taffy' and fly myself back across the Channel if I should run short of Marmite or PG Tips. But the Luscombe is a doddery old girl, restricted to fair-weather flying, and will only rattle away for about three hundred miles before the fuel runs out and the engine falls alarmingly silent. So that's another reason for not living too far south. But first I must find a likely aerodrome. For I cannot bring an old aeroplane to France until I have found room at the inn to hangar it.

The barman's moustache twitches as he slides a smoking coffee towards me.

'*Il n'y a pas d'aérodrome ici, Monsieur.*' He rolls his eyes at the other men in the bar as I struggle to unfold my damp chart, repeating a scenario I have played out in countless bars and *tabac*s all over France, where aerodrome denial is rife.

'But what's this?' I ask, pointing to the little star beside the name Jolibois on my aeronautical chart. He pulls a smile like the twitch of a suburban net curtain. I stare at the floor, feeling as if I have just asked Mr Bumble for a second bowl of gruel, and wishing that I hadn't.

At last, one of the early-morning drinkers clears his throat and murmurs something to the barman. The net curtain falls limp.

'Ah, you mean the landing-strip that the pilots use?' he huffs, sulkily polishing a glass.

I nod.

'Well, why didn't you *say* so, *Monsieur*?' he says. 'It's up the road, on the left-hand side.'

So I knock back my coffee, and head off in search of the landing-strip-that-the-pilots-use.

The caffeine is already drumming in my temples as I step outside. The rain has stopped and a trickle of sunlight seeps from a curdled-milk sky. I regard this as a good omen, and immediately set off on the wrong side of the road, straight into the path of a juggernaut with his lights on full beam and his horn blaring.

I swerve, buttocks clenched, as we pass each other, lances raised, like knights at a joust. Except that his horse is rather bigger than mine.

The landing-strip-that-the-pilots-use turns out to be a sloping grass track with a dank bog and a small green hangar at one end of it. Through a crack in the hangar doors, I can just make out the ghostly shapes of several microlights, packed together as tightly as crisps in a bag. No space there for a Luscombe. But at least these planes look as if they fly every once in a while, unlike the dusty spam-cans I have glimpsed through the cracks in hangar doors all over France.

I trudge past the frayed windsock – faded from orange to potato brown – and out on to the runway, trying to picture a bright yellow Luscombe Silvaire landing here.

Then I trek back into Jolibois, in search of the local

estate agent. Today is Monday. I've given myself a week to find a house near an aerodrome.

Jolibois is a drab medieval sprawl – more purposeful than quaint – wrapped in some grey outskirts that must have looked grim even when they were first built. I'm encouraged by the gleaming pipe-organ in the church, because I've been meaning to dust off my preludes and fugues. Besides that, there are several shops flogging health insurance; a hearing-aid centre; an evil 1960s fountain; a small yellow box called the Cinéma Lux; a tennis club beside a petite football stadium; and a swanky-looking theatre with posters for last year's plays curling on the notice-board outside.

The shops are all shut – perhaps it's a bank holiday – but there's a light on in the estate agency.

'We only have one old house that might suit you, and it's this one,' says the pretty estate agent in breathily accented English, after I've explained that I'm not quite sure what I'm looking for, but that it will probably be old and isolated and have a leafy view. Bright-eyed and petite, she reminds me of one of the woodland characters in a Disney cartoon. I'm busy thinking what a pretty town Jolibois is when she shows me a picture of a gloomy-looking farmhouse stuck to the side of a hill.

'Does it have any windows?' I ask, studying the picture.

'I think so,' she says, pursing her lips. 'Yes, look, there's one.'

'*J'ai vu la maison*,' says her colleague, Antoine, peering at me over his half-moons. 'It's a good house, but it needs a lot of work and the floors are all on a terrible slope. You'd have to do something about that, or you'd get sea-sick.'

'Can I go and see it today?' I ask the lady from the Disney cartoon.

'Sadly not,' shrugs Antoine, before she can reply. He

waves his spectacles at me. 'Not until the weekend. And there's another problem, too. It's the owner. The man's an ecologist. Polish, I think. Very gruff and difficult. Doesn't like visitors. You take your life into your own hands when you go up there.'

'Ah,' I say, encouraged.

'Émilie can take you on Saturday morning.'

The Disney lady and I smile uncertainly at each other. Then she pencils me into her diary for the following Saturday. So the first house will also be the last house, for I am booked to fly home on Sunday. In the meantime, I head off in search of my next aerodrome.

At St Juste, a small market town twenty-five minutes' drive from Jolibois, I discover a friendly little aeroclub whose members are in the process of building a new hangar. Waving me in out of the pouring rain, the club's genial president even helps me write a letter, requesting a place on the waiting-list for my Luscombe.

'To whom should I address it?' I ask, my pen poised above the paper he has provided, as we listen to the rain drumming on the roof of his office.

'*À moi*,' he guffaws, dictating his name and an appropriately high-flown salutation. 'And you, when are you moving to France?'

'Very soon,' I declare confidently.

'Then you must meet our other English pilot.'

I must have pulled a face, for the president bursts out laughing again.

'You English are so funny,' he says. 'Why is it that you always want to avoid each other?'

I shrug, embarrassed.

'Ah, but Peter Viola is just the same,' he continues. 'Flies his own microlight in all weathers, and speaks good French. You'll like him, I assure you.'

\*

French estate agents are not like English ones. In Britain, you just walk in, tell the man in the shiny suit how many bedrooms you want, and then you leap into his car and go and look at unsuitable properties. In France, estate agents are rounded professionals with strange things like rigorous training and qualifications. They expect you to make an appointment as if you were going to see the doctor. And, like good doctors, they give you a very thorough examination.

'In town or in the countryside, *Monsieur*?' asks the chain-smoking vamp – Cruella De Vil in a tight purple trouser-suit and with a sultry pout – who interrogates me in St Juste later that day.

'Well, the *edge* of a town would be all right, if it was leafy.'

'How much land, *Monsieur*?'

'*N'importe.*' I shrug. I really don't mind, just so long as the neighbours have some nice fields for the cat to depopulate.

'And water?'

'*Ah, bien sûr*. Water and electricity, too, please.'

Cruella eyes me wearily from behind a mascara portcullis. 'I mean, *Monsieur*, do you wish to be beside a lake or a river?'

'Sorry – yes, lovely. And not vital.'

'*Dépendances?*'

'No,' I say. 'I have no children. Just a cat.'

The sultry pout thins to just two strands of stuck spaghetti. '*Dépendances, Monsieur* . . . that is, how many outbuildings do you require?'

'Well, how many would *Madame* suggest?'

The tip of her cigarette glows as she takes a deep drag.

'How many square metres of living-space?'

25

In a panic, I try to guess the size of the little house in East Dulwich. I am about to say a hundred square metres, but that sounds like a football pitch, so I settle on sixty.

'*Soixante?*'

Cruella stops writing and begins screwing the lid on to her pen. I can see her mentally cancelling the holiday in the Bahamas she has been planning ever since I walked in. Rattled, I guess again.

'Seven hundred?'

'*Vous cherchez un château, Monsieur?*'

No, no. That's not right, either. So I split the difference and make a final stab.

'A hundred and seventy?'

With a smile like an iceberg, *Madame* writes down '200' in her notebook. And now we come to the virility test.

'*En quel état?*' she asks.

'*Excusez-moi?*' What's she saying now? Uncle is late?

'How – much – work – are – you – prepared – to – do – on – the – house?' she spits, each word shot out in a separate speech bubble.

I will soon learn that there are five levels of manhood in the French estate agent's virility test:

1. *Rénovée*: I am a rich cissy.
2. *Petits travaux*: I'll wield a paintbrush if you promise not to wobble the ladder.
3. *À finir*: I watch DIY shows on telly and have my own hammer drill.
4. *Habitable*: Who needs a bathroom when your tool-belt is as big as mine?
5. *À rénover*: I am a fearless caveman, skilled in the black arts of the mason, the roofer and the plumber, and only visit the blacksmith when I have a problem with my teeth.

My DIY prowess is strictly level 3 at best, although I do see myself as a testosterone-charged level 4 after half a bottle of wine with someone I'm trying to impress.

The fact is, I've always liked the idea of 'doing up' a house, heaving spade-loads of cement into a rumbling mixer, and splitting granite with nothing but a Swiss army knife and the sweat of my brow. I'm very keen and all that, for it is undoubtedly vital that the trainee hero chooses gruelling labour over cushy comfort every time. It's just that I've never done anything more complicated than putting up a few lights and painting a shed the wrong colour.

'If it's habitable, *ça va*,' I declare, puffing out my chest and banging my hand on the desk harder than intended.

'Oh, really?' Cruella blows a smoke ring at the ceiling. It looks strangely like a zero. I fear she has twigged that I don't even possess a tool-belt, let alone a laser gadget for levelling floors.

'Well, you know,' I add, attempting a graceful retreat without her noticing. 'I don't mind if the place looks a bit shabby.'

'*Petits travaux*,' she sniffs, making a clinical assessment of my manhood on her pad. 'In that case, *Monsieur*, I have nothing for you. Come back in a month, and I'll see what I can do.'

Bracelets jangle on a bony yellow wrist as she offers me her hand.

'*Bonne journée, Monsieur*.'

# 4

## THE OGRE

Saturday morning arrives at last, and I head off to meet Émilie, the Disney lady, in Jolibois. By now, I have been through a dozen Cruella-type interrogations, seen photographs of hundreds of properties, and been taken to view a surfeit of shambling houses built slap-bang in the middle of someone else's muddy farmyard. Émilie is already standing outside the estate agency when I arrive.

'Nice car,' I say as I slide into the passenger seat of her shiny Renault.

'Yes, my husband bought it for me as a birthday present,' she says, checking her make-up in the rear-view mirror.

'Nice husband.'

'Oh, Fred *is* good. I'm very lucky.'

'Unusual name, for a . . .'

'He's English,' laughs Émilie. 'You'll like him.'

The sky looks as blue as Wedgwood china as we follow the directions to the ogre's lair. The sunlight glitters on the road, still slick with last night's rain.

'So why do you want to live in France?' asks Émilie.

'For an adventure.'

She raises her eyebrows. 'Here, this must be it,' she says, turning off the road on to a track that seems to rise almost vertically into a dense wood.

'Are you sure this is a good idea?' I ask, clinging to the handle above my door as the track veers sharply right and left.

'No,' she giggles. 'But you said you wanted an adventure.'

'If he becomes violent, you're in charge,' I tell her. 'You have to protect the client at all costs.'

'OK . . .'

'That was a joke, by the way.'

'I know.'

'Oh, *this* is nice,' we chime, in our different accents.

The drive rises through a cathedral of trees, with great pillars of chestnut and oak. A soft glow suffuses the car, as the sun filters through the natural fan vaulting above us. On either side, strobing beyond the wooded curtain, I catch snapshot glimpses of bright open fields dotted with grazing sheep.

Onwards and upwards we glide, up this track which feels as if only the trees are stopping it from sliding down the hill. It reminds me of going up the drive to Windlesham at the beginning of term, only without that sinking feeling in the pit of my stomach.

Yes, this smells right.

And there, at the top, is a ramshackle house, with bright-blue windows in all the wrong places, and a foreboding pair of zinc-covered barn doors, and a garden so overgrown you could hide tanks in it, dominated by a lone pine as tall as a skyrocket.

And it is perfect.

We scramble up a steep bank towards the front door,

and I am a child of five, steaming my tricycle past the Old Ladies' house in a Guildford suburb, hoping the three sisters who hate children don't see me. Émilie grins like a child, too; blinking her astonishment at this wild, unkempt place.

But, oh golly: there is the shadowy figure of the ogre moving inside the house. He looks as big as a minotaur. Huge, hunched shoulders and a biblical beard, like a vision of Satan drawn by William Blake. I let Émilie go in front of me. I always used to let Nicholas, my little brother, go first, too, when we cycled past the Old Ladies.

A key rattles in the lock. The latch of the gentian-blue door is turning. Wood scrapes on stone.

The beast is before us.

Monsieur Zumbach appears more nervous than we are as he leads us from room to room. A big, burly man, whose heavy-lidded eyes appear to have been roughly chiselled out by a medieval wood-carver, he nevertheless treads lightly, with the hushed fervour of a druid welcoming visitors to Stonehenge. There is much bowing, much pressing together of palms, and frequent peals of tense laughter, which become more boomingly infectious as we progress through the house. Deep and rough as his voice sounds, it is musical, too, as if an organist were stomping out arpeggios on a pedal-reed. Sometimes he whispers with excitement at his own pronouncements.

Nevertheless, as we wander from room to room, I feel a growing sense of awe, tinged with dread. For it dawns on me that I am not merely being shown a house here; I am being offered a glimpse of my future. And I'm not sure I'm ready for it.

I feel it in the kitchen, where five black carriage-lamps are screwed to the rough-hewn walls, all at different heights, and two benches are set on either side of a simple wooden table in the middle of the stone floor. The combination of sandalwood incense and melancholy choral music gives the gloomy, heavy-beamed space the atmosphere almost of a chapel. I feel it as we step down into what the breathless ogre calls the *salon d'hiver* – the winter sitting-room – where chestnut logs are crackling and spitting in the wood-burning stove, next to an open fireplace big enough to roast a pair of oxen. And I feel it most as we walk through a pair of doors into the dusty shell of the cavernous *salon d'été*, when I gaze up at its great roof-beams, forty feet above our heads. The ogre slips outside to open up the zinc-covered barn doors, allowing light from across the valley to flood in through the tall French windows.

This place is like the defunct meeting-place of some secret sect. The roof is no more than a layer of bare tiles sitting upon beams of gnarled oak. Two of the walls appear to be composed largely of dust held together with ancient stones, and the other two are built out of sugarlump slabs; breezeblocks whose slathered mortar has oozed out of the joints like buttercream filling from a Victoria sponge. Two huge cattle-troughs project into the room on one side, with the old oak stalls still supporting the wall above them.

'A music room,' I murmur, and see the beast clasp his hands together, as if in prayer.

'Monsieur Wright, it makes me so happy to hear you say that,' he says, his eyelids crisping into a grin. But there is an unmistakable catch of sadness in his voice.

As we walk through rooms in various states of disrepair, and stumble through the jungle outside, the house weaves its spell, and I feel as if someone has just told me an awesome secret.

'What do you think?' asks Émilie, as we stand on a dusty cement floor, gazing up at the open roof of the cavernous summer sitting-room.

'I feel nervous. A sort of sinking feeling.'

'Nervous, why?'

'Because I have a horrible feeling that I am about to buy a house in France.'

'I know,' she smiles.

'How do you know?'

'Because I'd like to buy it, too.'

What disarms me is the fact that this place has everything I have been looking for, down to the smallest detail. It's like something a genie might have created, with a spell. And on top of this, it is surrounded by five acres of wild hillside studded with fruit trees and oaks. So I would be able to have my own sheep. Zumbach describes how he thinks the place may once have been an inn – *un relais* – on a tributary of the old pilgrims' route to Santiago de Compostela.

'You can still see the cairn marking the route on top of the hill behind the house,' he says, pointing at the wall behind the grease-encrusted gas stove.

But it is the aliveness of the place, as much as its history, that leaps at me. The way the house seems to grow out of the rock on which it is built. The vivid green shoots in the fields, on which the deer get drunk. The trio of goldfish lazing in the stone pool outside the back door. The riot of young trees, spreading within the protective boundary of their elders. The lone pine, tall as a church steeple, bisecting the view of the valley beyond. And the interior of the house itself, so ancient and yet so unfinished, because Monsieur Zumbach – from what I can tell – was interrupted by the departure of his wife just when he was in the middle of renovating it.

'I always . . . *mais ma femme* . . .' he says, shaking his head. We wait while he gathers his thoughts. 'It was a good joke the devil played when he made us desire each other.'

'I know I'm not meant to say this,' I tell the ogre, as he makes coffee for me and Émilie in a scarlet pot, 'but I can't quite believe I have found this place. Or that nobody else has already bought it.'

'*Je sais.* I could tell,' he says, his eyes sparkling with pleasure. 'The house has been waiting for you.'

Our eyes meet for a few seconds. Then he glances at Émilie, hesitates, and glances back at me.

'Monsieur Wright, I take it you are not entirely sane?'

'Quite correct,' I reply with a sigh.

'Good, good.' He presses his fingers together. 'Because I must tell you that you do have to be mad to live here. Are you married?'

'No, I'd be thinking of living here alone.'

The ogre roars with laughter. '*C'est parfait!*' he exclaims. It's perfect. '*Parce que ça, ça c'est La Folie.*'

'La Folie?'

'That's the name of this place: La Folie. And to think of living here all alone, *c'est de la folie*, too. Completely mad. That's all right for me, because I'm Polish, which comes to the same thing. But you . . .'

'Actually, I was thinking of bringing a cat, too.'

Monsieur Zumbach clasps his hands and shakes them vigorously, as he raises his eyes skywards. 'You will not regret such a decision,' he beams, though I am not really listening, so I miss the significance of his words.

I want to repay his frankness with an admission of my own. 'I suppose I'm also hoping I might find myself *une copine française* here in Jolibois. What do you reckon?'

'Monsieur Wright,' he says, suddenly serious, pouring

steaming coffee into three unglazed earthenware cups. 'I can honestly tell you that you will not find such a person here for you in Jolibois.'

'Are you sure?'

'Quite sure,' he says. And then emits a nervous laugh, with an apologetic wave at Émilie.

'I take it you are not from these parts, *Madame*?'

Émilie smiles and shakes her head.

'These are just right for this place,' I tell Zumbach, changing the subject, holding up my coffee cup: a plain earthenware beaker, with no handle or lip. I make a mental note that if I buy this house – *when* I buy this house – I must try to find some that are just the same. For they match the place perfectly.

Zumbach looks at me long and hard before breaking into a sunlit grin. 'So you're really thinking of living here all alone?' he asks.

I nod.

'*C'est de la folie*,' he repeats, in a peal of laughter.

In the car, Émilie and I are silent for a while.

'Well, he certainly liked *you*,' she says.

I don't reply. My head is jangling with images. The sparkling landscape has changed. The present has become the future. And I'm struggling to adjust, conscious that these great trees, that strip of grassy earth down the centre of the drive and this grey stone bridge over a French river will soon become more familiar to me than the graffitied lamp-posts and wheely-bins of East Dulwich.

Back at the estate agency, I confirm that I want to make an offer for La Folie, a house I only saw for the first time an hour ago. Not a cheeky offer, either, albeit that it undercuts the asking price. I want to pay what is right. Antoine and another lady in the office – a willowy thirtysomething in a rust silk dress – exchange glances.

'Monsieur Zumbach and I came to an understanding.' I cough.

'What understanding?' snaps Émilie, who heard everything. Seated behind her desk, the childlike fellow-explorer has metamorphosed, like Mr Benn, into Office Émilie.

'I can't really explain. All I know is that it doesn't feel appropriate to try to knock him down.'

Émilie can't rouse Zumbach on the phone. I imagine he knows with the same certainty I have that La Folie is sold, and is wandering the rugged hillside, beginning to make his farewells. So I head out to one of the restaurants in town – le Cheval Blanc – and ask the cheery *patron* if he has a table for one.

'*Bien sûr, Monsieur,*' he says, showing me to a table in the graceful old dining-room, complete with some very brown 1940s paintings depicting the place as the eighteenth-century coaching-inn it once was; the past refracted through a grimy lens. Nearby, a grey-haired couple in matching tracksuits are peering at each other in silence. The markings are unmistakable: *les Anglais*.

On the far side of the room, four young women in their early twenties are all talking at once around a table, as if they haven't seen each other for a long time. This is more encouraging. I am determined to prove Zumbach wrong.

I order a beer and my mobile phone rings.

'He's accepted your offer,' trills Émilie. 'He's on his way.'

'*Er, Monsieur,*' I say, waving apologetically at *le patron* and pulling a face of mortification. 'I'll be right back.'

And so, three hours after my first sight of La Folie, the Ogre and I are both signing the *compromis de vente* that commits us to the transaction: an ending for him; a beginning for me. We are to complete in July.

This is the biggest, fastest decision I have made in my life.

'Oh, that's not fast,' says Émilie, while the willowy lady in the rust silk dress guides me and Zumbach through the pages of the form.

'Put your initials here; your whole signature there,' she murmurs.

'We've just sold a house to an English couple who haven't even seen it yet,' continues Émilie. 'They just liked the picture on our website.'

'It's an invasion,' laughs the other lady. France must be changing so fast.

'The *fosse septique* won't need emptying until the autumn,' says Zumbach, as he sees my pen wavering.

'*Très bien.* I shan't forget.'

'You can hardly hear the train at the bottom of the hill,' he continues. 'And there are only four a day.'

'It's all right.' I smile. 'I like trains.'

# 5

# JULY: FAIR STOOD THE WIND FOR FRANCE

I'm still not entirely sure why I chose France for this adventure, rather than Spain or Chad or Patagonia.

There is a photograph of my great-grandfather looking severe in Paris at the dawn of the twentieth century, before he became an ice-cream salesman in Ealing.

My grandparents, Pa and Nanny, camped in the fields of Provence in the 1920s, sleeping in a leaky green bell-tent called Abdul the Damned. Even before they were married, the pair of them slipped away for a risqué holiday in St Tropez – and then swiftly raced home to Blighty, because Britain had 'gone off gold'. With only a trickle of news about abandoning the Gold Standard crackling on the wireless – and only a trickle of youthful abandon surging in their veins – I suppose Pa and Nanny were more bothered about their savings than fumbling for each other's secrets in the dark.

My mother fell for France, too, first as a teenager on a pen-pal exchange in Rouen, and then in Paris in 1956, smoking cigarettes with students in black polo-necks at the Sorbonne by night, and working in the offices of a company called Isolamiante by day, learning the dark secrets of *le plafond suspendu.* Suspended ceilings are still big business in France, and I like to think that my mother had something to do with it, simply by typing the words '*Veuillez agréer, Messieurs, l'expression de nos sentiments les plus distingués*' on to her blue carbon-paper a hundred times a day.

My father was in France at the same time, drinking his way through a rugby tour with his Cambridge college. 'The French cheated shamelessly,' he once told me. 'They would send one team to drink us under the table on the eve of a game. And then, when we were all nursing our sore heads the next day, they sent a fresh team to play in the match. But it was damn good fun.'

I am told that I was horizontal when I first saw France, gurgling in an expensive pram with a navy-blue hood and chrome-spoked wheels. When I was one, my parents took me with my older brother and sister on a family holiday to Brittany.

There are flickering cine films of me looking improbably beautiful at the time, a mass of golden curls and a dimpled beam as bright as a lighthouse. I like to think that my smiles reflect my love of this strange new land. Or is it that – as the camera whirrs – I have not yet discovered that I have no sense of direction, short sight, flat feet, and a hopeless tennis backhand?

Learning to be resourceful and self-reliant is all very well, but I'm jolly grateful when Simon from across the road in East Dulwich offers to help me load and drive the van with all my worldly goods to France.

Simon is one of my heroes, in that he sails through motorbike crashes, skiing accidents, lost car-keys and catastrophic engine-failures with spectacular élan, always with a smile and a wry wince of theatrical mortification. Although he works as a journalist, you'd think he was a 1950s racing driver. Tall, slim and eccentrically old-fashioned, here is a man who never seems happier than when he is giving up his time to help a friend, especially if the favour involves driving cars or vans, or – better still – riding ancient motorcycles on dusty foreign roads. With his collection of heavy old bicycles and wooden tennis racquets ('the Hazel Streamline has never been bettered,' he assures me), Simon belongs to an era when the world was simpler, chivalry was rife and people didn't react to every minor mishap as if it were a major crisis.

It takes us nearly five hours to heave everything into the rental van and tie it up in a cat's-cradle of string. The last thing to go in is one of Simon's vintage motorbikes. He says we may be glad of it. At midnight we finally slam the tail-gate and disappear into our opposing houses, like two duellers retreating their ten paces.

I don't sleep. At five in the morning, we are out there again, whispering so as not to wake the other neighbours in the street.

'As long as we get there by noon tomorrow, we'll be fine,' I declare. I turn the key in the ignition, and the van rumbles into life. 'That's when I have to sign the papers at the *notaire*'s office.'

Six minutes later, the beastly thing conks out on the corner of a dodgy Peckham housing estate, one mile into our six-hundred-mile journey from London to the Limousin. An amber warning light rages on the dash-board. Figures dart in the shadows. Turning the key in the ignition yields only an eerie silence. Our journey has ended, no sooner than begun.

'I'm afraid this is not a very good omen, Michael,' says Simon delicately.

'A little teething trouble, perhaps. I'm sure it's nothing you can't fix.'

Simon is good with engines, and I can't think of anyone with whom I would rather break down on a long and significant journey. We'll soon be on our way.

His face orange in the sodium glow of the streetlamps, Simon emerges from under the bonnet with a smile that could mean anything except that he has fixed the van.

'Electronic fault,' he mutters. 'It's not like with the old engines, where you can fix them yourself. They'll have to send out a replacement.'

We both stand motionless for a few seconds, listening to a distant police siren, and trying not to think about unloading the van.

'Oh well, it's good this happened close to home,' I declare, 'and not in a traffic jam on the *Périphérique*.'

Simon peers into the shadows. 'Yes, we're much better off surrounded by murderous drug-dealers than French lorry-drivers, aren't we?'

I glance at my watch. We must be in France by noon tomorrow, or I shall miss the completion date for La Folie.

'I'll just phone Helen and tell her to get the breakfast on,' continues Simon, sounding a bit like Paris on the eve of the Trojan War.

'Let's try it one last time,' I say. 'Just in case.' Simon folds his arms and watches from the pavement. I cross my fingers and nudge the accelerator.

'Come on,' I murmur, shutting my eyes. 'This time. Please.' I turn the key. A bird flits in front of the windscreen, making me jump. And the engine rumbles into life.

'How did you do that?' says Simon, with a slight edge in his voice.

'Hop in,' I shout, revving the engine till it screams like a jet. 'We can still make the ferry.'

No, we can't. Every time we slow down, the engine judders to a halt, the orange death lamp glows, and the rumbling swish of tyres on tarmac returns.

'What are you going to have for breakfast on the ferry?' I ask, in one of these silences. 'The ferry ticket includes a twenty-five-pound food voucher.'

Simon smiles and nods.

'I'm having the works,' he says, narrowing his eyes to peer into the far distance, as if he can see his breakfast hovering like a mirage above the horizon. 'Egg, bacon, sausage, mushrooms, tomato, baked beans, black pudding, fried bread, ketchup and a jolly good cup of builder's tea on the side.'

Against the odds, we manage to squeeze on to a ferry that puts us only an hour behind schedule. But the restaurant is full, so we end up in the bar, where we spend our voucher on a limp sandwich each and twenty quid's worth of crisps and fizzy drinks.

'Good sandwiches,' observes Simon. 'And at least I got my cup of tea.'

Greasy and burping, we stand at the back of the ferry, watching the propellers churn up the green-brown waters of the English Channel, and our wake stretching behind us like a chalk road. 'Goodbye, England,' I whisper to myself, as the white cliffs of Dover recede into a grey smudge on the horizon.

It is a long, sweaty trip beneath the baking French sun. Every journey's length is magnified by the heat inside the vehicle multiplied by the level of uncertainty of reaching one's destination. And this one feels very uncertain indeed. With the van as our patient, Simon and I are a pair of trainee paramedics, attempting to keep a heart-attack victim alive. By the end of it all, I feel as drained as the water bottles we have heaped behind our seats.

We have arrived, though not quite at La Folie. Our night-stop is a quaint *chambres d'hôte* a couple of miles up the road from my future, where I picture Monsieur Zumbach pacing the empty rooms, stroking the walls, bidding farewell to his past. The place I've booked is an ivy-clad farmhouse, whose gnarled antiques are garishly offset by the lurid orange wallpaper. Dinner is a communal affair at a long oak table with four other Brits who are passing through. All of them are house-hunting.

'Gosh, you *are* brave,' says one of the wives, peering at me as if I were an object in a glass case when I describe my plan.

'And so lucky, too,' replies the woman opposite her, a gaudy parakeet with dangly earrings and enormous breasts. 'Fancy finding your house just like that. Malcolm and I have been looking for months, but there are *so* few swimming-pools in the region. Isn't that right, Malcolm?'

'Yes, Maureen,' says Malcolm, dressed entirely in grey, not looking up from the duck leg he is attacking.

'I imagine that struggling French farmers don't have much time for practising the breast-stroke,' says Simon. 'But you could always buy a farm with a big sheep-dip, and convert that into an excellent pool.'

'Oh, no. We couldn't do that,' responds Maureen, shaking her head. 'Could we, Malcolm?'

'No, Maureen,' says Malcolm, staring at his plate.

'What's the betting that you end up with Malcolm and the lovely Maureen as your new neighbours?' asks Simon next morning, as we haul his motorbike out of the back of the van for the ride into Jolibois. Neither of us wants to climb back into that van ever again.

'Fortunately La Folie doesn't have any neighbours,' I reply. 'Would you mind doing this for me?' I point to my chin-strap.

'Told you the bike would come in useful.'

Émilie is seated at her desk, smartly dressed in a black suit, when we arrive for our meeting with the *notaire*.

'Ah, you must be the lovely Émilie. How very charming . . .' says Simon, who has a habit of turning into Terry-Thomas at the first sight of a pretty woman.

'Yes, yes, we'll see you later,' I reply, pushing him out of the door and ignoring his protestations about how he just wants to look at the property details on the wall.

Another old friend is waiting when Émilie and I reach the notaire's office: Monsieur Zumbach, breathless with nerves, all buttoned up in a shirt so well-pressed that someone else must have done it for him. A lady whom I take to be his ex-wife is there, too: a slim, birdlike woman with sculptor's hands. It was she, I suppose, who carved the worry lines into his medieval misericord. I'm happy to see them leaning their heads together to murmur between themselves; that their connection has not been entirely sundered. I knew that the sale of La Folie was the result of a broken marriage. I was hoping that all the fragments would not have been lost.

To my surprise, the birdlike woman tiptoes over to me and presents me with a huge bundle of keys. 'These are for you, *Monsieur*,' she says.

'*Merci.*'

I lay the bunch of keys carefully under my chair when we all tramp into the wood-panelled office of the notaire, and the woman gives me a quizzical look. But we haven't signed the papers yet. It feels too soon to take possession.

The *notaire* we were expecting – Yves-Pascal Pascaux – is on holiday. This one is a bald, studious man with a cold smile, glinting like flint. I follow everyone else's lead in treating him with exaggerated respect, which does not appear to dismay him. And then we are all shaking hands and emerge from the stuffy office like relieved cinema-goers at the end of a long and worthy documentary, blinking in the daylight and taking lungfuls of fresh air. Zumbach signals to me that he wants a private word.

'Er, Monsieur Wright,' he begins, with a nervousness that I find contagious. 'May I ask you a favour?'

'Of course.'

'It's the goldfish. Will you look after them?'

'*Bien sûr.*' I laugh, relieved. 'Is it difficult?'

'Just a little food, and some local gossip every now and then.'

'I'll do my best.'

He makes a little bow, presses his hands together in thanks, and avoids my gaze. Then he marches away with his head held high, as only a man who has lost everything he once held dear, and yet has held on to his pride, his compassion and his sense of humour, can.

'Are you all right?' asks Émilie, who has been standing just apart.

I nod, shaking myself out of my thoughts. 'He's quite something, isn't he?'

'The *notaire*?' Émilie wrinkles her nose.

'No, Monsieur Zumbach. He's become a bit of a hero of mine.'

'So what did he want?'

'He's left me the goldfish. And I've promised to feed them, even though I'm not going to be properly moving in for a couple of months.'

'Fred will look after them.'

'Are you sure your husband is going to want to drive all

the way out to La Folie, day after day, just to feed three goldfish?'

'Fred is good with fish,' she says firmly. And already I feel as if I am entering a different world.

# 6

## PA'S OMELETTE

My heart is thumping as I venture out of the furnace-heat of the afternoon, and into the dairy coolness of the dilapidated French house that I have just bought. Excitement mingles with dread as I tiptoe into each room. Simon strides behind, providing an excited commentary.

'Look at this!' he says. 'And look at that! It's incredible.'

I'm having the same thoughts. La Folie is such a higgledy-piggledy place that I can't even remember how many bedrooms there are, and I'm half afraid that a dead body is going to fall out of one of the cupboards.

'In fact, I wish I hadn't seen it,' declares Simon. 'Helen and I are never going to find anywhere as good as this. It's the perfect place.'

The French have a reputation for taking all the lightbulbs with them when they move house. Actually, that's unfair. They don't just take the lightbulbs. They also take the door handles, radiators, kitchen sink, the works. But it's not the things Zumbach has taken with him that make my mouth gape. It's the things he has left behind.

A ping-pong table encrusted with cement. One bent set of chimney-sweep's brushes and poles. An ornamental MDF throne, six feet high. A sugar bowl in the shape of a golf ball. Two dead bicycles, and one still fighting for breath. More than 150 Kilner preserving jars with perished rubber seals. Four pairs of Empire-building shorts (extra-large). A huge black-and-white television. Enough broken saucepans to cook *pot-au-feu* for a batallion. A quantity of gherkins. And so on.

'I can't believe it,' continues Simon. 'Are you sure he's already moved out?'

'His wife gave me the keys.'

'Even so.'

'This stuff was someone's life,' I say, ignoring him. 'It feels like it should be in the Louvre or the Smithsonian or something.'

To be fair, Zumbach did ask me on the phone if he could leave behind '*un ou deux trucs*'.

'*Mais oui, bien sûr,*' I replied, all innocence. I suppose I should have guessed from his tone that he was finding it a lot harder to fit the contents of La Folie into a one-bedroom flat in Limoges than he had expected.

I thought I was just buying a ramshackle house with three goldfish attached. But I have bought much, much more than that. I am now also the proud possessor of two rotting carts, one ox-drawn plough, the carcass of a 1930s threshing machine, a pigsty, six rabbit hutches, a fearsome dog-kennel, four acres of wild scrubland, an overgrown orchard and a ruined well.

'What exactly *is* a *truc*, then?' asks Simon.

'It's a whatchamacallit. A dooberry. A thingummyjig.'

At Simon's insistence, I telephone Zumbach on my mobile to check when he is planning to pick up the rest of his stuff.

'*Ah, non, Monsieur Wright*. These are little presents, for you.'

'*Ah, merci, Monsieur Zumbach. C'est très . . . gentil.*'

I walk into the kitchen and suddenly feel guilty rather than self-righteous. For there, on the kitchen table where Émilie and I sat sipping coffee four months ago, is a gift from the foul-tempered ogre: the three simple, unglazed earthenware cups that I had told him were just right for this place.

Simon is by now in clover. Here is a man who makes an artform out of collecting other people's discarded *trucs*. He has already expressed an interest in the MDF throne.

'Helen won't mind,' he murmurs. 'And what about this?' he asks, holding up the golf-ball sugar bowl. 'May I have it?'

'Of course,' I say. 'It feels more like we both just found all these *trucs* in a skip than that they're *mine*.' But I am ashamed to discover as soon as Simon expresses an interest in a greasy old teapot, or a wicker basket I had planned to discard, that I begin to wonder if I should keep it. I must learn to stop wanting things, just because someone else wants them. Otherwise, even now, I could end up with a stressful job in banking, two screaming children and a blonde wife who knows everything there is to know about daytime television and plastic surgery.

Poor Simon looks quite pale as we begin to make a pile of *trucs* for disposal. He really must learn to stop wanting things, just because no one else wants them.

'Are you *quite* sure you want to get rid of all this?' he asks, biting his lip. His eyes mist over as he surveys the broken treasure. 'Even the Kilner jars? Someone might want those for jam-making.'

'*Especially* the jars,' I reply.

The sky has turned golden and the crickets are whirring

in the long grass by the time we finish exploring. The blazing intensity of the afternoon has relented, like a cup of coffee finally cool enough to drink without burning yourself. I can feel the salt caking my face when I smile.

We sit on the low stone wall at the back of the terrace, drink cold beer out of bottles dripping with condensation, and ponder the mysteries of the universe. Beside us, the three goldfish swim silkily in the cool depths of their stone pool. In the distance, I can hear a train chugging through the trees. The lone pine casts its long shadow like a sundial into the field below and, across the valley, the tiny chapel of St Sauveur glows in the last rays of the disappearing sun.

'It's good here,' says Simon. 'You've done well.'

'But that's just it,' I reply. 'I don't feel I've done anything at all. It's too much. I don't feel worthy of this place.'

'I know what you mean.' Simon nods. 'And you will.'

The trip to the tip is a painful one. In the midday sun, we have sweated to load up the jinxed van, Simon wincing every time he glimpses one of Zumbach's 150 Kilner preserving jars.

And, once again, the beast conks out every time we apply the brakes. So we do not apply them.

'Have you ever seen the film *Speed*?' asks Simon.

'No.'

'Well, this is worse,' he pants, wiping his brow with his forearm as we scream across another roundabout.

Fortunately, the shimmering roads around Jolibois are very straight, and the local drivers don't seem much interested in braking, either.

'Do you live here, *Messieurs*?' asks the man at the tip, when we finally rattle through the gates. Leaning on a spade, he gazes at our English number-plate as if it were wearing stockings and suspenders.

'*Oui*,' I reassure him. I'm not some lightweight weekender; I'm here in France for the long haul. 'I live at Jolibois.'

'Then you can't leave your stuff here, *Monsieur*. This is the Magnac-Laval tip. You'll have to go back to Jolibois.'

'But there isn't a tip at Jolibois.'

'I know,' he says. 'It's too bad.' He wipes his face with the back of his glove, and looks genuinely sorry. Just not quite sorry enough. And then I tell a bare-faced lie. I know this is wrong. I know I shouldn't have. But I tell him that my parents live in Magnac-Laval, and this is their stuff. He raises his eyebrows.

'In that case, those must all be dismantled for recycling,' he says, jerking a thumb at our 150 Kilner jars, each with its thick wire hinge attaching the lid to the body.

'But what if someone wants them?' asks Simon, aghast.

'I know. It's too bad,' he says.

So Simon and I laboriously set about detaching the wire hinges from each jar. Glass into one dumpster. Metal into another. I can see how painful this is for him. It feels like I've asked a vegetarian to help me tear the wings off a flock of sparrows.

We have been dissecting Kilner jars for half an hour when, with an apocalyptic roar, a beige 2CV squeals to a halt beside us, and a man with a black beret and a face like Armageddon leaps out.

'You're not throwing those away, are you?' he barks, shaking his fist at the remaining eighty jars. His magnificent moustache twitches like a ferret. Simon and I stare at each other, mouths open. We've barely had time to respond before he is loading the jars into the back of the 2CV.

'You shouldn't throw such things away,' he shouts over his shoulder, as the car screams off in a cloud of black smoke.

'I *told* you we should have kept the jars,' murmurs Simon, gazing up at the clear French sky.

If you look up at the weather-beaten facade of La Folie, you can see that the house was built along practical, rather than aesthetic, lines. On the right-hand side are two huge barns for cows and other beasts, with space for hay on an upper level. On the left, tacked on almost as an afterthought, is the original human habitation: a primordial kitchen with a living-room attached, which Zumbach called his winter sitting-room, presumably because the temperature therein makes you think it must be winter, even in high summer.

This sloping, black-beamed space is dominated by the twin hulks of a huge, soot-blackened fireplace and a venerable Godin wood-burning stove, whose right-angled flue belches its smoke into the main chimney – or should do eventually, just as soon as I find a source of decent firewood.

At the back of the house, buried in the hillside, is the bathroom, which feels as if it will make a safe, if icy, shelter in the event of a nuclear war. This gelid place does have one tiny window, opening on to a narrow mineshaft – *une cour anglaise*, Zumbach called it – that allows no more than a trickle of milky light to penetrate from the world above.

Upstairs, now cleared of hay, is a huge open space that would make a good dormitory for monks, with a boxy little room carved out of one end of it, like the cab of a Luton van. This is the room I have chosen as my bedroom, though Zumbach constructed a much larger chamber at the back of the house, where Simon is camping during our stay. I prefer the smaller room, because it faces east, has white walls and no curtains. So as soon as the sun rises, I am dazzled into following suit. I like its compact solidity, and the fact that it looks out over the rocky track up to the house. If brigands come in the night, hoping to steal my *trucs*, I shall hear them. What I shall do after that, I have no idea.

Next door to these living-quarters is the first barn, the one that Zumbach had begun to renovate. Most of this has been converted into the shell of the projected *salon d'été* – the summer sitting-room, rising to the exposed rafters – and the rest, on two floors, forms the empty husk of the future *maison des amis*. On the far side of this is the second barn, home to my non-existent wood store, a complete food chain of scuttling creatures, and yet more rusty-dusty heaps of Zumbach's endless *trucs* – many of which, in fairness, must have been discarded by former inhabitants of La Folie, for the whole wretched gallimaufry has a strong whiff of the eighteenth century about it.

When Simon emerges from his room, already looking bright and ready to start the day, I make some muddy coffee in the scarlet tin pot that Zumbach has left behind. Simon scrambles eggs.

'You should really cook those more slowly,' I begin to tell him, and then stop myself as I remember that Simon once worked as a short-order breakfast chef in a greasy-spoon café.

'Have no fear,' chuckles Simon. 'They'll be the best you've ever tasted.'

'Did I ever tell you about Pa's omelette?' I ask.

He shakes his head; grinds more pepper into the pan.

'My grandfather, Pa, ordered an omelette in a

restaurant in Provence in the 1930s. A simple, unfussy omelette. And it haunted him for the rest of his life.'

'Was it the amoebas?'

'No, it was the best thing Pa had ever tasted. So at every restaurant he went to for the next fifty years, he would insist on ordering the same thing. And of course it just made him miserable.'

'*À la recherche de l'omelette perdue,*' interjects Simon.

'Well, precisely. It's a personal thing. Anyway, so Pa would sulk, and the concept of Pa's Omelette entered the family argot, to mean any unrepeatable experience that one cannot resist attempting to repeat.'

'These eggs are ready,' says Simon. 'But I don't know if I can handle the pressure.'

# 7

## DAEDALUS

After breakfast, we roar off on Simon's ancient motorbike in search of a second-hand car: a nag for Don Quixote. I'll be bringing my little red Peugeot 205 to France – le Pug Rouge, as Marisa used to call it – but I'm going to need something more van-like for hauling wardrobes and roof timbers around the countryside. And I'd frankly prefer to have an anonymous French number-plate to hide behind, instead of feeling like an English beacon on wheels.

From his kind, open face, Monsieur Poulenc the garage-owner looks as if he should be healing sick puppies or teaching the oboe to underprivileged children, rather than selling second-hand cars.

'Help yourself,' he tells us, waving out at his forecourt from the shadows of a dark office. 'It's too hot out there.'

The first car we try is a battered white Volvo, which runs very smoothly, and strikes me as a splendid bargain at six hundred euros.

'So what do you think?' asks Simon as we scream past a village pizzeria with gaudy window-boxes, and pull back on to the garage forecourt.

'I think we should take it.'

'And what do you think about that?' he asks, pointing at the dashboard.

'Ah. Bit hot, is it?' The water-temperature needle is trembling against its upper stop.

'Radiator's knackered.'

'You see, it's lucky you're here.'

Next up is a Nissan Bluebird, with about two hundred thousand kilometres on the clock.

'I love Japanese cars,' I declare as we strap ourselves in. 'Alfie has converted me.'

Alfie is a Honda Civic that Simon found for me a couple of years ago, when I was looking for a car for Marisa. Its owner, Alf, had carefully catalogued every oil change, every wiper-blade he'd replaced, every time he had put air into the tyres, in heavy blue biro in a spiral-bound notebook, over a ten-year period. I still wonder if he catalogued his own life – or his wife's – with such care.

'I'm not sure this is another Alfie,' murmurs Simon as we accelerate past the pizzeria with the gaudy window-boxes for the second time, and the car begins to judder and veer to the right.

The third option is a big green Renault Espace with bashed and dented bodywork, and large areas where the paint appears to have blistered in the sun.

'Looks a bit dodgy to me,' I declare, casting an expert eye over the wreck.

'Nothing wrong with that,' says Simon. 'The whole thing's made of fibreglass so it won't rust. And you can always respray it if you don't like the green.' So we climb in.

'Ugh. Smell that,' I groan. The inside of the Espace is carpeted in white dog hairs. It smells as if the dog is still in here somewhere, too, quietly decomposing.

'Two sun-roofs,' replies Simon. 'This is the deluxe model. Think of all the stuff you'll be able to fit in the back. And with a French car it'll be much easier to find parts.'

So the Espace wins it by a walrus's whisker, although my hopes of driving it home today are thwarted. It still needs its *contrôle technique* certificate – a bureaucratic bill of health – so there'll be a few days' wait before I can pick it up.

'Will you take an offer?' I ask good Monsieur Poulenc.

He shakes his head. 'I'm afraid the price has been set by the local notaire. It's being sold as part of someone's estate.'

'Dead man's wheels,' murmurs Simon.

My hunch is that it belonged to the dog.

And then we're loading up the van for the third time in three days, this time with all Simon's treasures bound for England: a rug he has found at the *déchetterie*, the golf-ball sugar bowl, some shiny black clogs which are only very slightly mouldy, Zumbach's MDF throne, and so on.

'Helen won't mind,' he declares firmly, as his trophies rattle around in the back. 'The clogs will cheer her up.'

'Don't you think she might prefer some perfume?'

'Well, he didn't leave any perfume behind, did he?'

Simon is silent for a while. He is driving; I am map-reading. I have made the mistake of attempting to route us around the west side of Paris, so the autoroute is now a distant memory, and – thanks to my ineptitude – we are stuck in a traffic-jam heading in the wrong direction through a grey housing estate somewhere near Versailles. Every time we slow down, the engine stops.

'Sorry sorry sorry,' I say, running my hand through my hair as I scan the map for a way out of the labyrinth.

Simon smiles to himself. 'It's fine,' he says, leaning

forward to peer up at the grey tower blocks on either side of us. 'This is the scenic route.'

The cars in front of us begin to amble forward, and he turns the key in the ignition yet again. I can see him turning something over in his mind.

'No,' he declares at last, as if he had cracked a complicated quadratic equation. 'Helen is going to love the clogs.'

Next morning, I gaze blearily out of my curtains in East Dulwich to see Simon lifting Zumbach's precious throne into the skip outside Dave and Audrey's house. Helen stands, arms folded, in the doorway behind him. The throne looks different in the grey murk of a London morning; like a theatre prop after the lights have been turned off. The shiny black clogs follow: placed as a pair, as carefully as flowers on a grave, not willy-nilly. Then, in matching crash-helmets, he and she mount Simon's bike for the commute to Bond Street, where Helen works at something glamorous. Good old Simon. The man never tires.

Half an hour later, I hear the familiar roar of the ancient Kawasaki and Simon returns. I watch him tiptoe to the skip. With a quick glance left and right, he grabs the clogs. Then, as if he can feel me watching him, he looks up at my window, grins and strides back inside.

July and August are spent in a London limbo; a no-man's-land in which I am not quite here and not quite there. My world is about to change, that much I know. But I don't seem to be able to let go of the old, and I cannot quite grasp the new.

I make frequent trips to the magical kingdom of La Folie, ferrying my last few possessions, and gradually equipping myself for my adventure as if I were a parent kitting out a child for a new school. Each time I return, the jungle around the empty house has grown a little deeper.

I have chosen the beginning of September as the start date for my adventure, for I am coming to France to learn, and this will mark the beginning of a new school year in my life. I have always associated September with the start of good new things. I loved my schooldays, and the month also contains the anniversaries of my parents' wedding and that of my best friend, Jon; my mother's birthday; the birthdays of several of my most special girlfriends; my first flying lesson; and Battle of Britain day, which fired my childish imagination with the possibilities of heroism at the controls of a Spitfire or Hurricane.

One Saturday morning in late July, I drive through Dulwich Village to say goodbye to my friends at the tennis club. Without the people, this place would be just three tarmac courts beside a cricket pitch, in the shadow of a railway bridge across which the Eurostar rumbles several times a day, and where I have lost more matches against other teams than I care to remember.

'It's a family club,' people like to say of our cheery little enclave of surgeons and journalists and ladies who lunch. 'Winning isn't important.' This is lucky, because we never do.

'Why are you going to live in France, Michael?' asks Lavinia, the tireless lady president, perfectly dressed as ever. 'You're awfully brave.'

'Because the cat has run out of mice here in Dulwich, and because I think it may improve my backhand.'

'So when can we come and stay?'

'If you saw the house I've bought, I'm not sure you'd want to.'

'Oh, I don't know. Are you doing it up yourself?'
Always that question, going straight to the goolies.

'Er, yes and no,' I reply.

It's hard to believe that we really are all saying goodbye. Today feels like just another Saturday morning, as if we'll be back here next Saturday, and the one after that. And the next, and the next. Life as an infinite series of repetitions: as secure and comfortable as a cat that has instinctively climbed into a cardboard box, although our box happens to consist of some white lines painted on the ground.

# 8

## AUGUST: IN LIMBO

I am a marooned sailor waiting for the trade winds, as I kick my heels and count off the days until September.

The sun beats down on La Folie, hard as drumsticks on a snare. The jungle is beginning to go brown at the edges. I am, too, even though I am still coming and going between England and France; not quite here and not quite there. In the burning heat, I return to good Monsieur Poulenc's garage to pick up the Espace. Ah, that smell again. The dead dog has been rotting in the sun, and wafts out to greet me in a reeking blast when I open the door.

A black cat is watching me from the shadows as I turn the key in the ignition. The engine fires first time. I wave goodbye to Monsieur Poulenc and head off on to the open road, whistling to make up for the lack of a radio, and because I don't want to listen too carefully to the sound of the engine. Too late for that now. Twin sun-roofs, I think to myself. The deluxe model.

'I want to move my account,' I say, in my best French, to the lady in the bank.

'Then let's make an appointment for you,' she says. Fortysomething, bright smile, shapely.

'But I only want to move from one branch to another,' I explain.

'You still need an appointment.'

'Later today?'

'Tuesdays are busy. Come back on Friday. Eleven a.m.'

So Friday it is.

'*Bonjour, Monsieur.*' The same bright smile, an outstretched hand.

'*C'est Michael. Bonjour.*' She's wearing a very pretty summer dress. White, with yellow-ochre flowers.

'*Bien. Michael,*' she says. '*Et je suis Marianne Marceau.*'

'*Marianne, enchanté.*' I smile. She raises her eyebrows. And smiles, too.

Now follows a game of twenty questions, except that the number of questions has been doubled. I can see why it has been necessary to set aside so much time for our interview, as I am quizzed on whether or not I wish to receive the bank's monthly magazine, which variety of overdraft insurance I shall require, and how I like living in France.

'Well, I'm not really living here yet,' I explain. 'I'm starting in a month's time.'

'But you speak very good French already.'

'So do you.'

Marianne finds this so funny that she has to hunt for a tissue in the drawer of her desk.

'And you,' I continue, warming to my theme. 'How do you like living in Jolibois?'

'Me? Oh! Me?' she says, wide-eyed. 'I like it very much.' And as she says it, she gives me a long, sad smile. We stare at each other for a second longer than feels comfortable, and then she perks up, pursing her lips. 'But today is a good day, because it's my birthday.'

'Wonderful. Are you going to celebrate tonight?'

'No.' She shrugs. 'But perhaps my son will be coming to visit.'

'Perhaps you should go dancing.'

'But I don't know how to dance.'

'Oh, that's ridiculous. Everyone can dance. I mean, I don't know *how* to dance, but I still have a go.'

'You're very brave. You must be a good dancer.'

'Not at all. I'm a terrible dancer. But there's nothing to learn: you just jiggle around in time to the music.'

'I don't think I could do that.'

'Nonsense. We could go dancing together one day,' I say, as you do when the sun is shining and you're talking to a lady in a pretty summer dress, 'and then you'd see that it's all a question of confidence.' It's fair to say that I have never said this to my English bank manager in the Waterloo branch of Lloyds.

'Really?' beams my French bank manager, opening her appointments book. 'When did you have in mind?'

Outside the bank, a pudgy old man with a bald head and tiny eyes like currants grabs me by the arm. He looks like a human snowman.

'Anglish? Anglish?' he hisses, in a hoarse rasp of sandpaper on stone.

'*Oui, je suis anglais*,' I reply, smiling, surprised at the strength in his fingers.

'Desert rats,' he hisses, jabbing his chest with the thumb of his free hand. 'Montgorrrry. Rommel. Afrika Korps.' Jab jab jab. 'London. Tottringham Hotspur. Buckingham Palais.' He is staring fiercely at me, searching for a flicker of recognition.

'*Ah, oui. Londres*,' I concede. A small crowd has

gathered to watch us. Possibly they think I'm being mugged.

'Margaret Tatcherr. Princess Dee. God save the kings.'

'God save the kings,' I nod, embarrassed. I unhook his clawed fingers from my forearm, and begin to walk backwards, away from him. '*Et vive la France.*'

Now he grabs his bicep and forcefully jerks his arm upwards in what I take to be not a sign of peace.

'Rommel. Afrika Korps,' he snarls. 'Desert rats.'

A distant church bell chimes as I duck into the papershop, relieved to be out of the incandescent sun, and out of range of the man with no voice.

It is peaceful in here, amongst the racks of white paperbacks, the postcards of Jolibois and of local cattle, with a faint whiff of tobacco sweetness mingling with the cabbage-pong of the newsprint.

'*Bonjour Monsieur,*' I mumble to the man behind the counter, whose grey cardigan and ever-so-slightly-troubled expression lend him the air of a prep-school headmaster.

'*Bonjour,*' he replies. 'I see you have met Édouard out there. Don't worry: he's quite harmless. I have English newspapers, if that's what you're looking for.'

'*Non, merci,*' I reply, defiantly holding up a copy of *Le Populaire*, the local French rag. My encounter with the snarling Édouard has unsettled me. Can people really see that I am English, just by looking at me? I gaze down at my faded white T-shirt, threadbare empire-building shorts (extra-large) and open sandals. And I think: Yes. Of course they can.

'*Donc ça fait quatre-vingts centimes.*'

'May I ask, *Monsieur* . . .'

'*Oui?*'

'. . . How you feel about all the English people who

are moving into the area. Does it bother the locals?'

'*Pas du tout*,' he replies, raising his eyebrows as if I'd just asked him if he minded my doing the cancan in his shop. 'We like the English. They renovate the old houses that nobody wants.' And then he lowers his voice. 'We'd much rather have *les Anglais* than all these immigrants from Lille. They cause no end of trouble.' He nods meaningfully. 'Whereas the English tend to keep to themselves.'

'But you do think it's possible for *un Anglais* . . . for someone like me to become integrated in the region?'

'*Mais oui*,' he replies. 'You speak good French. But you have to be patient. It will take six months. You'll see.'

The tennis club beside Jolibois's petite football stadium is deserted. I peer through the glass doors to see the empty wicker chairs; the reservations board dotted with yellow name-plates both alien and exotic; the glass tables scattered with dog-eared tennis magazines that have Henri Leconte and Guy Forget on the covers; the poster of Amélie Mauresmo hitting a leggy, sultry backhand, stapled to the cheap wood-panelling; the kitsch trophies on every available surface. And there, through another set of glass doors beyond, I can see the dusty pink peach-skin of the clay courts fading to burnt orange at the edges; the white lines like rails waiting for a train that will never arrive; the green chain-link fencing splashed with advertising hordings. Babolat. Banque de France. Roland Garros.

We don't have banner advertising around the tennis courts in East Dulwich. We don't have wicker chairs and magazines, nor expensive red clay baking in the afternoon sun. We don't have leggy Amélie Mauresmo on the wall, although Lavinia, the president, always looks immaculate.

We have tarmac slicked with afternoon drizzle, weak backhands and a surfeit of double-faults. We certainly don't have a problem finding trophy space.

A sudden flutter, a blur of brown beating wings against the far glass. A bird is trapped inside.

'If no one in office, apply to house next door,' says a sign. So I ring the doorbell. The house's shutters are closed.

I try the door of the tennis club again, more firmly this time. The bird stares down at me from a high window-ledge. Then I walk round the back, through the gates of the empty football stadium with its empty concrete grand-stand, grey as the National Theatre beside Waterloo, out across the empty cinder track, and round to the second set of doors beside the courts.

The bird is beating itself against the glass; and then, beady-eyed, is still as I approach.

I shake the doors. Locked.

Like Jolibois tennis club, the aeroclub at St Juste is spookily silent when I visit. A bright Sunday morning, and there's no one here. Have the French heard about my arrival, and already left in disgust?

I feel as I did when I was twelve, and my parents took me to look round Sherborne – my father's old school, where I was to go after Windlesham – during the summer holidays, to see if I would be happy there. And all I saw were high windows and empty classrooms and the morbid black walls of the deserted fives courts, and I felt hollow inside.

At Rochester airport, where my Luscombe waits on the banks of the River Medway, the place will – at this very moment – be alive with students practising their circuits alongside instructors still groggy from last night's beer;

with rental pilots heading off for a hundred-pound fry-up at North Weald; with aircraft owners taking girls they fancy across the Channel to Le Touquet, hoping to impress them enough to go a little further tonight.

And then, as I stand on the apron at St Juste, I catch a glint of sunshine on metal, far out in the blue void. The buzz of an aero engine, slowing as it turns downwind. A voice from on-high, crackling on the airport tannoy: '*St Juste, Golf-Kilo-Oscar, vent-arrière zéro-sept pour un complet.*'

So it's a British plane. Golf for Great Britain. Foxtrot for France. A solo game for eccentrics who enjoy hunting for lost objects in dense undergrowth (us), versus a stylish dance for couples sensually interwined (them).

From the ghost aerodrome, there comes no reply. But the crackling voice continues, cheerfully enough: '*St Juste, Golf-Kilo-Oscar, finale zéro-sept.*' This must be the 'other' English pilot they told me about. What was the name? Peter Feste? I know it was something from *Twelfth Night*.

The yellow insect of an aeroplane is descending fast in a heavy side-slip – too fast – and I have an impending sense of bursting tyres and bending metal. Standing in the shadows of the hangars, I hold my breath. But at the last moment the nose is kicked straight and the plane appears to hover for a second before settling gently on to the shimmering runway.

'Nice landing,' I say in English, as the pilot, brushing a few strands of white hair out of his eyes, climbs from the cockpit.

'Nearly wasn't,' he says, wandering away from me into the hangar, as if he'd just returned from a dangerous sortie with the Royal Flying Corps and didn't want to talk about it. 'But thanks anyway.'

'Peter Viola, I presume,' I say, to his back.

He freezes, like someone in a film who's just been shot.

'I say, you're not from the Inland Revenue, are you?' he says, turning round. He grins, regards me with growing interest. Tall, with bright-blue eyes that look younger than his crinkled skin, and a voice straight out of a black-and-white film. I guess he's about seventy; he looks like a child in a Hallowe'en costume.

'Just a fellow pilot,' I shrug, 'hoping to keep my plane here one day.'

'Oh, yes?' His eyes twinkle bluer than ever, as he narrows them. '*Tu parles français?*'

'*Oui, bien sûr,*' I reply, hoping not to be struck down by a thunderbolt.

'Well, that makes a change, I must say. I have a good feeling about this meeting. Let's go and have a coffee, shall we? I'll take you to the best place in town. By the way, how did you know my name?'

And so I make my first proper friend in France. Peter is not *un vrai français*, admittedly, but he's even more in love with France than I am, and we speak French to each other as we queue at the gleaming stainless-steel servery of the supermarket café opposite the aerodrome. I order a *café allongé*; Peter, a cappuccino with whipped cream, sugar, chocolate shavings, the works.

'Good evening, Peter,' trills the girl behind the till, fluttering her long eyelashes and pronouncing the words in such a heavy French accent that at first I don't even notice that she is speaking English. 'And 'ow are you?' Red-haired, petite, pretty as an autumn sunrise.

'Really spiffing, thanks,' he says.

'Speeffing?' She looks confused.

'Very useful word,' he assures her. 'And you, how are *you*?'

'Yes, I very speeffing also,' she giggles. 'Thank you.'

'All the girls here are lovely,' whispers Peter, as we carry our coffees to a table by the window. 'I'm teaching them English. We have some brilliant jokes.'

The place is almost deserted, save for a handful of grey-haired couples murmuring over the debris of their roast chicken, and as many waitresses wiping tables, beaming and waving at Peter when they spot him. I gaze around me; at the grey formica tables, distortedly reflected in the corrugated-chrome ceiling; at the black-and-purple office chairs, which must have looked dated on the day they were new; at the neon sign announcing *Toilettes* in racy italics, as if it were advertising a brand of beer. We are a long way from anyone's idea of an archetypal French rural café. And yet as I chat to Peter in the midst of this grey scene, and the shadows slowly lengthen outside, I can think of nowhere I would rather be.

'So what brings you to France?' he asks, wiping a moustache of whipped cream from his upper lip.

'I was too comfortable in London, if that doesn't sound smug,' I begin, searching his twinkling gaze for a response. 'I wanted to make my life interestingly difficult, and to see if I could integrate myself into a new culture. No disrespect to you, Peter, but I'm wary of becoming stuck in some English ghetto.'

'Fascinating.' He chuckles, folding and unfolding his arms. 'Do you know, I was just about to say the very same thing to you? I'm *so* pleased we've met. I really do have a good feeling about this. And I'm sure you'll have a hangar space for your plane in a jiffy. What did you say it was?'

'It's a Luscombe. 1946; fabric wings; sixty-five horse-power Continental.'

'A *Luscombe Silvaire*. How wonderful. I used to have an Auster myself. And you'll love the old boys at the club.

Excellent bunch. Oh, I know Marcel can be a bit of an oil-rag at times, but . . .'

'Marcel?'

'Of course, you haven't met him yet. I think "curmudgeonly" might be the general verdict, although he and I have had some tremendous laughs together. And he deserves some sort of a medal for all the planes he's crashed.'

'I'm already looking forward to meeting him.'

Later, after I have exchanged phone numbers with Peter, and he has promised to put in a good word for me with the committee, I drop into the supermarket next door to buy some fish for supper. And here I experience another small epiphany. For the lady behind the fish counter is the most beautiful lady-behind-a-fish-counter I have ever seen. Even in her white wellies and plastic apron, she dazzles. And she smiles at me in a way that no one in France, until today, has ever smiled at me before.

Our eyes meet and, distracted into largesse, I order two pounds of monkfish. I hope it doesn't look as if I'm buying for a wife and children. As she sticks the price on the bag and hands it to me, I am questing with my eyes for the gift of another smile, in the same way that the cat will claw at my trouser-leg in the hope of a few more morsels of diet food for porky cats. But my Botticelli in white wellies has already moved on to her next customer.

Back in England, there are still loose ends to knot, and people I want to see for the last time, before I dive into the deep-end of my French life. Despite the waitresses at the supermarket café, and the lady behind the fish counter, I still have Zumbach's warning ringing in my ears. In Jolibois, as far as I can see, women appear to go from fifteen to fifty, like caterpillars metamorphosing into moths. In between, they vanish; into marriage and children and jobs in Poitiers or Limoges.

It's not that I suddenly want to get married myself. But neither do I want to remain entirely marooned at La Folie; a hermit in his cave.

I phone a girl called Amy, who gave me her mobile number and email address at a party two years ago. I remember she was pretty and animated and wore a powder-blue dress, and said she was interested in living in France one day. I asked her if she'd like to come flying with me that summer, and yes, she said, yes, she'd love to. And I never phoned.

Now, with my French future looming, I phone Amy's mobile. 'We are sorry. The number dialled has not been recognized.' So I send an email to her work, little imagining that anyone in London could still be in the same job after two years. In cities, things change so fast.

I borrow Alfie from Marisa and drive down to Rochester, desperate to fly my Luscombe for one last time before my enforced separation from it. Today is a perfect English summer's day, and the two ground-staff in their fluorescent yellow waistcoats seem almost alarmingly cheerful as we manoeuvre the plane out of its hangar. Even Nigel, the gloomiest man in Britain, raises a smile when I thank him for his trouble. Amazing, what a difference a little sunshine makes.

I walk around the Luscombe, doing my pre-flight checks beneath the buzzing drone of aircraft arriving and departing from the busy circuit. Brakes on. Stick tied back. Wheels chocked. Standing in front of the propeller, I haul time after time on its twin blades, until the little Continental finally coughs into life.

After dragging away the chocks, I climb up into the cockpit and strap myself in, relieved to put on my headset to deaden the deafening clatter of the engine drumming snare-drum rudiments on the steel firewall at my feet. The oil pressure's good. And when the oil temperature finally begins to rise, I call up the tower.

'*Rochester Information, good afternoon. Golf-Bravo-Papa-Zulu-Alpha is a Luscombe on the apron; request taxi for VFR local to the south-east; one POB.*'

'*Golf Zulu-Alpha, this is Rochester Information.*' I recognize the confident, patrician drawl of Philip in the tower, who always reminds me of a ball-by-ball cricket commentator on Radio Four. '*Good afternoon to you, too. Taxi for runway two-zero via the eastern taxiway. QNH is 1021. Looks like a lovely day for it.*'

'*1021 and two-zero via the eastern. Thanks, Philip. Golf-Zulu-Alpha.*'

Lining up on the grass runway, stick held back, I make a final scan of the Luscombe's primitive instruments, remind myself to keep my heels well clear of the brakes, and slowly squeeze the throttle all the way forward. The roar of the engine surges to full power as we begin our bumpy acceleration across the grass. Revs good. Airspeed increasing. Temperatures and pressures still in the green. I push the stick forward to raise the tailwheel and, after a few more seconds of jolting, gently ease it backwards, just enough to allow the Luscombe to release itself from the cool grass and begin a steady climb at seventy mph.

And then I am soaring over the Kent and Sussex countryside at 2,400 feet, newly struck by the green loveliness of England, with its patchwork fields and dark woods and the tiny white dots of men playing village cricket on a Saturday afternoon.

My route, unconsciously planned, takes me up over the disused base at Tangmere where Pa used to train pilots in the war, in the days before a French omelette had blighted his life, and down over the white Hs of the rugby posts on the games pitches of Windlesham, where Clara Delaville never did fall in love with me and Amelia Blunt's breasts made me afraid. It all looks so different from up here.

In the distance, I can see the English Channel. Beyond it, close enough to imagine, yet too far away to see, is France.

An hour later, I am once again on the apron at Rochester, wiping flecks of oil from the Luscombe's cowling, still lost in my own world. Nigel waddles out from the café, muttering about his tea-break, and helps me push the plane back into its dark hangar. I wish I knew when I will fly again. For all Peter Viola's optimism, I know that the waiting list for the new hangar at St Juste is long. And vintage planes with fabric-covered wings do not enjoy camping outside.

The following day, amid the cardboard boxes and dusty receipts and wistful memories that litter the house Marisa and I shared in East Dulwich, I play my parents' old grand piano for one last time before it goes into storage, too. It will be a while before there is space for the instrument at La Folie. I'll need to turn the dusty stone shell of the summer sitting-room into a habitable music room, before it can make its enharmonic leap.

I shut my eyes as my fingers sink into the familiar weight of the gleaming keys. I play 'I Can't Help Falling In Love With You'. And then Chopin, the 3rd Ballade, and Schubert's A-major piano sonata. My parents used to have a scratchy Ashkenazy recording of the Schubert, and it was always the one piece I wanted to be able to play when I grew up. The next time I play it on this piano, we will both be in France.

There is a knock at the front door. It's Simon, my

heroic neighbour and fellow driver from across the road.

'I thought I heard the piano,' he says, grinning from the steps. 'Not getting too sentimental, are you? We're going to miss being woken up by that thing first thing on a Sunday morning.'

I grimace. 'And the drunken caterwauling of Abba songs in the early hours.'

'That too,' he nods. 'At least at La Folie you won't have any neighbours to disturb.'

'Oh, I'm sure I shall find a few sheep to torment.'

'Fancy a final game of tennis?' he asks. 'I know we took your racquets to France, but I'll let you borrow the Hazel Streamline.'

'Lovely idea,' I laugh, 'but I really don't have time.'

Simon rubs his chin. 'Need a bicycle?'

'Sorry?'

'I've got fourteen in the garden, and Helen's decreed that I get rid of them. Thought you might want one or two for La Folie.'

'I seem to remember that Monsieur Zumbach left me a couple in the barn. But where did you get them all?'

'Oh, you know. Teenage drug-dealers, mostly. They steal them and leave them against the railings in the street.'

'But Simon, just because a bicycle isn't locked doesn't mean it's stolen.'

'Around here it does,' he declares. 'And it seems such a shame just to leave them for someone else to steal again.'

'Whereas if you squirrel them away in your garden, that isn't stealing?'

'No, because I'm just looking after them until someone needs a bicycle. Such as you, for example, when friends come to stay at La Folie.'

'Simon, I really don't want your hot *bicyclettes*. But yes: I hope you and Helen will come and visit very soon.'

'Don't worry,' he says. 'We'll be there. I can't wait to see the transformation.'

A week before I begin my adventure, Amy and I meet for dinner. She received my email, after all. And yes, she wrote back, she'd love to meet up for a drink or whatever.

I'm glad we have agreed to meet under the statue of Julius Caesar at Tower Hill, as I'm not sure I would have recognized her. It didn't occur to me that she might not be wearing a powder-blue dress. But it's a perfect summer's evening, and the gentle breeze plays in Amy's hair as we sit on a restaurant terrace overlooking the Thames, sipping gin-and-tonics from heavy tumblers clinking with ice.

'I'm so grateful to have this perfect London moment,' I tell her. The meal is ended, and we are cradling our coffee cups as the darkness falls. 'You know, the river, Tower Bridge, this restaurant, the twinkling lights, dinner with a lovely someone I hardly know; the sense of life flowing by, that we're right in the middle of it all here.'

Amy smiles, staring into her coffee.

'The place in France where I will be living,' I continue, 'it's just so different. And I suppose that's what I'm appreciating, right now, here, with you. A moment in my life.'

I'm not trying to chat her up, and I don't think it's the gin-and-tonic speaking. I just feel unusually struck by how beautiful the city looks tonight, balanced as I am, Janus-like, on the threshold between two worlds; two different lives. It's like that moment, just before the end of a long transatlantic flight, when you dare to start talking to the person next to you, and discover that there is more to them than you would have thought possible. Amy, still silent, gazes out across the Thames.

'You know, I think of London as noisy and dirty and

full of concrete and stressed-out workers wishing they were somewhere else. But just look at this now. It's so perfect.'

'This river,' murmurs Amy at last. And then, brightening: 'Will you have a garden in France?'

'I will have a jungle which, gradually, I mean to tame.'

'That's sad. Better to leave it as a jungle.'

'Yes, but if you saw it . . .' The words linger in the air. 'Look, do you think you might come and visit one day?'

'I've only just met you,' laughs Amy, 'and now you're inviting me to your French love-nest.'

'I didn't say it was a love-nest.'

'Nevertheless.'

'Well, it was just an idea. No pressure. Just a thought.'

'We'll see,' says Amy gently, walking to the railings overlooking the river.

'Please don't jump.'

Amy doesn't reply. She is gazing down into the twinkling lights and skyscrapers bobbing and glimmering on the water's mirrored surface, a mirror flowing out and away, past Greenwich and Rotherhithe, past the shiny-faced men emerging from bars, past the wives looking at their watches as they flick through the channels one last time, carrying driftwood and plastic bottles and dead animals and broken dreams out into the wide estuary and the sea beyond.

Standing beside her, hands in my pockets, I lean ever so slightly to the right until our shoulders are just touching. London. This breeze on my face. As I gaze up at one of the gleaming office-blocks on the other side of the river, one of the lights in one of the dozens of windows is extinguished. And then, a few seconds later, the one next door lights up. I reach out with my fingers to touch Amy's hand.

Hers clasps mine, and we stand like that, watching the river glimmer. It might be minutes or seconds or hours. Then I put my arm around her shoulders, pull her towards me, and kiss her.

The river looks even more beautiful now, and Tower Bridge is white and purple and blue, glowing in the dazzling lights.

Goodbye, London. Farewell, ancient river. Adieu, Amy, whom – too late – I have only just met.

# 9

## SEPTEMBER: THE NEMEAN LION

I have a friend who is an eminent psychiatrist, a fact that would undoubtedly have had Great-Aunt Beryl tutting 'You *see*? You *see*?' into her teacup. And the eminent psychiatrist warns me that human beings tend not to fare well in isolation.

On the Friday before I finally depart for my new adventure, we are playing poker at his house, an event which always leaves me socially richer and economically poorer.

'We're worried about you, Michael,' says the eminent psychiatrist, laying three aces on the table and casually using his forearm to sweep another stack of my dwindling resources into his vast pile of chips. 'Are you sure you'll be able to cope?'

'With the next hand?'

'No, in France.' He shuffles the cards with the languor of someone who has won far too much already.

'To be quite honest, I have no idea,' I reply. 'It's an adventure. An experiment. A test.'

'What sort of test?'

'I don't know. A test of character. A chance to expl—' I can see his brain whirring. He must be wondering why I think I *need* a test of character. 'What?' I laugh. 'What is it?'

'We'll miss you on poker nights,' he says with an innocent shrug, beginning to sort his chips into phallic piles.

'You're very kind,' I say. 'But I really think you're earning enough money as it is without needing to fleece me every Friday night. And I promise to phone if I think I'm going batty.'

'But that's just it,' he says, shaking his head. 'You're likely to be the last to know.' For some reason the eminent psychiatrist appears to find this tremendously funny.

The cat doesn't know it yet, but she's coming to La Folie, too. Don Quixote must have his Sancho Panza, however furry. Especially since I have discovered that I am sharing the house with a large number of skittering rodents – which would explain why Zumbach looked so joyful when I told him I'd be bringing a mouser.

Worrying about the cat's transport is a good thing, because it takes my mind off my own last-minute jitters. Am I making a horrible mistake? In East Dulwich, I'm just packing the last few bags into the car when Simon's girlfriend, Helen, emerges from number five, opposite, and dumps two shiny black objects that look strangely familiar into the dustbin.

'I do think you're terribly brave, Michael,' she says, making chip-chop-good-riddance gestures with her hands.

'Taking a poor, defenceless cat to France?'

'No, going to live there on your own.'

The truth is that I don't feel very brave at all, nor do Helen's words swell my chest with pride. Many people over the past few weeks have told me that what I'm doing is scary and admirable and courageous and they wish they were brave enough to do the same thing. And it makes me wonder. My adventure may have seemed brave as an idea in prospect, but now that it is something that I – the non-brave, non-hero – am actually doing, it seems no more brave than waltzing across a dance-floor or going to the launderette. Indeed, it makes me nervous when people say what I'm doing is brave, because perhaps they know something I don't.

Brave is Ellen MacArthur setting off to sail around the world on her own, or Lance Armstrong lining up at the start of another Tour de France, knowing the pain that lies ahead. Brave is Émilie's husband Fred, who is not a builder, yet who is renovating a house at the very zenith of the estate agents' virility test, a house with no drains or water or electricity or anything. And he's doing it with his bare hands. Brave cannot be what I am doing, for I have always known that I am not.

I can see, however, that there is a difference between my adventure and the one that lies in prospect for the cat. I have made a choice, choosing action in favour of inaction, movement in place of stasis. She will be drugged and trapped in a box driven by someone else, en route to a place she wouldn't naturally choose for herself. Like all those people commuting to jobs they hate, who tell me I'm being brave.

Officially, Marisa and I share joint responsibility for the cat, following our parting of the ways. But by dint of the fact that I am moving to a mouseful house in the midst of a jungle wilderness, and she now lives in a first-floor flat on one of the scariest streets in South London, she has awarded me custody. Fortunately, Marisa retains a sense of quasi-parental responsibility towards the creature we chose together so many years ago.

'I'll hold her and you give her the pill,' she tells me, at the allotted hour of the appointed day, as we struggle to anaesthetize our unwilling traveller. Ryanair won't take pets, so we are to drive from London to La Folie in le Pug Rouge. This means nine hours in the car with a muzzy moggy. Thank goodness Marisa has agreed to come too.

The two of us still get on well; we rarely stoop to pushing each other's buttons, though we know exactly where they are located. No, Marisa feels like a comrade from a campaign fought long ago, or the other half of a double-act in which we both performed several seasons of the same end-of-pier show. I think the world of her.

The vet says the feline knock-out pill will take an hour to kick in, and should last three hours. By Dartford, the cat is already woozy. By the time we enter the Channel Tunnel she's snoring like a whoopee cushion. And shortly after Calais, she is motionless on her back with all four legs in the air, mouth and eyes wide open. Now I'm no vet, but I know a dead cat when I see one.

'Do you think she's OK?' I gulp, peering into the rear-view mirror.

'Oh my God,' gasps Marisa. 'I think we've killed her.'

Stricken, I stare at the Autoroute unfolding ahead of us. Thanks to my selfish desire for an adventure in France, I've just bumped off a perfectly decent cat. We drive on in silence, chain-sucking Vichy tablets. What's the French for pet cemetery?

By Paris, there are signs of a feline resurrection. A paw twitches; an eyelid blinks. A cheering aroma of ammonia wafts through the car. Cat pee never smelt so good. And when Marisa leans out of the window to pay the toll at the Autoroute's final *péage*, our little Lazarus even makes a woozy bid for escape. One life down. Eight to go.

It's past six p.m. by the time we bump up the drive to La Folie.

'Is this land all yours?' asks Marisa, impressed.

'No. It starts at these blue gates.'

'Even so . . .'

We're there, at La Folie. Marisa makes all the right 'ooh' and 'aah' noises as I show her round, while the cat – stiff-legged, tail held high as a periscope – displays exaggerated disgust.

I find myself making excuses to Marisa for all the things that aren't quite perfect yet. 'It'll look better without the crumpled zinc on the barn doors . . . I'm planning to mow that jungle . . .'

'I see the spiders have made themselves at home.' She shivers, gazing up at the grey candyfloss between the smoke-blackened beams in the winter sitting-room.

'That means there'll be fewer flies,' I declare confidently.

'So what are those?' Marisa is pointing at the brittle husks of perhaps a hundred bluebottles, laid out on the window-sill like Spartans after Thermopylae.

'Maybe French spiders are fussy about what they eat.'

'Let's sit outside.'

'That's where I usually sit,' I say, but Marisa has already vanished on to the terrace.

The cat looks alarmed. Her ears are going wild – twitching and twisting left and right, directed towards the latest threatening new sound of bird or insect or scuttling critter. She is hearing new noises and smelling new smells for the first time. She can probably hear mice whispering to each other in French.

Her reaction stops me in my tracks.

I imagined I would be wonderfully sensitive to my new surroundings, yet all I have done so far is stand and look at the trees and label them as beautiful. And, once labelled, things become invisible. It's so easy to label France as a surrogate England, only with better weather and proper tomatoes. But look: the cat is really listening.

And for the first time, as I sit on the terrace with Marisa, immersed in the whirring of the crickets, I am conscious – in a visceral, physical sense – that this is indeed another country; another countryside.

'I hope you're both going to be all right here,' she says, sounding as if this is exceedingly unlikely. 'No one will think less of you if it all gets a bit much and you want to come home.'

'We'll be all right. And I'll have the chickens for company.'

'Chickens?' She stares at me as if I were three years old and my face were covered in Chocolate Spread.

'I've always wanted chickens.'

'You never mentioned it.'

'You never asked,' I reply, and we both laugh.

Tomorrow I shall drive Marisa to Limoges airport, and she will return to her London life. And I shall come back alone to La Folie, and sit on my terrace with the cat, gazing out across the valley, and wonder what the hell we're doing here.

Hello. What the hell are *they* doing here? With Marisa safely dropped off at the airport, I am nudging my way up the drive in le Pug Rouge, when a white Citroën van – thoroughly beaten up and sprayed with orange mud – comes surging down in the opposite direction.

We both brake, with a squish of rubber on wet leaves. The collision avoided, the van-driver and I exchange smiles. I feel more relieved than he looks. Then he gestures at me, and begins to reverse so fast that I barely dare keep pace with him. Tucked into a corner, he waves me past. Two sheepdogs stare at me, bright-eyed, from behind his head.

Back at La Folie, I am relieved to find that the door is still locked. I have nothing of any value here, but still I run my eyes over the things that matter: my pilot's log-book; my lacquered fountain pen; the cat. It's all still here. So the man in the van wasn't a burglar. Besides, he didn't look like a burglar. Bright-eyed, like his dogs, and with a twinkly grin. Considering his familiarity with my drive, I can't help thinking that we shall meet again.

I have never been a fan of routines. Routines send the brain to sleep. But in the face of my daunting freedom and unbounded new life, I am surprised to find myself creating one or two of them after all. Each morning, for example, I swing my leg over the rusty old bicycle I found in the barn, and wish that I'd accepted Simon's offer of one of his whizzy reclaimed bikes. Then I freewheel down the drive, gazing at the jungle on my left and attempting to picture it as a vegetable patch full of spuds and tomatoes and aubergines, swelling in the sun. I must find a friendly gardener to advise me, I tell myself, as I prepare for the assault on the south face of the town. It's a steep hill, and my thighs burn as I push towards the summit and the *boulangerie.*

Yet the ride itself is not nearly such a challenge as try-ing to raise a smile from the sulky princess who works behind the counter. I suspect she is no more than eighteen, for she regards me with exaggerated disdain.

'*Ah, bonjour!*' I exclaim each day, louder than is strictly necessary. '*Et comment va la journée?*'

She regards me as blankly as if I were a croissant that hasn't quite risen.

'*Il fait beau, oui?*' I persist, wheeling out yet another of the brightest gems in my dazzling French repartee.

The princess frowns and shrugs. Beautiful eyelashes shading flashing dark eyes. Delicate lips curved into a tiny cupid's bow, which – day after day – fires arrows marked '*Non!*' in my direction. For the princess has her routine, too. And so, with a sigh in my heart, and a crusty *baguette de campagne* poking out of the top of my rucksack, I haul myself back on to my rusty charger, ready for the head-long hurtle back to La Folie.

Today, on my way down the Rue du Coq, I stop to look at the cards in the window of the *tabac*. A Franciscan monk called Frère Sébastien is looking for gardening work. This is almost too good to be true, I tell myself, as I stand on the pedals for the final, bumpy climb up the drive to the house. I have been wondering how to find someone to come and examine my jungle; someone not too expensively professional, to help me create a vegetable patch and teach me how to tend the many unidentified fruit trees. I am a stranger in this strange land, and my own ignorance scares me. But a monk: that's not scary at all.

Frère Sébastien is not wearing a cassock when he bundles up to La Folie in his white Citroën van. I'm disappointed about the cassocklessness – how can I be sure he's a real monk? – but clerical robes are presumably not practical for digging up spuds.

Nor does Frère Sébastien have a tonsure, nor Caesar sandals. Instead, he wears a yellow lifeboatman's anorak, sports a brillantined fifties quiff, and has a lined face that makes him look as if he probably did some hard-living before he found Jesus. I wonder if I should ask to see his monkish ID, and think better of it. From the way he greets me – pressing my palm between both of his – and the hushed tones in which he tells me how much he loves the savagery of my jungle and how Jesus loves us all, I think it's safe to say that he's a monk.

'*Quel beau terrain!*' he exclaims, with such rapture that I'm half wondering if he's going to kneel down and kiss the earth. Or, from the way he appears to have connected so immediately and intimately with the landscape of La Folie, if he will ask if he can come and live with me, in a willow cabin at my gate.

'Yes, I'm very lucky,' I reply. 'But I don't know much – in fact, *je ne sais rien* – about plants. I'm hoping you might be able to help me.'

'*Ah, bien sûr*,' he says, striding down to the broken fence – a confusion of rotting posts and mangled chicken-wire – that surrounds the old *potager*. 'We must get rid of this, and build a new one. The posts will be chestnut, their tips painted with tar so they do not rot in the earth. And there will be paths, here, and here. He maps out the shape of a cross. And over here . . .' – he strides off again – '. . . this will be the orchard.'

I prepare a simple lunch for us both – *pâté forestier*; pasta with fresh tomato sauce; a few cheeses – and from the way Frère Sébastien wolfs it down, I suspect it may be a while since he last ate. At first he makes me rather glad I never removed the gold papier-mâché Jesus that Zumbach – who is, I think, devoutly pagan – left hanging in the kitchen, and which I have decided somehow suits the place. And then I begin to regret it very much.

Daunted by Frère Sébastien's charismatic approach to gardening, I dare not contact him again.

The other white van – the one with the sheepdogs – passes me several times over the next fortnight. Our waving becomes more enthusiastic, and I stop resenting the fact that what had felt like my private driveway turns out to be a shared thoroughfare to nowhere. A small grass track snakes off it, just below La Folie, and it is down here that the twinkly smile vanishes, sometimes with a lady in the seat beside him. Perhaps it is a lovers' lane.

And then, one Saturday morning towards the end of September, the white van turns into the bottom of the drive just as I am rattling down it, en route to the market at St Juste. This time there is room for the two cars to pass. Room for us to stop, too.

I climb out of the Espace, staring at the ground, and wander over to the Citroën, doing my best not to look too threatening. The driver's door opens.

'*Bonjour*,' I say, reaching out my hand.

'*Bonjour*,' replies the twinkly smile, gazing into the distance. A stocky, sweet-faced man, he wears a ragged grey jumper over a faded tartan shirt that looks as if there must be some pyjama bottoms to go with it, too. The raffish wave in his greying hair, coupled with a roughly trimmed beard, make me think he should really be wearing a cloak and carrying a minstrel's harp. I'd guess he is in his mid-fifties, and that age agrees with him, like a stiff pair of shoes becoming softer with wear. He shakes my hand with what may be a Masonic grip. It feels odd, as if he's jamming his knuckle, hard, into my palm.

There's a silence, so I press on.

'*Er, je suis Michael. J'habite ici, à La Folie.*'

'*Ah, enchanté*,' he replies, sounding anything but enchanted.

'*Vous habitez là-haut?*' I ask, pointing up the drive.

'*Oh, non, non*,' he chuckles, with much shrugging, before adding something I don't catch and doing some pointing of his own in roughly the same direction.

'*Ah, d'accord*,' I reply, hoping that it is appropriate to

agree with whatever it was he said. 'And you, *Monsieur*. You are Monsieur . . . ?'

'Valette, Gilles Valette.'

'And we are neighbours?'

He shrugs. 'Josette and I live at the *moulin* just after the next bridge. So yes, I suppose we are neighbours.'

'Then it's especially good to meet you.'

'Would you, ah, would you like to drop round for *un apéro* at midday on Sunday?' he says, looking at Josette. At first I don't even notice that this is a question, let alone that it is aimed at me.

'*Eh, bien sûr! Avec plaisir!*' I reply with an enthusiasm which drives him a step backwards, and I see him gulp as if he were swallowing a pill. '*Merci bien, Monsieur Valette.*'

And then I motor off to St Juste yelling tuneless bits of *Die Walküre* to myself, for my neighbour has invited me for a drink on Sunday, which means that I am on my way.

# 10

## OCTOBER: CERBERUS

From the speed with which I come dashing out to greet him every morning, my specs still misted up from shaving in the murk of my subterranean bathroom, the postman – a grinning bald head in a yellow van – must think I'm barking mad.

The truth is that I am desperate for any human contact in the lunar landscape of La Folie. I have now notched up my first month of solitude, and feel absurdly grateful that the postman takes the trouble to come bumping up the drive at all. Especially when it's just to bring me this week's catalogue of special offers on pork from Netto and Champion, or the latest missive generated by France Telecom's bureaucracy-maximization department.

I can't wait for the telephone to be connected. I still use my old UK mobile for emergencies and monks, but a land-line will feel like an oxygen link between my lonely eyrie and the outside world. La Folie has no gas, no mains drainage, and only receives electricity thanks to an extension cable attached to the nearest farmhouse half a mile away.

*DANGER DE MORT* yells a cheery red sign just outside the back door. I'm glad the cat can't read French, or this would freak her out.

I have no television, and my radio appears to have a filter on it that excludes all stations except religious ones. The phone does have a dial tone, but since the line remains as dead as the local nightlife, this is a bit like having a purr with no cat attached. And Zumbach swears that he told France Telecom I was moving in. I should have sorted the thing out sooner, but it didn't seem terribly important at the start. Who wants a telephone on a desert island?

For 'security reasons', every new home-owner in France is assigned a new number. Unfortunately, security is so tight that France Telecom can't tell me what mine is. When I try to make a call, I am at first encouraged to hear a recorded female on the other end of the line. I listen to her message several times, partly because it's a voice – any voice – and partly because it takes me a few goes to work out what she's saying. I *think* she's telling me very firmly that I have no right to take such liberties, and that she'll come round and personally chop off my fingers if I don't hang up right now. Or words to that effect.

'We are pleased to inform you that today you spoke to one of our advisers,' says one of the many letters that arrive. 'We are pleased to inform you that you have a new number,' says another, before continuing: 'We are pleased to inform you that we will write to you soon and tell you what this number is.' I'm half expecting them to reveal the number digit by digit in bi-monthly instalments.

But after a few more letters, the phone rings and I almost jump out of my skin. It's my mother. 'Oh, you're *there*,' she says.

Yes, we are pleased to inform you that I'm here. And

I'm happy to learn that she and my father are already planning their first visit. This is good because it might just inspire me to clean the bathroom. Good, too, because I want them to be able to stop worrying about me. I'm trusting that when they see La Folie for themselves, they'll finally understand why I'm here.

'Should we bring Marmite?' asks my mum.

'No. Just survival gear and a torch.' She clearly doesn't realize how *French* I've become.

'And PG Tips?'

'Well, OK. A box of 160 wouldn't go amiss.'

Next day, I am lying in bed, staring at the mysterious knot-hole in the ceiling above my bed, while the early-morning sun comes blazing in through the window as if someone were making a film out there. Mornings are my secondary thinking time, at least until the cat stirs and starts yowling about the emptiness of the abyss that is her stomach. And this morning I am thinking about chickens.

There comes a time in every man's life when he must buy some chickens, and mine has come. Never mind that the sum total of my chicken knowledge comes from watching *Chicken Run* on video. I once knew a lady who kept budgerigars, and they can't be all that different.

Chickens will, I have no doubt, teach me something about life. And they will provide a gentle introduction to animal care, in preparation for the day – far into the future – when I may feel man enough to buy some sheep. Curiously, every shop in Jolibois sells great sacks of chicken-feed, with the exception of the paper shop and the *pompes funèbres*, which is currently advertising a sale of funerary monuments. Yet I have never seen a hen for sale.

More pressingly, the days are getting shorter, the evenings cooler, and still I have no firewood for the wood-burning stove. This is a worry, particularly with my parents' visit on the horizon. Apart from my thermals and a couple of blow-heaters that wouldn't heat a sausage, that stove will be my only weapon against the winter cold.

Trouble is, I cannot see how I am ever going to persuade anyone to reverse their tractor-plus-heavily-laden-trailer up the assault course of the drive. La Folie has stood on its foundations for nearly five hundred years. The place was designed for horses. So there's nowhere to turn around. My ideal visitor would arrive on a donkey.

I lie in bed, wondering where I am to find chickens, while the sunlight streams over me. Curled up against my chest, the cat lies purring like an unusually fluffy dial-tone. It's Sunday, and the day of my French social debut. But my mind keeps going back to chickens.

Down in the valley I hear the jangle of a distant electric bell, and then the approaching artillery of a train. That will be the 07.15 to Limoges. I must potter down to the railway line one morning, to take a proper look.

Later, at five minutes to midday, I climb into the Espace, tell myself that I shall one day get used to the smell, and rattle down the drive to Valette's raggle-taggle farmhouse. It's the first time I've been here, and I look both ways before bouncing across the tiny level-crossing – the one whose bell I must have heard this morning, and every morning – casually scrutinized by four cows in the field on my left. Even though it's only for a snifter before lunch, I have washed my face and put on a clean shirt.

From the level-crossing, the house looks as if it must once have been an old mill, powered by the same river that I am just beginning to hear splashing at the bottom of the hill on still days, now that the leaves have begun to fall. Rather like La Folie, most of the building is taken up with a pair of barns, while the small living quarters are bolted on at one end, like the engine of a two-carriage steam train on a rural branch line.

Smoke slants from the chimney as I roar into the farm-yard, my approach sending chickens flying in all directions. A pair of sheepdogs runs alongside the Espace, splashing through the mud, baying for my blood. But it's the smoke that holds my attention. Perhaps Monsieur Valette will be able to sell me some firewood.

Unfortunately, from the expression on his face when he comes out to see what the commotion's all about, it doesn't even look as if he's expecting me.

I wish he'd call off his dogs. His hounds leap up at my chest in a blatant attempt to amputate my nose. I flinch, turning my face away from the slavering jaws, though it turns out that the dogs want no more than to imprint my nice clean shirt with their gloopy paws.

''*Scusez les chiens*,' mutters Valette, shaking my hand, and giving one of the dogs a hearty kick. Again, that weird handshake, the knuckle in my palm. I don't know how to tell him that I'm not a member of the Rotary Club.

'*Pas de problème*,' I reply. 'It's kind of you to invite me.' I watch his face carefully, to see if he remembers.

'*Ahh-ouf*,' he says, with an unsmiling shrug, motioning me inside. Outside, the dogs cringe and cower as he barks something at them.

The kitchen is darker than I was expecting. I can see a woman in the shadows by the stove, which is throwing out the heat of a blast-furnace. A tall, dark-haired young man is sitting like a thundercloud at the table. He rises to shake my hand, murmurs something, frowns, and sits down again. The woman now shuffles over, and I recognize her as Josette, the other face in the white van. I shake her hand, too.

Perhaps they don't have any electricity, is my first, excited thought. Perhaps that ancient pump in the yard outside is all they have for running water. Perhaps the whole family sleeps in one bed, with the dogs, for warmth. We are as far from London as I could ever have dreamed. But when my eyes become accustomed to the gloom, my rapture at having stumbled upon some atavistic peasant hovel soon evaporates. An enormous wide-screen television dominates one end of the room, with twin video and DVD players beneath it. On the wall, proud young men pose in army uniforms, and Michael Schumacher raises his arms in a Ferrari. I am disappointed to note that the floor is of linoleum, not peat or straw or stone.

The strip-light above our heads flashes once, twice, on, and we all squint at each other, dazzled by the glare. Valette points to a chair, and I sit.

There is a selection of bottles on the table, most of whose labels I do not recognize. After the disappointment of the electrics, this is good. I feel very Abroad. I gaze expectantly at the bottles, then at my host, and then down at the paw-prints on my shirt. Nobody moves. Nobody speaks.

Unfortunately, given a silence, I always feel a strong urge to dive into it.

'And how are the sheep?' I ask Valette.

'*Ça va*,' he growls.

'Is it a lot of work?'

'Sometimes.' The silence deepens. I stare at the bottles, hoping that they will begin to pour themselves. The others exchange glances, the woman in the shadows looking accusingly at her husband, as if he'd tramped in with something evil on the sole of his shoe.

'*Et vous, Monsieur*,' I say, turning to the young thundercloud beside me. '*Vous habitez ici, aussi?*'

'No, I live elsewhere,' he replies, raising his eyebrows at the thought.

'And that would be where, exactly?'

'Châteaudun.'

'Oh, really? And what's that like?'

He shrugs and looks at Valette. '*Ça va.*'

I bite my lip and decide to go with the silence after all.

This turns out to be the right thing to do, because now Valette asks me what I'd like to drink. Eeny-meeny-miny-mo. I point at the bottle of Pastis – it's time I learned to like the stuff – and feel a twitch of relief as the taciturn young man follows suit. Valette pours a shot of something red and radioactive for Josette, while he himself settles for a bright-yellow liquid that looks like something you might use for cleaning the floor of an abattoir.

My drink is calling to me, but we are to do some more silent contemplation first, our filled glasses untouched on the plastic tablecloth before us. My mind is whizzing, and these three French people are – it dawns on me at last – dancing to an entirely different rhythm. There's no hurry, no need to fill every available split-second of time, every ticking moment, with my inane chatter. There will be time.

So I sit, and tell myself to relax my shoulders, and focus on my breathing like I do when the dentist's drill is squealing inside my mouth, and prepare to wait.

I wait, and absorb a silence broken only by the twittering of a caged canary in the shadows of the next room. I wait, and as I wait, I realize that I have absolutely nothing to say that needs to be said. This has never stopped me from speaking when I am in London. But now that my limited French is acting like a kink in the hose of my splurge to communicate, I am surprised to find that – far from feeling frustrated – I am strangely relieved. It is a silence I shall not forget.

Valette doesn't have any wood to spare. 'You don't buy wood in the autumn, you buy it in the spring,' he says, wagging his finger at me and heaving a mighty log into the firebox of the stove. 'That way, it has time to dry out. And it doesn't cost so much, either. Autumn wood . . . *ouff*.' He shakes his hand as if he'd burnt it, and chuckles for the first time. I explain that my main problem lies in finding someone willing to haul the wood up the drive.

'*Ah-ouff*,' he shrugs. 'I can help you with that. I'll hook a trailer to the back of the tractor.'

'Would you really?'

'Of course. *C'est normal*.'

Again, we all stare at our drinks, and wait.

'You know,' says Valette, 'there are other *Anglais*, just over the hill from you?'

My hand freezes in mid-air. Surely it's not possible, is it? I was convinced there was no other house within a mile of La Folie. It couldn't be . . . not Malcolm and Maureen, the couple from the *chambres d'hôte*? I ask Valette if he knows the people, or at least what they look like.

'*C'est un grand* . . . an enormous type,' he says. 'As big as two people.'

Relieved, I take a swig of Pastis.

'And hundreds of children,' continues Valette. Then he stops, and smiles at my expression. 'You don't like children?'

'*Ça dépend*,' I laugh.

Another silence. The others exchange glances. For the first time, I notice the pot steaming away on the hob. And register that everyone except me finished their drink some time ago.

Hastily draining my glass and rising from the table, I ask Valette where I might find some chickens. I'm half expecting him to tell me that I should have bought these in the spring, too.

'The first Saturday of the month,' he tells me, opening the door and shaking his foot at the dogs. 'You'll find them in the square outside the Mairie.'

'*Merci bien, Monsieur*.'

'And you can call me Gilles.'

As soon as I am back at La Folie, fired up with chicken enthusiasm, I pull my heavy-duty brush-cutter out of the barn. This is the first of my manly power-tools, bought for a hundred pounds on eBay. I have also bought a pair of steel-toe-capped boots and a plastic face-shield like a fencing mask, because I love Useful Gadgets, and because I know I'm bound to make a mess of things, like I did with the hedge-trimmer in East Dulwich. As I wobbled at the top of a metal ladder with my new toy in the grey London rain, I told myself that the one thing I must not do was to saw through the power cable. Two minutes later, I sawed through the power cable, in a spectacular shower of sparks.

Happy as I am to have graduated from a puny hedge-trimmer that makes a sound like an electric toothbrush, to a rusty brush-cutter with a two-stroke engine and a harness to help support its studly bulk, I'm ashamed to say that I have reached the age of thirty-seven without ever having started a two-stroke motor. I'm not even quite sure what a two-stroke motor is, although I know I need to add a glop of oil to the fuel, to stop the thing shaking itself to pieces. Standing on the broken flagstones of the workshop beside the barn, I make up the mixture in an empty Evian bottle, gushing unleaded petrol out of the can in heady torrents, before adding a capful of sleek oil from a green plastic container with a picture of a motorcycle on it.

Choke closed. Lay the engine of war on the damp grass, and take a firm hold of the metal shaft. A few good yanks on the starter-cord – we men love pulling on starter-cords – and I am in a sun-filled garden in Guildford, watching my father attempting to start his Flymo. The elbow of his maroon jumper jerks into the air with each whirring tug. A muttered euphemism every few pulls – 'Oh, blow' – and then a few more pulls – 'Oh, spit' – and then him straightening up and staring accusingly at the lifeless machine. My dad is good with machines.

I can feel him here with me now, as I tug away on the brush-cutter's fraying rope. And then, to my surprise, the thing fires. I don't quite catch it, and it dies. But with the very next pull it roars into full-blooded action. Blimey. Here we go, chaps.

The riot of brambles and shoulder-high nettles in the yard outside the pigsty – the one that will one day be a chicken house – resembles the kind of overgrown undergrowth that conceals magical kingdoms in children's stories. And, sure enough, after a couple of hours the whizzing blade begins to bounce and ping off something vast and metallic in the undergrowth.

I am rather hoping that this might be a battle-tank left behind after the occupation, or a discarded Rodin bronze, or perhaps an iron crate filled with 1945 Haut-Brion. I am not counting my chickens, however, partly because I do not yet have any, and partly because I have already found several dusty wine bottles half buried in the outbuildings at La Folie. Tragically, these are all empty. Some thirsty farmer, long ago, didn't want wifey to find out how he'd been spending the cow money.

Much huffing and puffing later, all is revealed: the Triffidish foliage conceals the iron tyres from a rotted wooden cart; one ox-drawn plough; one agricultural roller on a rusted chariot; and a fine horse-drawn harrow with brambles growing through the holes where the word

SEYFER has been stamped out of the seat. And then I hack away a bit more scrub, and see that it doesn't say SEYFER at all. It says MASSEY FERGUSON.

By mid-afternoon, my hands are a raspberry-ripple of pricks and scratches, and the brambles are still winning. I should have conquered them long ago, but am easily distracted. The children's swing beyond the goldfish pool looks so bare without a seat on it. I must just pick up some croissants from the princess in the *boulangerie*. That mouldy garden furniture needs to be carted to the forbidden tip at Magnac-Laval. I think I might just go and buy some more Useful Gadgets from Bricomarché, the local hardware store. I also make an expedition to the top of the hill, over a couple of barbed-wire fences, to steal a glimpse of the house where the Giant lives. There it is: a long, foreboding building with no ground-floor windows. Presumably the Giant doesn't like to bend down.

I walk, too, through the dust and detritus of the unrenovated part of La Folie, attempting to visualize how it will one day look. The granite-and-breezeblock box of the summer sitting-room where, in my dreams, I play Chopin's 3rd Ballade on a glossy black grand piano, gazing out through the French windows to the valley beyond, sunbeams gleaming on the polished oak floor. The unfinished rooms upstairs, still airless and windowless as in the days when they were no more than the fetid eaves of a cow byre. Here I propose to create a bedroom and a new bathroom too, so that guests do not have to clamber down a ladder and cross a building-site into the underworld when they fancy a tinkle.

Next morning, when the last bramble has finally been mulched into oblivion, I drive down to my new friend Gilles's farm, to ask what he thinks of my archaeological finds. He promises to come and take a look.

'Someone might want the cart-tyres,' he shrugs, as he surveys my rusting bone-yard. 'A pair of them will hold a hay-bale for sheep. You can drag them behind a tractor, too, to flatten mole hills. As for the rest . . .' He wrinkles his nose.

I explain that I had been thinking of keeping the picturesque harrow to hide the manhole covers of the *fosse septique* in front of the house.

'Oh, you don't want that rusty old thing.' He jabs his finger at my Massey Ferguson. 'Or if you keep it, you should paint it black. *C'est plus joli.*'

It's hard to persuade him that I actually quite like the rusted look, just as I prefer the appearance of crumbling stonework to modern render.

Not everyone wants to feel equally connected to the past. Last week I came across a man cutting down an avenue of two-hundred-year-old oaks with a chainsaw. He must have seen my jaw drop. 'It's all right, *Monsieur*,' he assured me. 'These trees are *old*. I shan't cut down any young ones.'

# 11

## THE GIRDLE OF HIPPOLYTA

Never mind the jungle. My search for a dishy *copine* has got off to a very bad start. Despite Zumbach's warning, I somehow expected Jolibois to be a town full of peachy French maidens in diaphanous summer dresses, just waiting for an invitation to come up and see my hypothetical chickens. Instead, I find a population of elegant walnuts; of mothers and matrons, unfailing in their kindness and – largely because they're all married – unthinkable in their birthday suits.

This is what makes my failure with the beaming temptress behind the fish counter at Carrefour in St Juste – my Botticelli in white wellies – all the more galling. I know she had me down as a two-kilos-of-monkfish type of fellow. But earlier this week I unwisely changed my mind about a single salmon fillet she'd wrapped for me. And she now has a special scowl reserved for the English cheapskate. *Angleterre, nul point.*

Worse, much worse, is to come with the girl in the tourist office. I've just popped in to ask for the number of the tennis-club president when I catch sight of this tousle-haired *coquette* with an irresistibly sulky expression and all sorts of tempting curves squeezed into a lacy top. I want to turn and flee; to catch my breath, plan what I'm going to say. But it's too late. She's already seen me.

'*Bonjour, Monsieur*,' she says, fixing me with two very bored green eyes. I've seen the cat gaze at cornered mice like this.

'*Vous avez le numéro du club de tennis?*' I stammer. Why didn't they teach us chat-up lines as part of French A-level? And why am I speaking in such a high voice?

The concept of supplying a single telephone number contravenes the French law of paperwork generation, so *Mademoiselle* fishes out a thick wad of A4 listing all the club presidents in Jolibois: voluntary gymnastics, former POWs, pigeon-fanciers, the works. *Les Français* love their clubs, because clubs mean committees. And committees, naturally, mean lots more lovely paperwork.

'*Voilà*,' she says, pointing at a name on the list. 'Jean-Michel Faure, *le président du club de tennis*.'

'*Ah, oui*,' I reply without enthusiasm. '*Merci*.' The truth is that, without quite knowing why, I want to stay longer in this glamorous woman's orbit; want to ask her more questions. Unfortunately, *Mademoiselle*'s list blows clean out of the water all the other spurious enquiries about clubs and associations and societies that have suddenly occurred to me in the face of such a thrilling cleavage.

'*C'est tout?*' she huffs, the cat prodding its half-dead prey with a clawed paw. 'Is that all?'

The silence between us opens up like an abyss. And in the very depths of the abyss, a lightbulb illuminates.

'Erm . . . evening classes.'

'*Quoi?*'

'That's right. I'm interested in doing some . . . some . . . pottery.'

'There are no evening classes in Jolibois.' She shrugs.

'Well, can you suggest . . . a decent go-karting track?' And so it goes on, I making ever-more-desperate enquiries, she responding with pamphlets and irritation.

We're getting on like a house on fire. I'm the house, and she's *les pompiers*, grimly pumping gallons of French pond-water into the blaze. I've got to do something; something brave. Man or mouse, Wrighty? 'Mouse,' squeaks a familiar voice in my head, just as I become aware of another man in the tourist office, saying something to the girl in an accent I vaguely recognize.

Oh my God. It's *me*.

'I don't suppose . . . perhaps . . . if you had the time . . . you would consider joining me for a drink . . . one evening?'

The eyes of the cat widen, as if the dying mouse between its paws had just begun a striptease to the tune of 'La Vie en Rose'. For a nasty moment, I think she's going to be sick. And then she replies with the magical three-letter word:

'*Non.*'

'*Très bien,*' I say cheerfully, the butt-naked mouse attempting to cover itself with a few shreds of dignity before racing for the door. '*Et merci pour tous ces papiers.*'

But the cat isn't listening. She adopts a look of regal disgust, huffs and stalks away in search of fresher game.

Back in the sanctuary of La Folie, I have a blinding epiphany: so *this* is why all *les Anglais* buying houses in France are already hitched. I'm still turning the thought over in my mind when the cat – my cat – comes crashing through the cat-flap at 120 mph, wild-eyed, electric-furred, as though it has seen a ghost. Rural France is going to take a lot of getting used to. For both of us.

# 12

## NOVEMBER: THE APPLES OF
## THE HESPERIDES

A puff of wind rustles through the acacias in front of the barn, and a single leaf falls. Then another, and another. When I first came to La Folie, I swore I would watch the passing of the seasons; that I would notice every detail of the cycle from birth to death and back again. Yet autumn has already started, and I never noticed it begin. In the straw-coloured frazzle of late summer, I never saw the first fox-mark of brown on the season's endpaper, the first tinge of gold smudging the brilliant green of the leaves all around.

With each shortened day, the house grows a shade cooler, as autumn begins to leech summer's warmth from its thick stone walls. I like being cold – I'd rather suffer in the frozen wastes of the Arctic than be scorched in the Sahara – but a warm blast now greets me when I open the back door, as if I were a cat shut in a fridge. And with only a week to go before Mum and Dad's visit, I still have no logs for the wood-burning stove.

Peter Viola, my new friend from the aeroclub, phones to ask if I want to go flying with him.

'Bit too nippy for the French, but I don't see why that should keep us on the ground,' he says, as casually as if he were leaning against a Sopwith Camel with a Woodbine between his teeth.

I know I should really be going through the local papers, phoning up farmers who have *bois de chauffage* for sale. But the chance to climb into that clear blue sky is irresistible. And I've never flown in a tiny microlight such as Peter's Thruster, which looks as if it has been bolted together from a Meccano set, and then given a set of wings that fell out of a Rice Krispies packet. I tell Peter I'll be there in half an hour.

'Bit of wind in your hair will do you a power of good, old boy,' he says.

On the way to the aerodrome at St Juste, I stop to buy bread at a village bakery. The door is open, though the shop is deserted. Lunchtime.

'*Je viens*,' calls a man's voice from next door, in the middle of a mouthful.

While I wait, I glance at the cards on the noticeboard: adverts for broken-down Renault 4s and chest freezers, for straw by the bail, and twin-bladed *girobroyeurs* to bolt to the back of your tractor for cutting the grass. At the bottom, beneath the neatly written cards, is a scrap of paper from a child's squared exercise book, scribbled with the words *Bois de chauffage* and a telephone number.

The baker emerges through a bead curtain, wiping his mouth with a napkin. '*Excusez-moi, Monsieur*,' he says, apologetically. '*Qu'est-ce que vous voulez?*'

I pay for one of his chestnut-coloured baguettes, and then point at the scrap of paper. Does he know the man who's selling the firewood?

He wanders over. '*Ah, oui, Jean-Louis*.' He nods. '*Il est super-sympa*.'

I jot down the number, fold up the paper and place it carefully in my wallet. Then I head on down to the aerodrome.

'Hop in, old boy,' says Peter, strands of his white hair blowing in the wind as he stands beside the Thruster. 'I'll just finish the pre-flight, and then we'll fire her up.'

So I strap myself into the leather bucket seat, and watch while Peter meticulously does his checks, pulls a small Argyll sock off the pitot tube, and bundles himself into the seat on my left. I watch as he scans the instruments, pointing his finger at each gauge and dial in turn. Then he points at the chart on his lap, its surface covered in an idiosyncratic array of coloured pins, and turns to me.

'My own patent navigation system,' he tells me with a wink. 'Never fails, even in thick fog.' Then he flicks two switches, presses the button on a yellow stopwatch attached to the corner of the chart, and turns the key in the ignition. The engine just above our heads kicks straight into life, and I reach for my headset to silence the din. I wish my Luscombe were that easy to start.

'*Saint Juste, Golf-Kilo-Oscar, je roule pour le point d'arrêt.*' That same English accent, the one I heard over the airport tannoy the very first time I came to St Juste and saw the yellow insect falling from the sky. And now here we are together, in that flimsy flying-machine of tubular steel and stretched nylon, about to commit aviation.

My low-slung seat feels so close to the ground that I could be in a rowing boat. If I were to reach out of the open doorway beside me, I could touch the tarmac with my fingertips. And then Peter opens the throttle, there is a furious roar, and we hurtle sideways down the runway.

'Blimey,' I announce, grabbing the strut beside me and clinging on.

Peter laughs as we soar skywards, still pointing sideways.

'Er . . . aren't you going to straighten up?' I gulp, still holding my strut.

'This *is* straight,' says Peter, his voice crackling in my headset. He taps the turn coordinator, and indicates the balance-ball perfectly centred in its spirit-filled tube.

'Righty-ho.'

'The struts do create some strange optical illusions,' he adds. 'For weeks I thought I'd never be able to land the thing.'

'I was the same with my Luscombe.'

'Yes, but at least you can land it now. Whereas I . . .' Peter's voice breaks off. 'I don't know why you're laughing,' he says, with a frown that finally breaks into a grin as bright as the sunlit clouds.

It feels so good to be in the sky again. Here, amid the scudding cumulus, I feel like I've come home.

That evening, I phone Jean-Louis, the man with the firewood, who is indeed *super-sympa*. I like the way he insists that I survey his logs first, so that I can be sure what I'm buying, before agreeing to purchase a stack of them. I am about to tell him about the problem of getting the wood up the drive, and then think better of it. I can always make a couple of trips in the Espace, if he won't deliver.

Next day, we are standing side by side in torrential rain, next to a pile of logs about the size of a railway carriage.

'*Oui*,' I say expertly. 'That's wood, all right.'

Jean-Louis laughs. He turns out to be a big, genial sheep-farmer, with an iron-age haircut and a beard so vast that I almost feel I'm talking to him through a hole in the hedge.

'I've had it with logs,' he says.

'Oh, really?' I haven't brought a coat, and the rain is

already beginning to drip down my neck. I've had it with logs, too.

'It's too much work. Maintaining the trees until they mature. Felling them. Shifting the trunks and branches. Sawing to length. Splitting into logs. Stacking them like this. Seasoning them for two or three years, because no one wants new wood.'

'But this looks like good wood. Is it all oak?'

'It's excellent wood. About ninety-five per cent oak, with a little chestnut and cherrywood thrown in. How much do you want?'

'Erm, enough for one winter, for one person.'

Somehow we agree on three *cordes*, or nine *stères*, which is the same as nine cubic metres. Except that in some villages locally, there are four *stères* to a *corde*. All I know is that it is a colossal amount of wood. Many fine trees have given up their lives for this. Several of the logs look too good for burning, and should really be carved into the statues of obscure saints.

'And how are you going to collect it?' asks Jean-Louis.

I nod ruefully at the Espace. 'Well, I was wondering . . .' I tell him about the vertiginous and labyrinthine drive to La Folie, about the way entire mule-trains have slipped and fallen to their deaths up there, and how it takes a Sherpa with crampons and an oxygen-mask just to deliver the post.

'It's all right,' he says, smiling. 'I can deliver it for you.'

I toy with the idea of falling to the ground and kissing his wellies, but in the end simply croak '*Impeccable, merci*,' and decide that Jean-Louis is the best person in the world.

'You'll need to clear those branches to get a trailer of logs through,' says Monsieur Valette – or Gilles, as I must now call him – when I drop in at his house to tell him my news. 'I'll bring the tractor,' he says.

'Are you sure?'

'Of course. You get in the front-loader with your chain-saw, and I'll lift you up to cut the branches.'

'You're joking.'

'*Non, non*, it's the best way,' he says, shaking his finger at me.

So there we are, the pair of us, looking like the driver and gunner of a secret weapon on *Dad's Army*, as our fearsome attack vehicle rumbles up the drive to La Folie. I'm Pike – fifteen-foot up in the air and wanting to come down – and Gilles is Captain Mainwaring, furiously gesturing at branches for me to massacre, and muttering whatever is the French for 'stupid boy'. My chainsaw is only my second manly power-tool, and I'm still rather scared of it. I'm sure it doesn't say anything in the safety notes about kneeling in the raised scoop of a tractor and swinging the razor-toothed roarer above your head. Afterwards, I make a big show of counting all my fingers. Gilles glares at me, but I don't know what he means.

A day before the arrival of my parents, the sun is blazing out of a clear autumn sky as another tractor labours up the drive, in a storm-cloud of groaning cogs and grinding gears.

Jean-Louis the woodsman beams at me through the dense foliage of his beard, and I wave back at him. He mouths the word '*Ici?*'

'*Oui.*' I nod. '*Là.*'

With a hiss and a clunk, the trailer rises. Two tonnes of seasoned oak thunders off the back of it, sending up a cloud of dust that shimmers in the sunlight.

Six o'clock, and the cat and I are sitting on the terrace,

admiring the gold and rust and russet and ochre and chestnut colours of the trees across the valley.

This is our primary thinking time. Tonight, with the logs all stacked in the barn, I have that pleasant muscular tiredness which comes of having done heavy work, and that blissful mental sense of having deserved a break. It's not a feeling I remember ever having had as a theatre critic, however late into the night I worked.

Six o'clock has always been my favourite time of day. Six o'clock in my imagination is drinks before dinner, the whole family gathered in the kitchen as my mother cooks something from Elizabeth David and the evening lies ahead of us like the prospect of summer. Even in Bogotá, when I was ten years old, and slurping Pepsi through a straw rather than sipping *pineau* or Pastis. A quarter of a century after my parents left Colombia, I can still picture the dusk beginning to silhouette the flowers outside, and the guard slouched in his box by the gate. Probably drunk again. Indoors, the maids bustle around, drawing curtains and lighting lamps.

Aged ten, I am plump and bespectacled, with a head too big for my bumptious body. My favourite things are Spitfires, pipe organs and Greek irregular verbs. My father, home from the office, looks at his watch and clinks ice into two glasses. With his pewter measure, he pours a tot of Johnny Walker into each. Then a splash of water for him, and rather more soda for Mum.

'Why do you measure it, Dad?' I ask, watching him from the piano stool.

'Because then I know it's just the right amount.'

'So why don't you measure the water?'

He grins at me. '*Touché.*' And I know what this means, because we have learned it in fencing at Windlesham. I like fencing, because it is like the sword-fights they do in

*The Four Musketeers.* But one boy – a wild, red-haired lad from Australia – stomped out of our first lesson, because he thought it was going to be about how to build fences, and he couldn't see how sword-fighting would ever be useful. Now that I am contemplating keeping chickens and even sheep, I think he may have had a point.

Each night in Bogotá, my father switches on the short-wave radio, and he and my mother listen to the seven o'clock news on the World Service. Except that it isn't seven o'clock in England. It is midnight, and I shiver as – in another universe – the funereal bong of Big Ben strikes the hours. I suppose Mum and Dad listen to the dark, serious voice of the newsreader because it makes them feel closer to home. But something about it makes me feel hollow inside.

A few times, I think I hear a car on the drive up to La Folie. And then it's definitely them. It must be, because the car's headlights are on full beam, even though it's a dazzling afternoon.

In the passenger seat, Mum smiles and waves. I point out a parking spot for my father, under the ancient box tree in front of the house, even though I know he won't sleep until his Volvo is safely garaged in the barn.

They climb out of the car, looking tired and happy. Mum and I do our kiss-hug thing, and then I hug my dad, too. Dad and I haven't been doing this very long, and I suspect he thinks it's a bit modern, but – standing stiff as a board – he humours me, nonetheless.

'Golly,' exclaims Mum, knuckles on hips, gazing out across the valley.

'Gosh,' exclaims Dad, looking up at the house.

'So you found it all right, then?' I say, not yet ready to face their struggle to find something polite to say about La

Folie. Better to allow them to debrief fully about the traffic-jams en route, and the cunning shortcuts that Dad found to avoid them, and the unsporting dead-ends that weren't marked on their 1973 Michelin road-map. Which is, I presume, why they're only three-quarters of an hour early.

'It's certainly remote, isn't it?' says Mum.

'That's what I was looking for,' I reply, already on the defensive.

'The stonework's very fine,' says my dad. 'And I'm sure that big crack is nothing to worry about.' He points at a tiny chink in the crumbling render of the facade. My mother is staring at le Pug Rouge, her old car.

'How funny,' she says. 'I'd forgotten you had it.'

'Right, yes, well, you must be ready for a drink,' I declare, rubbing my hands as I walk backwards towards the house. 'And then I'll show you round.'

'*After* we've unpacked the car,' says Mum, in such a way that the grass around her blackens and begins to smoke gently in the breeze.

'Can't it wait, Anne?' pleads my father.

'There are things that need to go into the fridge,' she says, glaring at him.

'What things, precisely, Mum?' I ask, knowing full well that I shall be expected to find space in the fridge for all the bits of their half-eaten picnic that must not be thrown away until after they have left.

Never mind that the fridge is already full. Out come the screwed-up freezer bags, the creased tin-foil, from the depths of the car.

'But I already *have* plenty of cheese,' I protest, as my mother proffers the remnants of a cross-Channel Camembert from Waitrose. 'And France does have bakers.' My mother is threatening me with the end of an English baguette she defrosted yesterday morning.

'Well, what about this milk?' she asks, waving a Unigate carton that has just spent several hours in a Volvo climatically controlled to evoke the tropical Palm House at Kew Gardens.

My mother relaxes considerably once all her manky leftovers are safely stored in the fridge and their suitcases are upstairs.

'Right, six o'clock,' I announce, not even looking at my watch. 'Now it's *definitely* time for a drink.'

I uncork a chilled bottle of Saumur, extracted from behind my mother's Unigate carton like a prize in one of those fairground crane games, and pour her a glass of wine.

'Would you like me to measure yours, Dad?' I ask.

'Ha ha. Very funny,' he says. 'No, thank you.'

It feels strange to be a grown-up, looking after my parents in my own house in a foreign country.

'So here you are, in France, again . . .' I say.

'Yes, and very nice it is, too,' responds Mum quickly.

'We like your house very much,' adds Dad, making me wonder how they can already have had time to discuss it. 'But I do admire your courage, because the state of it is . . . rather more daunting that we'd realized.'

I frown, to stop myself smiling. For this is just what I wanted to hear. 'It's simply a question of finishing the work that's already been started,' I reply. And I might just as easily be talking of all they have done for me.

The following morning is a fine and frosty one as I rattle down to Jolibois in the Espace. The Espace is no chick-magnet, even now that I have removed some of the rear seats which make me feel like an absent father. But it only cost me nine hundred euros, and I do like having a French number-plate with an 87 for Haute-Vienne at the end of it. I can now wave gaily at everyone I pass, making them turn and peer after me. *C'est qui?*

On the pretext of a bread-run, I'm going to recce the market for chicken sightings, before returning to La Folie for breakfast with my parents. Then we'll all ride back down to Jolibois together, for the epochal moment when I purchase the first chickens to have been in my family for two generations. It turns out that Dad's mother – a closet alcoholic I never met – kept chickens in Southampton during the war. When she died, he says they found bottles hidden all over the house. No one knows what happened to the chickens.

Jolibois is all a-bustle with its monthly market. Groups of beaming women kiss and wag their fingers at each other on every corner, while men in berets lean on their sticks to watch the traffic. An excitable policeman in white gloves stands in the middle of the road, waving the cars ahead whenever the lights go green, and stopping them with a flat palm when the lights go red. Presumably this is helpful, if you're colour-blind.

The monthly market is smaller than I was expecting, and there appear to be more people selling mattresses and cheap anoraks than goat's cheese or artichokes. But Gilles was right about the chickens.

Two lorries have already set up just outside the estate agency where Émilie works, with chickens, ducks and geese packed so tightly into cages that their down squeezes out between the bars like fat thighs in fishnets.

Bingo. Chickens ahoy, skipper. I barely stop to look. My sortie accomplished, my heart fluttering, I gun the Espace's tired old engine and head back to La Folie.

It must have rained in the night, for the fallen leaves have turned into a wet porridge on the side of the road. I takè the steep first hairpin on the drive carefully. I don't want to skid.

Then comes the shallower uphill stretch, and I'm going just fast enough to change up to second, before I let the Espace cruise gently down the other side. Oops: not too fast. I can hear the tyres hissing through the leaf-porridge.

Just to be on the safe side, I dab the brakes. The front of the car dips and skids right, towards the curtain of trees that pins the lane to the hillside, stopping it from sliding down the steep bank and crashing on to the sheep below.

The car's not slowing down. Steer left, left. Brake harder. No, *pump* the brakes. It's all happening so fast, but in slow motion. And then comes the crunch of fibre-glass on young oak, the sickening tinkle of breaking glass, and I so wish I hadn't done that.

I switch off the engine, and open my door in the silence. This means lifting it almost vertically towards the canopy of trees, as the Espace has come to rest at a steep angle, like an aeroplane crashed nose-first in the jungle. I jump down with a splash and let the door slam shut behind me.

The damage isn't as bad as I feared: one smashed head-lamp and some crunching distortion to the front-bumper. For a while, I attempt to push the thing out, standing in the mulch of leaves and heaving with all my strength. Stacking all those logs in the barn has given me Atlas-type delusions. But there's no way to keep a foothold, and the car is going nowhere. Perhaps I can persuade Gilles to come and drag me out with his tractor. First I have to face my parents. I feel like a child again as I stomp up to make my confession. I hope they didn't hear the smash.

'Morning, Mum,' I say, as I march into the kitchen. I lay the bread on the table and head straight for the fridge. I have a surprising need to eat some strawberry yoghurt, fast.

'Oh, hello,' she replies. 'Are you back already? I didn't hear the car.'

'Hm, yes.' I select a teaspoon from the draining-board and begin to shovel the creamy sweetness into my mouth.

'Would you like coffee? And were there any chickens?'

'Yes, please. And yes, absolutely. There were chickens.'

The coffee tastes so good that I burn my mouth and have to eat a second yoghurt. I didn't even like yoghurt before I came to France.

'Are you all right?' asks my mother.

'I'm fine. Where's Dad?'

I'd rather start by fixing the problem, and deal with the sarcastic comments afterwards. I already know exactly what Mum's going to say, and the amused tone in which she will say it.

I find Dad in the barn, where he is rearranging objects in the boot of his car so that they will occupy a smaller space than the volume of the objects themselves. Packing cars is one of Dad's gifts, like finding brilliant-yet-flawed shortcuts, and it is another thing that I have not inherited from him.

'Dad, I'm proud to say that I have just crashed the Espace.'

He turns and looks at me, to see if I'm joking or bleeding.

'Ah. Bad luck. I take it you haven't told your mother.'

I shake my head.

'Where is it now?'

I point towards the trees in the distance. 'Can you see that green shape, nosing down sharply into the trees? The engine still runs, but it's stuck. I could get my neighbour, Gilles, to tow me out,' I say, with bogus nonchalance, 'but I was wondering if with the Volvo . . . you might be willing?'

'Have you got a tow rope?' he asks, smiling at being able to be a proper dad again.

Mum comes to the kitchen door as Dad reverses; wants to know where we're going.

'I've had a little skid in the Espace, and Dad's just coming to help pull it out of the mud,' I say, not wanting to open a discussion about how it's lucky Dad's here.

Mum smiles. 'Do be careful,' she says. 'What would you have done if your father weren't here?'

To give my parents credit, they do not even mention the smell in the Espace, let alone the smashed headlamp. In town, I beg them to keep a low profile while I make my chicken purchase. Sticking out my belly and adopting a swagger I consider to be authentically Jolibois, I do my best to look expert as I approach one of the big moustaches who is busy stacking cages. I hope Émilie isn't watching through the window of the estate agency, too.

'*Elles pondent bien?*' I murmur, kicking an imaginary stone. Do they lay well? I'm not sure what I'm expecting the man to say, but from the way he waves his arms around and mimes an excited squatting action, I take it that either his chickens are indeed splendid layers, or else he's been overdoing the stewed apricots.

The hens cost a few euros each, with some smart white *poules de Bresse* for a tad more. These look huge and heraldic: more like albino vultures than hens. I gesture that I'd like a couple, on the expert basis that if they cost more, they must be good. Then I point to a couple of medium-sized black ones, and a couple of little brown ones.

'Is it all right to mix them?' I ask, in French.

'*Ah oui, bien sûr, Monsieur.*' The two little brown hens, eyeing the white vultures, don't look quite so sure. I wince as the man grabs all six birds by the feet and stuffs them into two tiny cardboard boxes like dirty laundry. I have never seen chickens looking so *alive*.

'I'll need some feed, too, if you have any.'

'*Pas de problème*,' he says, dumping a large white sack at my feet.

But now I have a problem. Sudden lack of cash. And the man won't take a cheque. I turn to the lady behind me, who has been pretending to admire the partridges. 'Er, Mum . . . any chance you could lend me forty euros?'

Mum chuckles, and examines – with excruciating slowness – the contents of her wallet.

As I hand over the forty euros to the chicken man, I can see Émilie waving excitedly at me from inside her office. I nod and hold up my two boxes in shy triumph.

I drive us back to La Folie so slowly that we are hooted from behind by a tractor. But it's only Gilles, waving at our stately progress. In the back, my mother gasps with exaggerated horror every time I dab the accelerator. Finally we are at the top of the hill, and – while Mum and Dad watch from a safe distance – I lay my boxes on the ground in the enclosed yard outside the pigsty, open them, and hastily retreat, as if I'd just lit two mighty rockets.

A head pokes up. Then another. And another. I'd expected the chickens all to leap out and rush off to start laying eggs, but they look too shocked and dishevelled for that. So I attempt to lift them out. I've all but grabbed the first one – one of the two big white *poules de Bresse* – when she manages to break away in a terrifying explosion of shrieking and flapping and flying feathers, making a sound like someone shaking an empty paper bag right beside your ear.

Now all hell breaks loose. There are chickens everywhere, running, hopping, squawking, panicking, in a fearsome chain reaction. One of the white bruisers ends up on top of the wall, glaring down at me with undisguised hatred, like something out of Du Maurier via Hitchcock. The two little brown hens huddle in the corner of the yard, visibly shaking. The other three stand, heads to the wall, feathers ruffled, as if they have all volunteered themselves for detention.

'I think I've changed my mind about having chickens,' says my mum, watching from the safety of the other side of the wall.

'Thank God,' mutters Dad.

'They're just settling in,' I say authoritatively, channelling my inner farmer. At this, the white bird that was on top of the wall hops down the other side and starts running away, heading for the trees and freedom.

'Is it meant to be going over there?' giggles my mother, with a snort.

Early evening, and we are out on the terrace, sipping our wine. It's chilly, but the low sun offers a last vestige of late summer. And we *are* English, after all. I ask my father about his parents, whom I never met, and his grandparents, whom he hardly knew. Questions I've never asked before. God knows why I had to come to France before I could ask my dad where he came from.

'My grandfather was a plate-layer on the railways,' he says. 'I believe that's something to do with building steam trains.'

'He built steam trains?' I splutter. 'I can't believe you never told me that.'

'I suppose it never seemed important. It was all in the past.'

'But you know how I felt about steam trains.'

'How could we forget about the Royal Queen?' says my

mother, gazing dreamily at the cat, which is stretched out in a Superman pose across her lap.

'And the past *does* matter,' I continue, my voice coming out louder than intended. I hate hearing other people lecture their parents. 'It's what makes the present happen. It's the foundations of the house.'

'You're probably right,' says my dad gently. 'But your mother and I grew up in the war, and perhaps that—'

'And that just makes it all the more fascinating,' I interrupt. We are all silent for a moment.

'Sometimes you really can be rather aggressive, Michael,' says my mum.

'Sorry. You're right. Sorry.' And we all sip our wine in silence.

'Did your father have any brothers and sisters, Dad?' I ask, trying another tack.

'I had an uncle . . . I believe he used to make Spitfires, in the Supermarine factory near Southampton.'

'Spitfires? You're *joking*. Spitfires! And you never told me.'

'Well, I *think* it was Spitfires,' replies my father hastily. 'It was hard to be sure, because he was always very hush-hush about it. He used to tell us that he was making the wooden pips to go into wartime strawberries.'

'I love it.' Because I do love it, when everything fits together. When the past and the present make sense of each other, and history isn't just something that happens to other people.

My dad smiles, takes a sip of wine, and gazes out across the valley at the huge oaks, and the leaves that are continuing to fall.

By nightfall, things have calmed down on the poultry front. But there's still a problem. Not one of the girls has shown the slightest inclination to lay any eggs. Instead, they are now all squeezed into the corners of the *poulailler*, wretchedly trembling. Nor do they show any interest in occupying the fine perches I have provided for them. They simply hunch themselves at the edges of the cold cement floor, looking glum as teenagers at an icy disco. Strange. An hour later, and it's the same story: still *pas d'oeufs*.

Next morning, I march out to the nesting boxes, armed with a large basket to collect all my farmhouse produce. In the nesting boxes: nothing. Not a *saucisson*. But – ignoring the feed I've poured out for them from the big white sack – the girls do at least come scuttling out of the chicken house to scratch and peck at the weeds in their yard. And it's hilarious.

Quite clearly at the top of the pecking order are my two white *poules de Bresse*. That means yesterday's clucking escapee – caught after a marathon pursuit employing the tactics of the Schlieffen Plan by me and my father – and her even more vocal sister, whose scarlet comb is so big that it flops at a rakish angle reminiscent of a Rembrandt self-portrait. Of the two, the latter shall be Mildred, self-styled trumpet queen of the roost, with Melissa the Fugitive as her regal consort. Then come the two black-and-gold birds, Margot – a Spanish galleon, complete with foredeck and poop-deck – and Martha, my instant friend.

Martha appears to have decided that I am her kin, and comes hurrying to greet me whenever I set foot in the yard, tugging at my shoelaces with her beak and flapping her wings in look-at-*me*-Papa fashion.

Bringing up the rear are Mary and Meg, already the hen-pecked squaddies of the troop. These two are both so brown and small and plain that I cannot easily tell the difference between them. Meg makes the occasional cluck. Mary breathes not a sound.

Day three: Eureka. My heart swells with pride when I spy a tiny brown egg lying in the straw. Granted, this egg is some distance from my luxury nesting boxes, but greater accuracy will, I assume, come with time. And it's an egg. A proper, egg-shaped egg. It even has a shell and everything. Since all the chickens make defiant clucking noises when I remove the precious artefact, I assume it must have been a joint effort. I can't wait to show Mum and Dad how clever I am.

Never mind the fact that, when ceremonially boiled, this first egg tastes about as interesting as polenta and yields a yolk approximately the size and colour of a sherbet lemon. It is an egg. And even though I didn't lay it myself, I almost feel that I did.

Saying goodbye to Mum and Dad is difficult. We've never been very demonstrative – Surrey people aren't – but that doesn't mean we're any less attached to each other than those who go in for more histrionic farewells. I hug my dad and kiss my mum, and almost conquer my embarrassment enough to tell them that I love them. I manage to say this to them about once every five years, at which moments they generally blush and fumble for words and swiftly reassure me that such things don't need to be said, before wondering aloud if it is going to rain this afternoon.

Our goodbye makes me understand now how hard it must have been for them to send my brothers and sister and me away to boarding school in England, when they were living in Colombia, five thousand miles away. It is a sacrifice for which I shall always feel grateful. I cannot imagine what it must have been like for them, waving us off at the airport with our teddies and our sunburn, as we headed off across the Atlantic for a new term.

Years later, when I returned to Windlesham to teach for a while, one of the most disturbing scenes I witnessed was a mother saying goodbye to her eight-year-old son on his first day at my old school. The little chap stood there on the front steps, lip trembling as he attempted to comfort his mother, who was clinging to him, weeping and wailing like an amateur thesp in a bad production of you-know-what. What does Mummy know about this place that I don't, the brave child must have been thinking, as he waited for the blubbering to cease.

Standing on the steps outside La Folie, it doesn't occur to me until after my parents have driven away that they must have been as lump-in-throat sad to leave as I was to see them go. I suppose we try to be brave for each other, because it's what the English do. Stiff upper lip and all that.

# 13

## THE HYDRA

Alone again, and without method or masterplan, I am doing my best to *m'intégrer avec les Français*. I have now conquered my fear of entering the smoky, all-male cafés in town, where leather-faced farmers stand hunched over their ten a.m. beers at the bar. The secret, I discover after a series of botched visits and bottomless silences, is to stride in with a cheery '*Bonjour, Messieurs,*' and to shake hands with anything that moves.

This is the French way, and appears to be disarming when practised by *un Anglais*. As the weeks pass, I am even beginning to recognize some of the late-bottled Oliver Reed lookalikes whose chalky paws I am shaking. We don't exactly then start singing 'Knees Up, Mother Brown' together, but we don't get into a sword-fight, either. Echoing the man in the paper shop, Gilles has told me that any newcomer must expect to wait six months before local people begin to accept them. So that leaves me another three and a half months until the beginning of March, to sit out my time in Coventry, or one of its friendlier suburbs.

After driving into town to deliver some eggs to Émilie at the estate agency – the production line is now in full swing, and I already have far too many for personal consumption – I stop off for a coffee at the Café Colibri, shake hands with each moustache in turn, and then wander down to the church.

The mystery of the church in Jolibois is that it is always deserted: dark and sombre as a tomb. And yet, each time I visit, there are always two or three votive candles burning which appear to have only just been lit.

Today, however, the door is open, and a chatter of ladies is arranging flowers in gaudy vases. Light creeps through the stained-glass windows, casting green, red and golden ghosts on to the pale stonework. I've come to ask about playing the organ.

I have practised my organ-playing little since school, after the poetry of Chopin and Schubert led me away from Bach's meticulous prose. But I'm hoping that here, finally, may be my chance to brush up my massacring of Widor's Toccata, and make some small contribution to Jolibois life.

'You play the organ, *Monsieur*?' asks a trembling bunch of carnations, before calling out to the vast display of lilies beside it: 'Céline, there's *un Anglais* here. (That's right, isn't it, *Monsieur*?) Wants to play the organ.'

'You're in luck,' giggle the lilies. 'Fabrice the organist is my son-in-law.' A lady I recognize from the *boulangerie* emerges from behind the froth of petals. I am beginning to think that everyone in Jolibois is, in the nicest possible way, related.

I'm also fully prepared to wait until the beginning of March before I hear from Fabrice, but he telephones me the following morning, and we arrange to meet at the church.

I can already hear the organ bucketing off the twelfth-century stonework as I climb out of the Espace. That's quite a beast he's got in there. I don't recognize the piece, but it sounds like the baddies are winning.

As I clump up the steep wooden stairs to the tribune, the racket stops. A small boy with chocolate smeared around his mouth comes racing round the corner, and reaches out to shake my hand. Good Lord. Fabrice is younger than I imagined.

'*Bonjour*,' I say. The boy makes no reply, but turns and scuttles back around the corner of the tribune, his fingers leaving two dark trails on the dusty panelling. I follow, and almost bump into the figure who has climbed off the organ stool to greet me.

'Fabrice?' I mumble.

'*Bonjour*,' he mumbles back. Organists are not a talkative bunch.

Fabrice cuts a pale and otherworldly figure; an overgrown schoolboy in corduroy trousers and a baggy black sweatshirt, who looks as if he may not have seen daylight in the last thirty years. He regards me with a liquid stare for a few seconds, before digging out a dusty book of *chants* and motioning for me to play one.

'I see that you have already met my son,' he says, while the little boy peers out at me from behind his legs. Fabrice's voice is high and soft, and he sings very beautifully, leaning out from the balcony like a flying buttress, as I sight-read the *chant*.

So follows a series of Sunday mornings in the organ loft with Fabrice, attempting to learn how to accompany the Mass. Like most of France, Jolibois is Catholic. I, for my sins, am a lapsed Anglican in mufti. My entire Catholic experience amounts to a few Masses dutifully attended with Marisa, and watching *The Thorn Birds* on ITV with my mum. So I really don't know my Anamnesis from my Agnus Dei. I could be found out at any moment.

To make matters worse, Fabrice plays everything from memory, with not a scrap of music in sight. So I'm lost in a jungle without a map. There's no hymn book, and no 'We shall now sing hymn 385: "Let Us Winkle Out Impostors".' No, the organist is expected to divine what comes next by instinct alone, like a pig snuffling for truffles.

'*C'est maintenant?*' I rasp at Fabrice in a panic, one Sunday, when he invites me to take over for the Gloria. '*Je commence?*' I can see the lights glinting off the specs of Raphaël, our young priest, as he glares up at the organ loft, wondering what the *diable* is the delay. I like Raphaël. Tall and solid, he used to farm cattle and strawberries before he found his priestly vocation, yet he has a veneer of city sophistication, too, that seems at once out of place and strangely familiar to me.

Even worse than not knowing what to play when is the improvising; a central pillar of the French organ tradition. Fabrice's resonant extemporizations for the *offertoire* or the communion sound like Handel meets César Franck. My glib noodlings sound like Pinky and Perky meet a sticky end.

'How long have you been the organist here, Fabrice?' I ask him despondently, as we stand by the church door.

'Thirty years.'

'But if . . . how *old* are you?'

'I'm thirty-eight,' he shrugs.

Overhearing our conversation, an elderly lady, bright-eyed, grabs my arm as she passes.

'They called him *le petit Mozart*,' she whispers.

Characters abound in Jolibois, and many of them have been bundling up the drive to La Folie in their white vans to give me quotes for my renovations. The first of these, simply for pointing the walls of the summer sitting-room, is for fourteen thousand euros, which would swallow more than half of my entire budget. I can see that finding the right mason is going to be a challenge in itself.

Today, Monsieur Étang – a handsome caveman in a yellow anorak, hopping around on tiptoes – arrives to quote for plumbing a new bathroom in the *maison des amis*. Now anyone I've asked about plumbing tells me that Étang is the best plumber for miles around, and one of the cheapest, too. The trouble is that everyone knows this, and poor Monsieur Étang cannot be very good at saying no. His shining reputation is clearly taking its toll. He runs upstairs with his tape-measure, runs from wall to wall, measuring and panting, runs down to examine the water-heater, scratches his head, asks me about the *fosse septique*, and then runs away again. All on tiptoe. The frenzied stress of the man is alarming. I want to sit him down, make him a fortifying cup of PG Tips, and tell him to think of cool, wet grass. But there is no time for this when the water-pipes of Jolibois have need of him.

'I'm so sorry, *Monsieur*,' he says, looking pained as he jumps into his car. 'I will write to you next year. There are so many people to please.'

Various fine moustaches have already driven up the hill to La Folie to consider the question of insulating the two hundred square metres of exposed roofing in the summer sitting-room and *maison des amis*. Several more will appear over the next few weeks. After Monsieur Étang, the running plumber, comes an electrician the size of Blackpool, to examine the wiring.

'*C'est Charlot*,' he says, opening yet another junction box and shaking his head. I recognize this as a reference to Charlie Chaplin, who was not, I think, a world-renowned

electrician. 'You need to find out who did this crazy instal-
lation, so he can explain where all the wires go.'

I telephone Zumbach, who sounds nervous.

'*Tout va . . . bien à la Folie?*' he asks.

'Yes, absolutely. I don't suppose you happen to have a
number for the man who did the wiring in the *maison des
amis*, do you?'

'Er, I think it was someone from . . . Lille,' he says. Lille
is about the furthest, largest, most anonymous town in
France. I do not press the question.

In between waiting for other *ouvriers* to come and
examine the various renovation works to be done, I make
frequent trips to Limoges, mostly to the *grands espaces* of
Monsieur Bricolage and Castorama, where I buy wall-
lamps and draught-excluders and various lengths of
timber for ambitious projects that I am much better at
starting than finishing. Mostly I like gawping at the manly
power-tools, and wondering if I could justify a router or a
band-saw or *un raboteur*.

And then Raphaël the priest telephones.

'We wondered if you'd be willing to accompany the
Mass this Saturday evening,' he asks, without preamble.

'*Mais oui . . . bien sûr,*' I reply. 'But Fabrice . . . ?'

'Fabrice only plays for the Sunday-morning Mass,' says
Raphaël firmly.

'But I don't want . . .' I falter, for I have no idea
how to say 'I really don't want to tread on his toes' in
French.

'Fear not,' says Raphaël, several steps ahead of me. 'It
was Fabrice who suggested it.'

My first reaction is to feel thrilled, for here – at last – is
my chance to make a local contribution. And then I feel
terrified, because I'm not ready. I wonder if I ought to
come clean to Raphaël about not even being a proper

Catholic. But it's too late to worry about that now. I've already said yes.

I have never been good at saying no. The day I first fell in love with the organ was the day I discovered what it is to be thoroughly and rottenly drunk. I was five years old. My parents had been invited to a christening at Eton College, where one of their friends was a housemaster. I don't recall hearing any music. But in the soaring chapel, the faded beauty of the huge organ pipes – etched with green and red and gold – gave me an unusual thrill. They reminded me of the steam trains I loved, their boilers gleaming in the rich Victorian liveries of the regional networks.

All too vividly, I remember how, after the christening, we children in our awful shorts had tea in a different room from the grown-ups. Here, I discovered that Babycham was a most unusual fizzy drink. It wasn't like Coke or Fanta, because it came in tiny bottles and it gave you a strange whooshing sensation in your head. I don't remember much after that, except that it was a baking hot day and I was sick all over the fountain in the middle of Eton's quad.

Seven years later – aged twelve – I attempted to persuade Mr Lorraine-White, Windlesham's director of music, to teach me how to play the organ. I had a hunch that this might just impress Clara Delaville. I told Mr Lorraine-White that my favourite record in the world was *The World of the Organ*, and that I badly needed to learn Bach's Toccata and Fugue in D minor, the chorale prelude *Wachet Auf, Ruft Uns die Stimme*, and Widor's Toccata. He rolled his eyes, lit a cigarette, examined my legs to see if they were long enough to reach the pedals, and let me loose on the school organ. I was in heaven, even if the music he fed me – the easiest of Bach's Eight Short

Preludes and Fugues and some childlike snippets from the Anna Magdalena Notebook – exuded not quite the coruscating brilliance that I had in mind.

Clara Delaville was not visibly impressed. But one half-term, when Pa and Nanny gave in to my pleas to take me to the music shop in Weybridge, I finally laid hands on the coveted sheet-music for Widor's Fifth Organ Symphony, with the ten triple-staved pages of its final Toccata black with notes. Buying this artefact took all my pocket-money, and I couldn't play a single bar of its hurtling splendour with my clumsy child's hands. Nevertheless, this huge score, with its mottled green paper cover and crude French printing – all the words in heavy-serifed capitals, all the notes looking almost too big for the stave – became one of my special treasures. I still remember how much it hurt when an American boy at Sherborne, a few years later, crept into my study and – in a calculated act of cultural vandalism – carefully poured the contents of a bottle of Ribena from my mother all over the cover.

Twenty-five years on, that mottled green cover is still stained with purple. But I can play all the notes now, with my creased adult hands. And I find a strange delight in playing the same short preludes and fugues, those same childlike snippets that Mr Lorraine-White taught me at Windlesham, in an empty church in rural France, while the dusty sunlight streams through the stained-glass windows on to the lilies and carnations arranged beside the altar by Céline and her friends.

Since school, I've lost count of the number of pipe-organs I have played. You can usually find where the churchwarden has hidden the key, if you look hard enough. The most beautiful was an instrument in Strasbourg, on which Mozart had played. The biggest was at Guildford Cathedral, where the organist said I could spend an hour practising as long as I didn't play too loud. So I didn't play too loud, for at least the first ten minutes, when my purple-stained Widor began to call to me. And the most fun was the vast 1930s cinema organ of my uncle's cinema, the Regal in Eastleigh, complete with fire-bells and police whistles, silver paintwork, art deco lighting and a pneumatic hoist. This organ had been installed by my dad's dad, who – I finally learned, while my parents were at La Folie – started out as a cellist accompanying silent films, and ended up as the owner of multiple cinemas, became mayor of Eastleigh, and won England two gold medals for lawn bowls in the Empire Games of 1930 and 1934.

It's hard to describe what a joy it is – when you are ten years old, with a pudding-bowl haircut and tortoiseshell National Health specs – to ride on a burnished-silver organ console that is rising from the depths of a 1930s cinema on a pneumatic hoist, while you rattle out a flutey version of 'A, You're Adorable' with your right hand, and wave at an imaginary audience with your left. Add this to royal-train driving and Spitfire flying: another vocation missed.

# 14

## DAVID AND GOLIATH

In the midst of my frequent trips to the church to practise the organ, and my various stilted phone conversations with French carpenters and plumbers, I have been spending a lot of time watching the chickens. I love the way they come rushing to greet me each time I bump up the drive in the Espace: six fat madams in feather boas, racing to catch a bus with their hands tied behind their backs.

Their pecking order is now firmly established, so that the perches in the chicken house have as clear a social delineation as the stalls, dress circle and gods of a Victorian theatre. And the order in which the girls emerge through the pop-hole each morning tells its own story of bullies and victims. I see the expression 'hen-pecked' in a whole new light as I watch Meg and Silent Mary being remorselessly taunted by Mildred and Melissa, my strapping white *poules de Bresse*. But Mildred has her own problems. Never mind her exalted social status, I have a nasty suspicion that she is egg-bound.

The poor dear has been jumping in and out of her nesting box, clucking with frustration, to no avail. And my chicken book tells me that I must now smear Vaseline on her bum and squirt pharmaceutical-grade liquid paraffin into her beak to help get things moving. *Quel plaisir.* When I came to France to learn how to be tough, this wasn't the kind of tough I had in mind.

I leap into the Espace and head down to Jolibois to see Monsieur Chabrier the pharmacist. Finding his gleaming shop heaving with elderly ladies browsing for suppositories, I lurk behind the homoeopathic display and pray for them to leave before I request my hen lubricants.

'*Il me faut de la Vaseline, et de l'huile de paraffine aussi, s'il vous plaît,*' I say quietly, slamming a toothbrush I don't want on to the counter.

Chabrier narrows his eyes and looks at me carefully. I can see he wants to tell me that this is modern France – *vous pauvres Anglais!* – and that over here these days they have more advanced ways of dealing with my problem.

'Do you have a prescription?' he asks.

'*Non, c'est pour . . . une poule.*'

'*Une poule?*' Chabrier pulls his best now-I've-heard-everything expression and gazes around the shop, just to make sure that all the old ladies have heard what the *drôle* Englishman just said. I can see the frown-muscles in his face fighting a losing battle against an appalled leer. '*Une poule,*' he repeats quietly to himself.

I stare hard at the toothbrush.

Finally, he lays two shiny blue boxes in front of me. '*C'est tout?*'

'*Er . . . j'ai besoin d'un . . .*' Here I mime the action of filling a syringe, which I need for administering the paraffin into Mildred's beak.

'*Une poire?*' asks Chabrier, raising his eyebrows still further.

'*C'est quoi?*'

'An enema?' he murmurs, switching into heavily accented English.

'*Non, non*,' I exclaim. '*Quelque chose plus petit que ça . . .*'

Chabrier pulls a thin smile. Was it for this that he spent all those years studying his pharmacology textbooks?

I can't get out of there fast enough. Scooping up my purchases, I scuttle out into the street. And then realize that I have left the toothbrush behind on the counter.

It's the middle of the afternoon, and Mildred is crouched like a fat snowball, half in and half out of her nesting box, by the time I return to La Folie. We stare at one another in the half-light of the chicken house. I'm glad none of the other girls is about. This is going to be embarrassing for both of us.

'You lay one finger on me . . .' she mouths.

I scoop out a big glob of Vaseline from the jar and clench my teeth.

'Not a word of this to anyone,' blinks Mildred, with the slightly brittle self-confidence of a public-school head-mistress who has mislaid her spectacles and doesn't want you to know it.

Holding my breath, I feel my way through the fluffy down around her back end, and – gulp – smear the Vaseline on what I hope is the right place. Mildred, unflinching, gazes back at me with suppressed outrage. Then the moment comes for me to squirt the paraffin into her beak. But the patient is having none of it, like a baby faced with a spoonful of purée it is determined not to swallow.

This stage of the treatment *has* to work. Because if it doesn't, the book tells me that I must hold Mildred over a cauldron of boiling water, to relax her bum in the steam.

I don't like the idea of this any more than I like the sound of stage four, which involves attempting to puncture the egg inside her and hoik it out with my fingers. Delia doesn't say anything about this in her recipe for foolproof scrambled eggs.

Fortunately I now have a moment of inspiration. I cluck very loudly at Mildred. This she considers for a moment. And clucks back. *Squissssssshh* goes the paraffin into the open beak. And poor Mildred becomes very still and pensive, as if I had just told her a terrible secret.

A few hours later, with much excited clucking from Mildred, the long-awaited egg pops out.

But Mildred has her revenge. For later that week, I am alarmed to find that I'm suffering a rather similar and uncomfortable condition, no doubt caused by a surfeit of scrambled eggs for breakfast. So there I am, down at Chabrier's pharmacy once again, requesting substances that may provide a little light relief.

'Don't tell me,' says Monsieur Chabrier beadily, as I show him my prescription. 'It's for a chicken, right?'

Today is my big day: I am to accompany the Mass for the first time. Alone in the tribune, I open the fuse-box and click the five *interrupteurs* to 'on'. The leather bellows creak and fill like an old man's lungs. Half an hour before the Mass, the church is still deserted. There's just a lady lighting the candles on the altar, who waved at me when I came in.

I play a couple of nervy Bach preludes as the church fills up. And then the Angelus tinkles from the sacristy, and the Mass is hurtling by in a flurry of mounting panic, ecclesiastical French and excruciating silences.

All at sea in a morass of meaningless photocopies, I am fumbling to find the right music in time for the next bit, and mostly find it about ten seconds late, when an uneasy rustling has already started down below and, out of the corner of my eye, I am dimly aware of upturned white faces looking to see what's wrong.

Somehow I manage to mix up the Kyrie and the Gloria, sink the Sanctus, and then – dripping with sweat, my pulse racing – launch boldly into the *Prière Universelle* when Raphaël announces the *Notre Père*. Well, I thought the Lord's Prayer *was* the Universal Prayer. Apparently not, from the way the light glinting on the priestly spectacles suddenly flashes like an Aldis lamp. *Non, non, non.*

Standing at a microphone in front of the congregation, a lovely old fellow called Henri does his best to lead the singing. Now Henri has the voice of a rugby player calling for the ball, and beats time as if he were guiding a helicopter in to land on the deck of an aircraft carrier in a force-eight gale. Yet the heroic gusto of his presence, and the rubicund cheer with which he belts out every note, somehow carries me through the storm. Though he is not required to sing the *Anamnèse*, Henri still comes trundling out from behind a pillar to give me one of his radiant nods as my signal to start playing. He reminds me of a retired cherubim in tweeds. If ever I am chained to a radiator by terrorists for several months, I should like someone like Henri to be there with me.

From time to time in the service, he and I even manage to arrive at the same note at the same time, and his rapturous smile illuminates the church.

Even so: I know I'm going to be found out. They're going to burn me at the stake in the square outside the church, *pour encourager les autres*. I think I might sleep in the chicken house tonight.

The Mass thus massacred, I play a skittery postlude

before staggering down the stairs, wondering if I'm about to be *excommunié* by a church I don't even belong to. Sure enough, there's quite a mob waiting to lynch me outside.

'*Bien joué, Michael*,' announces Henri, the retired cherubim, amid a gentle ripple of applause. As our eyes meet for a second, I can see that he knows what I've just been through.

'*Je suis désolé*,' I exclaim.

'*Non, c'était très bien*,' coos Françoise, Henri's wife, taking his arm. Her smiling face reminds me of a beautiful wrinkled peach. And to see these two old souls so happy together somehow makes everything OK.

'But I got it all wrong,' I say.

'Not *all* of it,' chuckles Henri. 'And you'll find it easier next Saturday.'

'*Ah, bien sûr*,' I hear myself say, when what I really mean is, 'Are you telling me we have to go through that all over again next week?'

Suddenly a wiry old man in a grey suit bowls up. '*Mes félicitations* to the young Anglican organist,' he chirrups in French, his eyes bulging from their sockets.

I'm about to beg him to keep his voice down when I become aware that I haven't gone up in a puff of smoke, and that no one seems remotely surprised.

'*Merci, Monsieur*,' I hear myself saying, though inwardly I'm thinking, 'How the hell did you work that one out?'

The landscape fades from gold to grey, as the trees give up their last shards of shrivelled foliage. I hear the hiss of the distant river more clearly now, and the rattle of the two-coach trains rumbling through the cutting at the bottom of the hill, their diesel engines churning as they begin the climb towards the viaduct that spans the valley behind the church.

My breath fogs in front of me as I trudge out to the barn to fetch another armful of logs for the wood-burning stove. Tonight, I have just fixed myself a Pastis and poured a heap of pistachio nuts into a bowl when Jean-Michel Faure, the president of the tennis club, phones. I left him a message a fortnight ago, in the traumatic aftermath of my debacle with the lady from the tourist office. And now, without preamble and in a voice booming enough to make me hold the receiver away from my ear, he wants to know if I'd like to take part in a game of doubles on Tuesday evening.

'*Bien sûr*,' I reply, feeling the familiar fear grip my insides. 'But won't it be dark?'

Jean-Michel laughs so hard that the phone vibrates in my hand. 'There are lights in the gymnasium. We play indoors at this time of year, unlike *les Anglais*.' I wonder how he knows this. At the little tennis club in Dulwich, Simon and I would often play tennis in midwinter, slipping and sliding on the frosty courts.

'*Ah, très bien*. But there's one other thing, Jean-Michel.'

'Yes?'

'I'm really not very good.'

'Nonsense,' he barks. 'That's what everyone says about themselves. You'll be fine. *À mardi, bonne soirée*,' he barks, and hangs up.

Another chance to make a fool of myself. I hang up the phone, sip my milky Pastis, and settle down to my six o'clock think. Except that I don't seem to be able to think, for my mind is racing, cluttered with images from long ago.

Aged seven, my best subject is English, and my

worst subject is PE. In my dreams, I fantasize nightly about being given an off-games chit by matron.

Football is the thing I dread most of all, because I am so useless. Yet it is the one thing that all the other boys seem to care about.

I cannot understand why I am so bad at games, because when my father was at school, he was some kind of sports hero. He was captain of everything and – before a vast crowd, silent with excitement – took the decisive kick in the Public School Rugby Sevens of 1953, earning a write-up in *The Times* as Sherborne celebrated its first and only national victory on the rugby pitch.

Twenty years later, in 1973, twenty boys of different shapes and sizes are shivering on the touchline of a muddy football pitch beside a railway line in Woking. Behind my back, I cross my fingers. Please let me not be the last, not again.

Mr Bishop, the PE teacher, raises himself on to his toes, blows his whistle even though nobody is talking, and tells the two biggest boys to pick teams. I hate Mr Bishop, and I know that he hates me. I can see the scorn in his eyes, and the derision flowing in the veins that stand out on his temples.

A train rumbles past the pitch, and I wonder if the passengers have any idea how much it hurts to be here, waiting to be picked, knowing you will be the last, once again.

Aged eleven, my best subject is Latin, and my worst subject is PE. In the first round of the Windlesham tennis tournament – which I have entered in the deluded hope of impressing Clara Delaville – I am drawn against Norman Handley, who is the best player in the school.

There I stand, with my stubby little racquet and regulation itchy-navy shorts, grey Aertex shirt and plimsolls.

My opponent arrives with three Dunlop Maxply racquets, a smartly ironed Fred Perry ensemble in dazzling white and – most covetable of all – a brand-new pair of Dunlop Green Flash shoes.

Really, Handley is thoroughly decent about the whole thing. He doesn't hit the ball too hard at me during the knock-up, and he doesn't complain each time he has to jog on to the football pitches to fetch my latest skyer.

I have decided that I will be satisfied if I win at least one game in the whole match. And then we begin, and I am forced swiftly to revise my ambitions. Now I shall be thankful to win at least one point.

But I can't. Not a single point. Not a blessed sausage.

Handley, damn him, doesn't make one error. Not one. I can *tell* that he doesn't want me to win a single point. He just hits four out of every five shots to my backhand, and I hit five out of every five of these into the net. He doesn't even have the common decency to hit one double-fault, to salve my embarrassment. What makes this worse is that he smiles – not at me, but to himself – throughout our encounter. It is a beastly sort of smile; the smile of someone who wants you to know that he knows a secret, but doesn't want you to know what it is. If he were any less good-natured, it would be a smirk. But what makes my drubbing even more mortifying is that we are playing on one of the courts opposite the girls' dormitories. So my shame is visible for all the world – and, more particularly, for Clara and her friends – to see.

'Bad luck, Michael,' says Handley, glancing up at the dormitories and leaping the net to shake my hand after I have fluffed my last backhand.

But there was no luck involved. I am hopeless, that's all there is to it. And as I drain my Pastis in a smoky old kitchen in France, twenty-seven years later, I have no reason to revise my opinion. I am, quite possibly, the worst desperately keen tennis player in northern Europe.

Tuesday night, and the gymnasium at Jolibois doesn't appear to have a door. I can hear tennis being played within, but as I circumnavigate the place, I begin to think that the players must have started playing before the builders walled them up inside. Eventually I stumble in through a fire-exit, and come face to face with three blank stares.

'*Monsieur Wright!*' roars a hawkish man in square glasses and a red tracksuit, as he strides forward to shake my hand. I'd guess he is about sixty. He introduces himself as Jean-Michel, the club president. Though he appears hard, there is an effusive quality about him, too, like water gushing from a rock in midwinter. Two other players amble up to us, and I feel a twinge of surprise because *they are both roughly my age.* This is a bit of a breakthrough: youngish blokes in Jolibois.

The taller of the two – a toothy grin beneath a spiky outcrop of black hair – beams at me, shakes my hand, and goes back to bouncing a ball on the edge of his racquet, pacing in circles like a welterweight boxer limbering up for a fight. The other looks more intense: stocky and combative as a pit-bull, with a hint of moroseness lurking behind his frown.

The welterweight boxer strikes the ball with a silky smoothness, knees bent, perfect as a demonstration video. The pit-bull is more punchy, racing around the court like a speeded-up cartoon, and making me feel a whole lot better as he hits shot after shot into the net or – with a crash of pressurized felt on metal – at the ceiling.

They are all considerably better than me. I've played indoors before, at Queen's Club with the eminent psychiatrist, but the gentle moon-balling we do there is nothing compared with the hustling smash-and-grab of tennis in the doorless Jolibois gym. The ball seems to ricochet off the shiny floor like the puck in a game of air-hockey, and I miss it completely with my first shot, my racquet arriving at the allotted spot in mid-air about a second after the ball has flown past me.

Yet tonight is one of those rare times when, against all the laws of physics and natural justice, I do not utterly disgrace myself. We play a game of doubles: the boxer and the pit-bull against the rock in midwinter and the funny Englishman. There is a lot more cut-and-thrust, and a little less good-natured joshing, than I am used to from the little club in Dulwich, where the smell of barbecuing sausages would waft over our friendly mixed doubles. But the god of double-faults and fluffed smashes smiles upon me and – to my surprise and relief – I even hit one or two good shots. It doesn't matter to me that Jean-Michel and I lose, although I think from the way he grinds his teeth that it matters to him. No, what counts is that I have passed a kind of test – a sporting test – and that I feel involved and part of something.

'I do find it amazing,' I tell them as we walk back to our cars afterwards, 'that it is possible for someone like me to come here from Angleterre – from abroad – and none of us have met before, yet we can play a game together, following the same rules, all with the same idea. And it works, just like that.'

The boxer and the pit-bull exchange glances. My epiphany has been a private one. I shouldn't have attempted to try to explain it. But Jean-Michel, relenting, helps me out.

'*Le sport, c'est international.*' He shrugs, his glasses glinting in the moonlight as he swigs water from a bottle of Evian. 'Now you just have to learn to win.'

'Our first international victory,' laughs the pit-bull, making a fist and shaking it at the boxer. Then he gives me a friendly thump on the shoulder. 'And Tim Henman will be back next week.'

I wake up at two o'clock in the morning, still in my tennis kit on a rug at the top of the stairs. Last night, my success – or at least my failure to fail – on the tennis court inspired me to a private celebration involving a very cheap bottle of red wine from Netto. Coming on top of the beer and Pastis which preceded it, this has not proved a tremendous panacea for my health.

My head feels as if it is full of boiling marmalade. I wish I could remove my brain and rinse it gently under a cold tap for a few seconds. That might help.

Seven o'clock and things have not improved. Cool hands on my forehead, that's what I want. These not being avail-able, I fry myself some egg and bacon. And a tomato. And butter some toast. Sometimes an English breakfast is the only thing that will do the job. I'd love a cup of tea, too, but that would sock my temples something rotten.

The two tomato halves are just beginning to sizzle in the pan when I hear the sound of a diesel engine out-side the back door. It's my neighbour, Gilles.

'Are you all right?' he asks, peering at me and reaching forward to shake my hand with his masonic grip.

I nod carefully. 'Just a little too much *vin rouge* last night.'

He strokes his beard and chuckles. '*Ah, les Anglais aiment bien boire.*'

There is not much I can say to this, so Gilles continues. 'Do you want a cockerel?' he asks. As you do.

I blink; glance at his van. 'Is it in the back? Is it . . . *alive*?'

'No, no, he's not in the van. But he's a fine cockerel,' says Gilles. 'I have two, and this one's being bullied. So I wondered . . .'

Well, yes, I do like the idea of being woken by a trumpeted *cocorico* – French cockerels don't doodle-do like their English cousins – albeit not in my current state, which makes even Gilles's soft voice sound like a meat-slicer. But what will my six girls think?

In the end, a visit to view Gilles's cockerel after break-fast fixes everything. The strutting fellow turns out to be so splendid that I make the decision on the girls' behalf. This, for reasons I cannot explain, shall be Titus.

Twice the size of my smallest hens, and resplendent in his golden breeches, Titus is a dead ringer for Holbein's Henry VIII. He arrives that evening, upside-down, legs strapped together with a length of bandage, swinging like a nightwatchman's lantern from Gilles's outstretched arm. It's not the most dignified entrance, but – wincing – I take comfort from the thought of the dishy harem that awaits him. We put him into the chickens' enclosure, watch for a few moments as he scampers around, vainly attempting to avoid being bullied by his new wives, and then I walk Gilles to his car.

Five minutes later, we are standing there discussing sheep houses when we hear the pit-pat-pit-pat of a scampering biped. *Titus.* Legs akimbo, the little blighter is pounding down the drive, throwing up clods of mud in his wake. My girls, it seems, are not good enough for him. Or did the sisterhood freeze him out? Either way, he's off.

'Shouldn't we *do* something, Gilles?' I ask.

'He's your cockerel now,' laughs Gilles, with the air of a man who has chased a lot of chickens in his time. 'Maybe you'll find him up a tree in the morning, if a fox doesn't get him.'

Next day, I am woken from a fitful sleep by a joyous sound. It's Titus, crowing in the far distance. Now I don't speak fluent cockerel, but the young bugler sounds decidedly anxious as he tootles out the reveille. Donning my wellies over my stripey pyjamas, I grab a bucket of chicken feed and stumble out to coax him home.

So begins a chase scene that lasts considerably longer than Titus's entire time in captivity at La Folie. Unimpressed by the lure of my chicken feed, the escapee is soon three fields away and heading for St Tropez.

I chase Titus over hill and dale; I gallop after him through hedges and bramble bushes. He flops across a stream; I fall into the stream. Wellies squishing, ripped pyjamas dripping and dropping – the elastic seems to have gone west somewhere in those brambles – I stagger onward, feeling a bit like the Terminator after he's been through the car-crusher.

A good thirty-five minutes later, I am so fed up that I head back to the house and resort to an underhand tactic. Delving into the mildewed cupboards in the kitchen, amid the pea-like husks of dead wood-lice and the sticky white globs of spider spawn, I draw out a fearsome weapon: the domestic equivalent of the European nuclear deterrent. It's not much, but it's the biggest cooking pot I can find.

Returning to the fray, I wave the pot meaningfully at Titus. Panicked, he makes a dash for a distant hedgerow. I sprint after him, brandishing my saucepan in one hand, whilst doing my best to hold up my jim-jams with the other.

This is when the postman's van comes round the corner of the drive.

'*Bon . . . jour . . . Mon . . . sieur*,' he murmurs, winding down the window of his yellow van just halfway.

'*Bonjour*,' I pant, holding out my saucepan to receive a

pile of leaflets about pork bargains from Netto. '*Er . . . j'essaie d'attraper un poulet . . .*'

'*Oui?*' He eyes my pyjamas suspiciously. '*Eh bien, bonne chance . . . et bon appétit,*' he says, leaving me choking on his exhaust as he zooms off in a cloud of diesel smoke.

It's now that Titus makes his big mistake. He attempts to dive through a hole in a fence that is about the size of a ten-euro note. And gets stuck. I narrow my eyes and wish I had a pair of spurs jingling on my boots and a cheroot to chew between my teeth as I advance upon my quarry. Yet Titus still has some fight left in him. The poor chap almost shakes himself to pieces in a froth of red-and-green feathers when I grab him and do my best to contain his thick beating wings.

By the following morning, and after a night with my gorgeous girls, Titus has come to his senses. He struts out of the chicken house behind them, proud as you like, before leaping up on to a gate and bellowing his lungs out. *Cocorico! Cocorico!*

This sound gives me a ridiculous thrill every time I hear it, and the girls seem happy enough, too. They have even stopped bullying each other, now that they have a bloke who makes them feel wanted on an hourly basis. Titus has made his mark. At the start, and in a manner that absolutely does not make me think of the femme fatale in the tourist office, I take it they were just playing hard to get.

# 15

## SPACE INVADERS

One morning, the cat and I are woken from our beauty sleep at the crack of dawn, and not by Titus. Outside my bedroom window, I can hear a jeering mob. *Mon Dieu.* It's those women again. And more of them than ever before.

I know why they're here. The fat trollops want what's left of the shrubs at the front of the house. I rub my eyes, and there they are, smugly gazing up at me from below the window, chewing away like bored teenagers. So this is how Potiphar felt. But all he got were seven fat cows, whereas I've got twenty-seven fat sheep. And this is not a dream.

A pair of these buxom Marys – escapees, no doubt, from Old Boulesteix's place over the hill – turned up yesterday morning. By the afternoon, they were back with a couple of friends. And now the gossip has spread: tasty foliage on offer up at La Folie. Coach parties welcome. Foxgloves and chips all round, please, Mavis.

As one who had a knack of killing every house-plant I touched in London, I feel strangely protective of these

French fronds that are still stretching towards the sky in spite of me and the encroaching russet of autumn. I've noticed that Nature manages very much better when I resist the urge to intervene. But I'm not prepared to apply this rule to marauding *moutons*.

Hurrying downstairs in my dressing-gown, I dodge the mouse entrails lined up for my approval on the bottom step, and confront the bleating throng. This is considerably more exciting than rushing down to switch off a car alarm in East Dulwich.

'*Va-t'en! Va-t'en!*' I yell, scampering around the back of the invaders and clapping wildly at them. The result is instant. The cat rockets up a tree. And the sheep tuck into their breakfast more hungrily than ever. I suppose I just have a way with animals.

A few minutes later, having found my inner sheepdog, I manage to hurry all the sheep down the drive and they hustle back through their hole in the fence. Afterwards, I feel strangely deflated. It was good having sheep at La Folie, if only for a moment.

A few days later, Gilles and Josette come to lunch. I've invited Old Boulesteix and his wife, too, but Gilles tells me that he'll be very surprised if Monsieur Boulesteix ever sets foot in La Folie.

'Boulesteix can't stand *les Anglais*,' he coughs.

'*Mais pourquoi?*' I ask, opening the oven of the wood-burning stove and taking out the shepherd's pie that I have cooked. I've never met Boulesteix, but his wife always say a friendly *Bonjour* when I see her in the fields above the house.

'Because he used to rent a farm not far from here, until an Englishman bought it for an amazing price.'

'A bargain?'

'No, a rip-off. That's why many people around here

have lost respect for the English. They pay too much. *Il faut marchander*. You have to haggle.'

Like the colours at La Folie, France is changing, too, as the English invaders rush in.

'We do like you, Michael,' says Gilles. 'But thanks to the English, the young here can't afford to buy houses any more.'

I don't know what to say to this. I put the shepherd's pie on the table, and fetch three plates from the wood-burning stove.

'It's the same for me,' continues Gilles. 'When I retire in two years' time, I'll have to stop renting the farm. We were going to buy a house with a little piece of land. But now there's nothing we can afford.'

I'm thinking about all this when Gilles jumps up and starts waving his hand in the air. Is this what French haggling looks like, I wonder?

'*Ah, merde . . .*' he yells. I notice that the top half of one of his fingers is missing. *Mon Dieu*. I leap up, too, glancing around for a cat with a French finger in its mouth. But there doesn't appear to be any blood.

'Those plates are hot!' he says, glaring at me.

'Er, yes. I've heated them.'

'Is that an English thing?'

I'm not sure how to answer this. I am too busy staring at Gilles's hand, and the gap where the middle finger should be. Has he burnt it off?

'An accident with a chainsaw,' he explains. 'Years ago. It hurt like hell; still does, on cold wet days.' He doesn't have much control, he says, over the nerveless severed stump.

We all think about this for a moment.

'So in France, you never heat the plates?' I ask.

Gilles and Josette stare at each other as if I'd just proposed a game of Twister.

'No, we don't,' he says slowly. 'But it's an interesting idea.'

And again we sit in silence, basking in simple wonder at our differences as I serve up the shepherd's pie. Like sodium in a swimming-pool, it fizzes and splutters when it hits the white-hot plates.

'What do you think about me buying some sheep, Gilles?' I ask, as we stand and survey my jungle pasture after lunch.

'You? Sheep?' Gilles whistles. I can see him rifling through the first ten things that spring to mind, until he comes up with an acceptably polite way of deflecting my folly. 'But you haven't any grass.'

'So what's that?' I ask, pointing at the shrubby chaos before us.

'*C'est pas joli*,' says Gilles, shaking his head.

Not pretty? Not pretty! I am stunned. I like my jungle. It looks wild and rustic. Clearly there is a gulf between French and English notions of what a proper field should look like.

'Suppose I come and mow just one strip with my tractor,' suggests Gilles, 'and you see what you think.'

'But won't that spoil it? And what about all the little creatures who must be living in there?'

'*Ah, bof*,' he replies, wagging his finger at me. 'I won't cut it too short.'

'Let me think about it,' I beg. It's hard to deny that mowing just one strip of jungle would really do no great harm to La Folie's savage ecosystem, but I'm terrified that Zumbach may turn up for a surprise visit, and see how I've violated his wilderness. Months after the sale, it still feels as if La Folie is more his than mine.

# 16

## DECEMBER: THE OXEN OF GERYON

Titus and the Egg Squad are still confined to the small yard outside the pigsty. This seems hard on them, when there is so much other land that they might explore: the grassy haven of what must once have been a beautiful orchard, rough scrub, the depths of the jungle; atavistic chicken heaven. Melissa and Mildred, my big white *poules de Bresse*, appear to have had the same idea, for – just as on that very first day – they have begun to make repeated flapping forays on to the wall of the yard and out into the field beyond, where the abandoned rabbit-hutches and the broken-down old ploughs and harrows lurk in the returning brambles like silted ships on the sea-bed.

So I build a fence around the field.

Quite possibly this fence will one day be listed as the worst-constructed fence in the Limousin, except that it is unlikely to last long enough for that. It looks about as taut as a set of curtains held up with half a dozen drawing pins. But at least it is, recognizably, a fence.

With due pomp and circumstance, I open the gate of the

pig-yard and let the girls into their lavish new enclosure. Out they potter, tottering on their high heels, handbags flying, heads perked on the qui vive. There is some low-grade pecking at my shoelaces, and then Melissa's off, like the brassiest ladette on a vodka-fuelled hen night. She's not interested in staying put. No, with the blood of Napoleon coursing through her veins, she is ready for fresh conquests. Up on to the gate that encloses the new field, cluck, cluck, cluck, come on girls, *veni, vidi, vici, je ne regrette rien*, and all that.

'Oh, blimey . . .' I begin to exclaim. In a flurry of feathers, they all follow Melissa: up on to the gate, then over and out.

At last, only poor Mary is left behind in the new enclosure. Flapping and fluttering, she is unable to make the jump to freedom. She doesn't even seem to be able to cluck, bless her. I feel so bad for her, I lift her up, too. On the top of the gate she turns her head and gives me an apologetic blink before jumping down on the other side and charging after her sisters. Together, the six of them waddle into the distance like the Magnificent Seven with one missing.

I think we can call that a success, I say to myself, peering after them.

Later the same day, I am in the queue for the check-out at Champion, and the old Frenchman in front of me is struggling with his shopping. I can tell from the way he is eyeing the long queue behind him, and doing his best to hurry – fumbling in his purse, struggling to find the opening in the carrier bag, dropping his courgettes – that he's not local. I shuffle forward and start to help him.

'There's no hurry, *Monsieur*,' I tell him in French. 'And these carrier bags are tricky.'

'*Ah, merci bien, Monsieur. C'est très gentil.*' He sighs. 'I'm not as young as I used to be.'

When I walk out of the supermarket, the old man is waiting for me.

'*Vous êtes anglais, Monsieur?*' he asks, with an amused smile.

'Ah, you guessed.' I laugh.

'*Et vous habitez ici, à Jolibois?*'

'I'm doing my best.'

The old man hesitates. 'It's just that I am having some local people for drinks tonight. Some of the more cultured local farmers. And I thought you might like to join us. Are you free?'

'You Frenchmen are very spontaneous,' I reply, chuckling.

'That's settled, then. Here, I'll draw you a map.'

And so I meet Jérôme, seventy-three, a former banker from Paris who has nine grandchildren, nine horses, nine bicycles, several donkeys, four hundred acres of beautiful wooded hillside, and a mind as quick as an escaped cockerel.

Inviting a complete stranger to your house for drinks with the locals is – I think – more a Jérôme thing than a Limousin thing, where the official social-quarantine period for interlopers is, as I am only too well aware, six months.

But when dusk falls, I drive up to a grand farmhouse with a big square tower that looks like it ought to have bells in it, and Jérôme ushers me in as if I were an old friend. Which is almost how I feel, when I recognize one of the cheery faces glowing in front of the fire. It's Jean-Louis, the great oak of a man who delivered my logs back in October, whose WG Grace beard and yo-ho-ho geniality lend him the air of a young Father Christmas. Beside him stands his wife, the willowy Chantal, whom I have to stand on tiptoe to kiss, and who seems unusually poised and elegant compared with the more earthily pragmatic women I tend to see in Jolibois.

Jérôme turns out to be, like me, a former townie who has come to *la France profonde* in search of a more authentic existence. In my case, because I am hoping to learn what it takes to be a wise old man. In Jérôme's case, because he is already a wise old man, and he wants to create a haven for his grandchildren, secluded from the fever and fret of city life.

'I want the family to have a base,' he says, puffing on a manky cigarette he has rolled for himself, 'so that the question "Where do you come from?" will mean something again. These days people live everywhere, which is the same as living nowhere.'

Jean-Louis and Chantal nod.

I sip the Pastis that Jérôme has poured for me, feeling at once everywhere and nowhere. When people in Jolibois ask me from where I come, I always say '*Londres*', because they have heard of London, and it seems to reassure them to be able to put me into this neat box. Whereas 'Surrey' troubles them, because they learned at school that that's what you say when you sit on someone's *baguette* by mistake.

Soon after I moved into La Folie and gazed up at its crumbling walls, exposed roofs and dangling cables, I decided that I'd attack the renovation work myself. I came here to learn to be strong and practical and resourceful, after all.

It wasn't just that I couldn't find any French workmen to do it for me before Doomsday. I felt it was important for me to move up from a level-three handyman to the giddy heights of a level-five *bricoleur*. And I had all my London friends asking 'Are you planning to do it up yourself?' as if restoring an ancient farmhouse were as simple as fastening the back of a lady's dress.

I think I've made a jolly good start. After ten minutes of hacking away with a chisel at the 120 square metres of ancient French stonework that need repointing in the summer sitting-room – the soaring space that will one day house the grand piano – I have already completed an area the size of a table-tennis bat. Only another 119.98 square metres to go, and then I can go out and buy two tons of mortar and a trowel. This seems like an ideal moment to break for lunch. God knows, I've earned it.

La Grange is one of my favourite local restaurants. There is no choosing between *poisson* or *viande*; between *saignant* or *à point*. Vast dishes of food simply arrive, to be shared between friends. And it's ten euros for five courses, including a carafe of drinkable *rouge*. Four workers in blue overalls are already getting stuck in when I arrive.

'*Bonjour, Monsieur,*' they growl, with a quartet of nods. I love this about rural France, the way everyone says *bonjour*. In the last month alone, I must have shaken hands with more strangers than the Queen.

Two hours later, as I stagger out into the bar to pay, I feel like Humpty Dumpty before his tumble. But even in my feast-dazed state, I can't help but notice the bar's finely pointed stonework.

'*Qui a fait ça, Monsieur?*' I ask *le patron*, examining the masonry. 'It's good, isn't it?'

He laughs. 'You should have said so earlier. That's Jou-Jou. He was sitting right behind you. He does good work, and not expensive, either.'

In the evenings, I always make an effort to cook myself something – perhaps a lamb chop and some green beans, pasta with chicken and peppers, or a piece of fish. Tonight, hungry again after an afternoon spent sawing logs, I grill myself an *entrecôte*, and light two candles. Special occasions demand at least one more candle than the number of people dining. And so, night after night, I light two candles. For I have reason to celebrate.

Mine, after all, is not an enforced loneliness, and I know I am blessed to have the freedom to experience this strange new life. I am healthy in body and – *pace* Great-Aunt Beryl – in mind. I have no hungry mouths to feed. I am not suffocated with debt. I am simply a bloke at the beginning of the twenty-first century, attempting to learn what it means to be a man.

Unfortunately, laziness appears to come as part of the package. No doubt I was lazy in London, too, but idleness is more easily hidden there, amid the helpful niggle of deadlines and the buzz of other people's activity. Here at La Folie, there is no place for my laziness to hide. I can saw logs, build fences, feed chickens and heave rubble out of the summer sitting-room until the cows come home. Yet there is no escaping my failure to address *The Labours of Jack Larry*, the dazzling first novel I was meaning to write here in France. With plenty of time to write, and a daunting absence of distractions, I have finally run out of excuses. Yet I still don't know how to begin.

One day, I am staring at my blank computer screen and sipping my third mug of PG Tips when I hear the sound of a tractor grinding up the drive. Just as I feared: it's Gilles.

Despite my misgivings about his mowing my jungle, my neighbour is surging up the drive in a tractor the size of Poitiers, towing a machine that makes me very glad I'm not herbaceous.

'I'm not so sure about this, Gilles,' I yell above the din.

But the war-machine is already enveloping the hill in a cloud of destruction, from which fly clods of earth and the departed souls of mulched rodents.

In the silence that follows, I contemplate the strip of yellow devastation that I have sanctioned. It's the Rape of the Lock, the shaving of Aslan's mane and Delilah's betrayal of Samson all rolled into one.

'So what do you think?' asks Gilles, rubbing his hands.

'*Très impressionnant,*' I gulp.

Some days later, however, I take another look at Gilles's Strip of Death. Despite the season, it is beginning to look almost green, and tufts of late-autumn grass, not weeds, are beginning to appear. Birds are scratching for grubs. The demon barber appears, brandishing a local news-paper called *ParuVendu*. 'Look, Ouessant sheep for sale,' he chirrups.

'But I'm not ready for sheep, Gilles. I don't have any grass. And why Ouessants?'

'I've already rung the lady,' he says. 'There's one ram and three ewes, with four extra rams thrown in as a *donné*. Ouessants are really tiny and easy to look after. You should go and see them.'

So I phone the lady about the sheep, and arrange to go and see them. I don't really want to go, because I know I'm not going to buy them, and Aubusson is a long way away. I'm not *ready* to buy them, because sheep need fences and feed troughs and water-drinkers and all sorts of other things that I currently know nothing about. My *Sheep for Beginners* book is quite clear on this point: don't go buying a flock of sheep until you're ready to house them.

My first brush with sheep, as a child, was not propitious. I was eight years old and firmly in my Spitfire phase, when

Mum and Dad decided that they wanted to give up the rat race in Surrey, buy a huge house in Scotland and run it as a bed-and-breakfast. So we drove all the way up to the Highlands for the weekend and camped in a big tent – Abdul the Damned II – in the pouring rain.

I remember that all the fields were full of sheep, and Mum and Dad stayed up late drinking whisky with a German couple they met at the campsite. But their sulkiness next day could not compare with the rage of the farmer who came shaking his fist at us as we were about to drive off, his face the colour of beetroot, his yellow spittle spraying the car window, after our sausage-dog, Ceilidh, made the mistake of chasing his pregnant ewes.

'Yerra wee duggie has been baiting my sheep,' he roared. 'They'll all be losing thurra wee lambs a-cause a-ye.'

I was shocked, for this was the first and only time I have ever heard anyone shouting at my parents. I didn't think you could talk to grown-ups like that.

We never did hear if Ceilidh's antics ultimately proved fatal to those unborn lambs. But I was left with a sense of the fragility of young sheep, and the irascibility of farmers. Here was an entirely different world from my narrow Surrey universe, with a different set of rules and rhythms and facial expressions. Even people's spit was a different colour.

In Guildford a fortnight later, Ceilidh climbed through a fence and ate both our neighbours' guinea-pigs. The neighbours said not a word, as dictated by Surrey protocol. And my parents decided not to move to Scotland after all.

Throughout the two-hour drive down to Aubusson in le Pug Rouge, I promise myself I will not be swayed into buying any sheep.

On the way, a *gendarme* with an outsize moustache stops me, and gives me a forty-euro fine for not carrying a spare brake-lamp bulb. I hope he doesn't notice that I am also chewing gum and didn't brush my hair this morning.

The farm outside Aubusson must have been deserted for weeks. Even the '*En Vente*' sign is cracked and faded. The stable doors hang open, and any horses have presumably bolted. Weeds a foot high mark out the paving-stones in the yard, and a frayed halyard slaps against a broken flagpole in the wind. The empty windows of the house gape like groaning mouths. I shiver, and dial the number the sheep lady gave me when I spoke to her. Inside the dead house, I hear a phone jangle, unanswered.

Behind the stables is a lush hillside. A squat cabin, like a ski chalet for children, breaks the horizon. Perhaps the sheep are hiding in there, although it doesn't appear to have a door or any windows. A light rain is starting to fall.

I'm toying with wandering over to the cabin when a car with a broken exhaust draws up, unseen, on the other side of the buildings. I hurry round to meet it, anxious not to look too much like a snooper, even though that's what I am.

'*Bonjour, Madame*,' I say, extending my hand to a fierce-faced woman with an untamed scramble of black-and-peroxide curls. A handsome man shaped like a crooked drainpipe lurks in the background, steps forward to say hello, then fades away again.

'*Les moutons sont déjà vendus?*' I ask hopefully.

'So you've come to buy my babies,' barks the woman. She is clad head-to-foot in khaki, with a fake-leather jacket bursting at the seams that completes the destitute-storm-trooper effect.

'Well, just to have a look, really,' I burble. 'As I explained on the phone.'

'I've driven a long way to be here,' she grumbles, peering into the carrier-bag she's holding.

'So have I,' I remind her.

She considers this for a moment, frowns, nods and goes striding round the back of the house.

'You'll see that they come to their mother,' she says, motioning me to follow. Now she launches into a complex series of whoops and whistles and hollers. And then we both wait. I can hear a stream rustling at the bottom of the hill. But nothing stirs.

'Probably it's because it's wet,' she harrumphs. 'They don't like the rain. But they love bread.'

She begins to shake the carrier bag, loudly, in the breeze.

A brown muzzle appears on one side of the cabin. On the other side, another. And then, in a thudding, flying, waggling, galloping melee, eight tiny sheep come hurtling over the hillside towards us.

Oh. My. God. These creatures look like some extinct species dreamt up by Darwin to explain evolution. Each is the size of a microwave on legs. Their prehistoric mahogany wool reaches down to the ground in matted dreadlocks; a primordial fire glitters in their bright eyes, and there is something bewitchingly pagan about the curled horns of the chief ram, and the sheer aliveness of their twitching flanks.

These are not sheep. They are microdinosaurs; proto-*moutons* sun-bleached to almost the same colour as the Woolly Mammoth in the Ladybird book about the Stone Age.

'*Mes bébés! Mes bébés!*' cries the woman, causing the eight galloping missing links to hesitate in mid-stride. But

161

then she shakes the bag, and they're racing towards us again, my heart racing with them.

I must not buy any sheep. I cannot buy any sheep. I don't have any fences. And I certainly don't need eight of the things. A couple of old ewes, that would do nicely.

'Just look at the ram,' she says, snapping pieces off the baguette in her bag, and feeding them to the nuzzling muzzles. 'Have you ever seen such a fine beast?'

'*Non*,' I agree, marvelling at the satanic horns, and wondering what is the French for 'But that's not saying much.'

'And this little one,' she adds, struggling to catch hold of an even smaller ram, whose curled horns are as tiny as tiger prawns. Caught, the young creature flails as if in fear for its life.

'*Mon bébé! Mon bébé!*' she cries.

'Do they like being held?' I ask.

'They haven't forgotten me,' she says, breathless with the strain.

'Looks like they haven't been shorn for a long time,' I observe, my head on one side. *I must not buy any sheep.*

'Oh, they only need to be shorn every two years, because they're wild creatures. And look . . .' – she points at the chief ram – '. . . I did him myself, with scissors, last year.' No kidding. The poor fellow's fleece looks like what's left of a half-knitted jumper after it's been sucked into a vacuum-cleaner. My heart goes out to him as he gazes at me, side on, his head held high. I know he's daring me to laugh.

'He's worth at least a hundred euros, alone,' says the woman, tossing her own dreadlocks, fixing me with her own fierce stare.

'I'm surprised he's so thin, compared with the others. I thought rams were usually bigger.'

'Oh, that's just because the ewes are coming on heat and he's been chasing them.'

I nod, not really listening. No, no, you mustn't, yelps a voice in my head.

'So you want three hundred and sixty euros for the lot of them?' I ask.

'*Oui*,' she says, setting her jaw. 'That's for the ram and the three ewes. The other four rams are a gift.'

'It still seems a lot of money . . .'

'Ouessants are very rare,' she snaps. 'They easily fetch eighty euros each. But these are not sheep for eating. You do understand that, *Monsieur*?'

'Absolutely.' I'm not interested in eating them, any more than I'm interested in questioning her maths. I just want to learn something about animals. Mind you, I should have started off by learning about sheep before dashing out to not-buy some. I know I'm supposed to look at their teeth. But what am I looking for?

'I'll give you three hundred,' I say, my toes curling in my shoes. I am the world's worst haggler. And I'm not meant to be buying any sheep, anyway. Just as I feared, she is disgusted at my offer.

'You're saying you'll give me three hundred for these sheep?' Not so much disgusted; more like incredulous. I shift uneasily from foot to foot.

'That's right,' I say, sticking manfully to my guns.

'Is that francs or euros?' she asks, cogs visibly ticking in her brain as she flounders in mental-arithmetic land.

'Euros, obviously.'

'Étienne!' she yells. From nowhere, the drainpipe man appears, shambling out of the shadows, grinning shyly at me. 'The Englishman is offering me three hundred euros for my sheep. What do you think?'

'They're your sheep,' he says, trying to hide his smile by stroking his chin.

'Of course they're my sheep.'

'And I assure you that I will not eat them,' I add, the expert haggler twisting the knife in the bosom of his helpless victim.

'You promise?' That glinting glare again. This lady would make an excellent gypsy fortune-teller, if she didn't frighten all her customers away.

'*Oui, je promets.*'

We have a deal. I even give her twenty euros cash, there and then, as a sign of my good faith. It's going to take me a fortnight to create a properly fenced field for her babies, and I don't want her thinking I might try and back out now. Nor do I want her selling my sheep to anyone else.

I drive away, singing. For I am a sheep farmer in spite of myself. Never mind that what I have bought is a ramshackle bunch of munchkins of uncertain parentage. Unloved, overpriced and trailing their manky black dreadlocks, they resemble nothing so much as a gang of Rastafarian street kids. And I now have just a fortnight to fence my jungle, freshly mown for their arrival.

# 17

## THE MAN-EATING HORSES
## OF DIOMEDES

'The first and biggest hurdle to keeping animals,' Jean-Louis the woodsman told me when we were at Jérôme's for drinks, 'is enclosing the land on which to keep them. In the city, hedges and fences are for keeping people out. In the countryside, fences are all about keeping animals in.'

'How big are your sheep, *Monsieur*?' asks the smiley blonde assistant in Alliance Pastorale, the farmers' wholesaler from which Gilles has recommended that I buy my fencing sundries, including *grillage*. This is the squared wire mesh that is to be stretched between my wooden posts. I am determined to do better with this fence than the last one.

I hold my palm out flat, about two foot off the ground.

'*Ah, c'est une blague*,' she giggles.

'*Non, non*, it's not a joke,' I reply. 'They're Ouessants, the smallest sheep in the world. From the isle of Ouessant, just off the coast of Brittany.'

'Ah, so they're *dwarf* sheep!' she says, brutally conjuring up a world of garden gnomes and toy windmills. 'In that case I should think eighty centimetres should do you.'

'But won't they jump over it?'

'Well, how much grass do you have?'

'About a hectare.'

'Only *one* hectare?' She stifles a guffaw. 'For how many sheep?'

'Eight,' I declare, trying to sound modest as I straighten up and expand my chest.

She examines my face carefully. 'Quite honestly, *Monsieur*, for eight little sheep, I think that will be plenty.'

While the smiley lady looks up the codes for the *grillage*, I wander around the racks of syringes and pincers and powders and pessaries, wondering what other Useful Gadgets I can justify. What about all those sticks of dye, the buckets with half a dozen teats sticking out, the shepherd's crooks? Shan't I need a crook?

Next, I head off to Beaumarin to buy my fence-posts. Acacia is best, Gilles tells me, but chestnut is most common. He's told me to use concrete posts for the corners, and to set these in concrete, too.

The snag here is that I know about as much about making concrete as I know about two-stroke motors. At Windlesham, hatchet-faced Mrs Smollett taught us how to bake a sponge cake, and mine did achieve a startling evocation of concrete, but it wasn't the real thing.

Seeking concrete wisdom, I go and see Émilie's husband, Fred the Viking. Now Fred is always covered in a fine coating of masonry dust, so he is sure to know all about concrete. Especially since he has just bought himself a cement-mixer, the manliest power-tool of all.

'Yeah, no problem,' he says, lowering his sledge-hammer

and pushing his fair hair out of his eyes with the back of his hand. We are standing in what Fred describes as the kitchen of the house he is rebuilding, though it reminds me of the dungeon of a ruined castle. 'You're welcome to borrow the cement-mixer. I'll come and give you a hand, if you like. I'm no expert, but Douglas has shown me how to do it.'

'Douglas?'

'Huge bloke, from London. Built like a brick privy.'

'He doesn't live just over the hill from me, does he? My neighbour, Gilles, mentioned an English giant.'

'That would be him,' laughs Fred. 'I thought you'd already have met.'

Douglas, it emerges, is an ex-City boy who lost all his teeth and nearly lost his eyesight playing rugby, and now supports his wife and four children by working as a plasterer. 'He's huge and looks a bit scary,' explains Fred, 'but he's very gentle when you get to know him.'

Fred sends me off to the builders' merchants to buy sand, gravel and four sacks of cement. For once in my life, I feel positively gritty. In London, at B&Q or Homebase on the Old Kent Road, I never bought anything more hardcore than a few pots of paint and some wood to build a house for the cat; a complex, sloping-roofed bungalow which took me several days to construct, and which she has never deigned to enter. This, from a cat who cannot resist a cardboard box, even the ones so small that she can hardly fit one cheek of her vast bum inside.

Today, back at La Folie, Fred and I are manfully hauling two dustbins full of sand and gravel out of the car and firing up a cement-mixer. This makes me want to beat my chest and roar, or at least to swagger just a little, as proper workmen do, with their arms held stiffly away from their sides to imply the vast muscles that prevent them from lowering them, like toddlers zipped into quilted anoraks.

Spots of rain are beginning to fall from an iron-grey sky. Into the juddering mixer go the sand and gravel, then the cement, and Fred sloshes in water from a bucket until the required consistency is reached. It's just like making a cake with sulky Mrs Smollett, only with manlier ingredients.

'I think I would enjoy working on a building site,' I declare, leaning on my shovel.

Fred narrows his eyes at me.

'Well, maybe for a week or so,' I correct myself.

He keeps on staring, his head on one side.

'All right, for about a day and a half, then.' I laugh. 'But you know what I mean. There's something about manual work . . . it just feels more honest to me than sitting in front of a computer and writing about *Macbeth*.'

'It's atoms and bits, isn't it? With your PC, you're just manipulating digital impulses. Whereas here we're actually shifting *stuff*. And it feels better to me, too.'

'It must be a lot of atoms,' I say, pressing my fist into the small of my back.

'On a computer, it's a lot of bits. Is that your phone?'

I hurry inside, leaving a trail of white footprints on the tiles of the winter sitting-room, like a page from a ballroom-dancing manual.

It's my brother, Nicholas, on the phone. I can picture him sitting there in his swanky office in Farringdon, meditating on computer networks and partitioning hard drives while our cement-mixer thunders out its *musique concrète* in the rain.

Last night I left a message to see if Nicholas would be willing to come and help me collect my sheep – I'm already beginning to fret about the journey back from

Aubusson – and he sounds only slightly suspicious about what will be required of him.

'Do they *bite*?' is his first question, intoned with the whispered theatricality of a 1970s wildlife presenter. I picture him raising one eyebrow. Nicholas has never taken anything too seriously, and tends to live his life as if it were a movie. I suspect he regards my adventure at La Folie as he might regard a spoof documentary about the hunt for the Loch Ness Monster.

'No, of course not. They're very tame.' I've read that Ouessants are extremely wild, and I've no idea how the sheep will react to a two-hour car journey. Apparently the stress can sometimes kill them. But I'm not about to tell Nicholas that.

'So where do I come in?' I can hear he is eating a sand-wich. Probably an All-Day Breakfast from Prêt-à-Manger, although it might be the chicken-and-bacon club. I suddenly feel very, very hungry.

'Well, perhaps they're not *that* tame. And I need you to stop them trying to climb into the front while I'm driving.'

'Rrrrright. By speaking firmly to them?'

'By giving them a good slap across the chops.'

'Ah. Perhaps Steven will be free next weekend?' Steven is my other brother, but he is an Artist, and probably allergic to sheep, as Nicholas well knows. I can tell that he likes the idea of being a shepherd for a day, but wants to make me suffer a little. He prides himself, with complete justification, on being the one practical member of the family.

'There may be a little bit of fence-building, too,' I add, just to seal his enthusiasm.

'All right, I'll be there at the end of the week,' he sighs, his enthusiasm still expertly hidden.

'Thanks, Nick. What are you eating, incidentally?'

'Chicken Caesar sandwich from Prêt. Why?'
'Oh, you know. Just curious.'

Next day, the midday sky is black and it pours with rain as I set to work on setting the last three corner-posts. This is what I came to France for, I tell myself, as I struggle to push the wheelbarrow full of concrete up the soggy hillside, while Mildred and the girls shelter in the barn, clucking at the rain thundering on to the roof above them, before it tick-tick-ticks on to my precious wood-store in the places where it has found a way through the lichen-encrusted tiles.

I can see the cat gazing at me from the window-sill inside the house, idly licking a paw as I stagger past with one of the concrete posts across my shoulders as if I were a peasant in a pillory.

I've already painted evil black tar on to the tips of all my wooden posts. On the phone, my father tells me I need a post-hole borer (his favourite Useful Gadget) to make the holes for these, before adding – as he always does – that 'Your mother cooked something really first-class last night,' as if he were letting me in on a secret. But both Gilles and Frère Sébastien have told me I must use a heavy iron bar to make the holes. And when I find just such a weapon in the barn, apparently left behind after the Hundred Years War, I take another step further from Surrey; another step deeper into darkest France.

*Wham, wham, clang* goes the iron spear into the earth, juddering my spine every time it hits a chalk-seam, forcing a readjustment to right or left. My hands are soon numb. Sweat and rainwater are running into my eyes. And I'm enjoying this. The rain eases off, and a gentle mist that appears to be falling sideways keeps me cool, as I roughly set post after post in place. I think back to my conversation with Fred, when we were mixing concrete. Somewhere along the way through my comfortable existence, I lost touch with just how satisfying hard physical work can be. Especially when the only person making me do it is myself.

And then I'm whacking in the fence-posts with my sledgehammer, and watching the tops split after the first ten or fifteen hits.

'You need a different kind of *masse*,' sighs Gilles, dropping by to check on my progress and pulling a disgusted look as he examines my narrow sledgehammer. Then he leans forward to squint down my latest row of fence-posts, to see if it's straight.

'Not bad?' I say, panting like a happy spaniel.

'Not good,' he says, shaking his head. 'These should soon be fully set,' he adds, kicking one of the concrete posts. 'Let me know when you're ready to stretch the *grillage*. I'll come and show you how it's done.'

So it's back to the nice ladies at Alliance Pastorale for a new sledgehammer, one with a plastic shaft and a huge flat head. This is much massier than the first one, and does the job in half the time.

A day later, I'm so stiff from heaving all those atoms, I can hardly move. And time is running out. It's Thursday already. Nicholas arrives tomorrow afternoon, and we're to collect the sheep on Saturday.

Another ten wooden posts done. Gilles and Josette appear again, this time bringing with them the fence-stretcher: a couple of stout pieces of wood to grip the fence, two rusty iron chains, and a lever. I bring out the roll of *grillage* and we unfurl it, inquisitive chickens watching in awe as it rolls down the hill like a playful child.

With a haste that makes me think he must have left his

best trousers just in front of the fire, Gilles now begins to lever the *grillage* into a state of tension. This is amazing. After a few pulls, the fence begins to rise off the ground and stand all by itself. And then – as the wire tightens – it begins to look like a real fence.

Suddenly Josette shrieks, '*Arrête! Arrête!*' The concrete end-post has started to shift in its foundations. The concrete is solid enough. It's the hillside that appears to be moving. Gilles must be stronger than I thought. He stops tightening the *grillage* and the post holds. But the damage is done, for it now leans down the slope at a Pisa-type angle, almost perpendicular to the hill.

'It's not good,' says Gilles ruefully, looking at my botched fence.

'No, but it's another good lesson for me,' I reply. 'I'll do better with the next one.'

Nicholas is sitting on his luggage in front of the 1960s-style terminal building when I arrive at Limoges airport in le Pug Rouge.

'Am I late?' I ask, looking at my watch.

'The flight was half an hour early,' he shrugs. 'Jolly little airport, isn't it?'

'They're about to knock it down and put up a bigger one. This one was designed long before *les Anglais* discovered the Limousin.'

'There were so many English voices on the plane, it's hard to believe I'm in France.'

'Just wait till we collect the sheep,' I tell him. 'You will.'

The next morning dawns bright and clear, and Nicholas and I wander out to the barn to examine the vehicle I have selected for our mission.

'You can't be serious,' he says, gazing in awe at the Espace.

'What's the problem?'

'Michael, it's a *car*.'

'Yes, I know it's a car. But there's plenty of room in the back.'

'For eight sheep?'

'Well, they're very *small* sheep. And my neighbour Gilles says it's better if they're packed in tightly, because they won't charge around so much.'

'They won't *what*?' Nicholas's sheep experience is strictly confined to grilling and basting. He's not accustomed to being attacked by his own pot-roast.

As we rumble down the drive, I click a Blues Brothers tape into the stereo and Nicholas dons his shades.

'Right,' he says, perking up. 'It's a hundred kilometres to Aubusson. We've got a full tank of gas, no cigarettes, it's dark and we're wearing sunglasses. Hit it!'

En route, I declare that it's important we keep the sheep as calm as possible. 'And you'll need to give them a good slap, Nick, if they try to climb into the front.'

'Oh great,' he mutters.

Two hours later, and we are contemplating eight little dreadlocked thunderclouds – five rams and three ewes – as they rage and tear around inside their sheep house.

'I'm afraid they're a bit over-excited, *Monsieur*,' whispers the peroxide *Madame*. The drainpipe man attempts to tie up the hooves of the chief ram and then thinks better of it, as the panicked creature flails wildly to escape.

'We'll just have to put them in as they are,' he says through gritted teeth. 'But I'm worried about them smashing a window with their horns. If one jumps out, they'll all follow.'

'What did he say?' asks Nicholas.

'He said French sheep love car journeys.'

One by one we bundle the struggling animals into the back of the car, and then I'm writing a cheque for 280 euros and reassuring *Madame* that I won't turn her precious darlings into cutlets.

'One last thing, *Monsieur*,' she calls, as we drive off. 'The ewes are on heat.'

I'm not listening. I'm too busy concentrating on every bump in the road ahead, my pulse racing with concern for the creatures now in my care.

'What are they doing, Nick?' I bark every five seconds.

'They're still fighting. Does it matter that one of them's got a runny nose? Oh, hello . . .'

'*What?*'

Alarmed, I peer into the rear-view mirror. And there, peering back at me with an embarrassed grin, is the face of a small black ram, visibly jiggling. I raise myself higher in my seat to investigate, only to spy that the rest of the woolly scrum are all equally bent on doing what comes naturally. Ah, the joys of driving through rural France, while a flock of randy sheep stages a mass orgy in the back of your car.

As our travelling sex-show rumbles through sleepy villages, I gaily wave and smile at the walnut-faced matrons who stare at us in gap-toothed disbelief. The one blessing is that Ouessant sheep are so very small. So it's only when the lusty dwarves are actually up and at it on their hind legs that passers-by can see them participating in the sordid scene.

'Down, down,' hisses Nick, and I instinctively duck. But it's the sheep he's addressing. Just up ahead are a couple of *gendarmes* on motorbikes. I clench everything, concentrate very hard on the road ahead, and start chanting the thirteen-times table in French for the benefit of the lads in the back.

Somehow, we make it back to La Folie, and I lift the sheep over the newly constructed fence into their field. The place is slowly coming to life. Nick says he's right off lamb chops. I am an emotional wreck. And the Renault Espace will never be the same again.

# 18

## THE CERYNEIAN HIND

Jérôme – the old man I helped with his shopping in the supermarket – and I have become friends. We seem to understand one another, across the gap in our ages and language and culture. Our solitariness is a bond. And I think to myself how lucky his nine grandchildren are to have him, waiting for them in such a perfect place, with a horse and a bicycle for each of them.

But, as Jérôme explains to me one day, after he has patiently listened to my excited chatter about my new-found role as a shepherd, the mere fact of having horses and bicycles does not guarantee the presence of grandchildren.

'You have a piano in England that you do not play, and an aeroplane that you do not fly,' he says. We are chatting in his stableyard, where he has been showing me his donkeys. 'For me it's the same.'

'Not really, because those things are both far away. I'd have them here, if I could,' I reply. 'I will do, one day.'

'*Peut-être*,' he says with a gloomy shrug, opening another door in the ancient stone wall of the stables.

And, too late, I begin to understand the truth: that the grandchildren rarely come, and the nine horses wait in vain for their child riders, and the saddles of the nine bicycles are gathering dust, and the four hundred acres of beautiful wooded hillside do not rustle with the sound of children kicking their way through autumn leaves, because – as Jérôme acknowledges, chewing on a soggy cigarette that looks as if he rolled it in about 1934 – today's children do not always appreciate these things.

'Perhaps they will come next year, Perce-Neige,' he whispers, as we stand in the half-light of the stables and he strokes the neck of one of his unridden horses. The horse lowers its head and gazes at him. And to judge from the glances that they exchange, neither of them really believes this is true.

A fortnight after Nicholas's departure, a few days of late-autumn sunshine have lit up the landscape, so tonight the cat and I are out on the terrace again, having our twilight think. I sip a beer. She licks her paws.

I can't imagine how empty this place would feel without another living, breathing presence building its life around mine (although the cat would probably say that I am building mine around hers).

Each morning, round about six o'clock, she comes into my bedroom, jumps on to the bed and gently claws at my head until I outstretch one arm so that she can nestle against it. This I can bear. It's when she tries to clean her mouse-encrusted tongue by rasping it on my unshaven chin that I find myself grimacing and holding my breath.

Hard as it is for me to believe, we have only been here at La Folie for three months, and already she has chalked up at least thirty kills (excluding probables and lizards). Even now, as I stand at the wood-burning stove to sizzle myself a mushroom omelette, she rediscovers – and begins to chew – a forgotten mouse head on the kitchen floor. It's a sound that makes my shoulder-blades twitch. I remove it from her with a few words about the merits of dining al fresco, and she slinks out through the cat-flap looking (I like to think) guilty and embarrassed. Five minutes later she's back with another mouse, its two ends dangling from her jaws like one of the outsize moustaches in the *Colibri*.

I know that being in France hasn't been all plain sailing for the cat. I knew she might struggle to understand French-speaking mice. But I hadn't twigged how creepy the whirring of a hundred thousand French crickets might be to a London moggie brought up on traffic noise and police sirens. The spooked creature can spend hours peering out of her cat-flap with flattened ears and, on the rare occasions when she does summon up the courage to venture outside, expects me to keep guard while she performs her little *devoirs* under the cover of the lone pine.

I begin to share the cat's disquiet about what might be lurking out there, waiting for us. And tonight my vague foreboding ratchets up into something closer to alarm when – haunted by the scuttlings and scamperings around the knot-hole in the ceiling of my bedroom, directly above my pillow – I climb a ladder to investigate. What I find up there is worse than I feared. Between the roof beams, someone has left a rusty man-trap with jagged metal jaws, big enough to catch a young wildebeest, on a heavy iron chain. What did Zumbach know that I don't?

The chickens help keep me company, too – especially Mildred, because she always has so much to say, and Martha, because she appears to have decided that I am her best friend in the whole world. While the others are having their dust baths around the lone pine – traumatizing the cat, who would like nothing more than to answer her calls of nature in peace – the dear girl spends hours on the window-sill each day, gazing in at me. I gaze back. I think we must be in love.

Even the goldfish add to my social picture, in their dreamy, silent way, their three bright-orange shapes gliding in the depths of the pool, permanently searching for something they've already forgotten they've lost.

The sheep are something else. Ouessants, I discover, are not like the big white sheep in the fields all around La Folie, docile beasts bred to fatten as fast as possible. No, Ouessants are wild, ancient creatures, their blood coursing with the salt air of their rocky island home. Chase a flock of meat sheep, and they huddle together, scared and unthinking. Chase a band of Ouessants, and they scarper in all directions, eyes flashing, tails flying, making a nonsense of those ignorant souls who say that sheep are stupid. Mine are jinking, nimble athletes, with a ferocious side-step. So I don't chase them. I just stand and wonder at them as they lie in the grass, digesting their lunch, learning to accept their new surroundings.

I see now why *Madame* in her stormtrooper trousers gave me those four extra males as *un donné*, rather than expecting me to pay for them. Little Ramekin is no trouble, but his three brothers are fighting amongst themselves, and poor old Gaston – my chief ram, he of the satanic horns – has his work cut out defending his ewes from the Oedipal attentions of the youngsters. *Madame* assured me that Gaston alone would mate with the ewes, but the old boy cannot be everywhere at once. Worse still, the young rams – wonky-horned Charlie and his two thuggish henchmen – are much the greediest when it comes to snuffling up all the granulated feed I put out for the sheep, so the lads grow bigger while Gaston and the girls starve.

I place an advert on the notice-board in Champion, and pray that someone in Jolibois will be interested in providing a good home for two or three wayward Rastafarians ('*jeunes, noirs, en bonne santé*'). If not, the time may come when I have to take them to market.

My ambition for both the sheep and the chickens is for them to produce lambs and chicks in the spring, and – if possible – that those lambs and chicks should produce their own young the following year: a generation for which I will have been entirely responsible.

Day after day, I sit at my desk, looking out across the valley, worrying about the sheep, and thinking about starting the novel that I always thought I'd be able to start, just as soon as I was free of the distractions of the city. It never occurred to me that I might find a new and very much more pressing set of distractions in the rhythms of nature in darkest France. I think about Christmas in a few weeks' time, too, because I have decided to spend it here at La Folie, alone.

This will be my first Christmas away from home, and the thought makes me uncomfortable. In a way, that's why I've decided to do it. But there are also the Rastafarians, the cat and the chickens to think about. And Fabrice has asked me to play the organ for Midnight Mass, which is the Jolibois equivalent of playing Wembley. While I play, he will lead the singing.

Last week, Raphaël convened a meeting to decide which *chants* to include at Christmas, and I lobbied for 'Once in Royal' and 'O Come All Ye Faithful', albeit with French words. 'Silent Night' is in the mix, too. So my French Christmas will have an English soundtrack.

I want to rouse Jolibois with the traditional descants for the carols, the ones we used to sing in the choir at Windlesham, when the trumpets in the gallery would send tingles up my spine with their searing octave leaps in *Adeste Fideles*. But I can't remember how the melody goes in the penultimate line. So I phone my friend Jason in Dorset, who went to Charterhouse and writes music for television thrillers. He is sure to know. Jason laughs and performs the descant down the phone.

'*Glo-o-o-o-o-ria, in excelsis deo*,' he growls.

'If your phone is being tapped, someone at MI6 is going to be very worried,' I tell him.

'Ha ha ha. And you'll have Inspector Clouseau round in the morning.' He sounds very far away. 'What the hell are you doing in France?'

'I'm having an adventure. I'm learning to be brave.'

'I'll say. Are you all alone out there, then?'

'Apart from the cat and the chickens and the sheep. And the goldfish.'

'Chickens!' The word explodes in my ear, and I almost drop the receiver. 'I *love* chickens. But all ours were eaten by a bloody fox. On a beautiful, clear night with a full moon. Almost as bright as daylight, it was. They all decided to go for a walk. And we heard the fox picking them off, one by one, every few minutes, starting at about four a.m. The screams were horrendous. Deeply sad. Have you lost any of yours?'

'None yet, touch wood.' And I'm not planning to lose any, either.

'Well, good luck. And happy Christmas to you.'

I shiver. Outside, a chill wind has begun to hiss through the long grass beside the terrace. The cat comes and sits on my lap, eyes soon closed in a blissed-out ecstasy, kneading rhythmically at my jumper as if she were smoothing the lumps out of a cake mix.

Living in France makes perfect sense when the sun is shining and the air is warm on a cat's fur. But I suspect that the worst events in her life are the frosty days when I'm too mean to light the wood-burning stove. Anxious to preserve the integrity of my railway-carriage of a wood supply, I am currently refusing to burn a twig of it until the temperature in the kitchen has dropped below thirteen degrees (a concession, after we both found that waiting for it to drop below twelve degrees was just too parky for comfort). Parsimony apart, this is part of my process of attempting to harden myself up, although I don't suppose the cat sees it that way. Nor do the one or two unexpected guests who arrive at La Folie, like Raphaël le Prêtre, who reacts to my question 'May I take your coat?' as if it were a personal threat. And no wonder. The locals keep their houses so warm that you can slow-cook a *coq-au-vin* simply by leaving it on the kitchen table. If the cat ever visits such a place, I know I shall never see her again.

All this is what makes me nervous about the fact that my friend Zuleika is coming to stay.

She and I met at a journalism evening class I was teaching in London: fifteen adults buzzing in a grey classroom, while the night gathered and sparkled outside. Like the second-rate conjuror in Max Beerbohm's novel, Zuleika is one of those women who can make men fall in love with her at will. Not classically beautiful, she nevertheless has an ability to dazzle that could stop an elephant at a hundred paces.

Her aliveness was what first drew me to her: a wicked brilliance offset by the lost, almost melancholy face she presented to the world. She seemed fun and funky and altogether more worldly than I had been at twenty-six. She took me to cool bars without names, and with doors you wouldn't spot unless someone showed them to you. It was a brittle London thing, but there was a warmth and a connectedness, too, about our friendship that filled some of the gaps I could feel inside myself after Marisa and I had parted. It was no surprise to discover that she had the same birthday as me: 8 June. Or that her grandfather was killed in a celebrated crash in a Tiger Moth biplane. My grandfather, Pa, flew Tiger Moths, too, before the war.

One day, in one of the nameless, shady Soho bars with invisible doors, I took Zuleika's hand in mine and examined her palm.

'Do you know anything about palm-reading?' she asked, as I traced the lines with my finger. Her face glowed pale in the candlelight.

'No. I just wanted to hold your hand.'

'You're a silly man,' she laughed, drawing her hand away.

And then over the next few weeks of early summer, we grew closer, once the forcefield between us was broken by that first touch.

'You're one of my three favourite people in the world,' Zuleika told me one day. It didn't occur to me to ask who the other two were. And I couldn't reciprocate with similar precision, because I don't carry around a list in my head of my favourite people, like clubs in a league-table. But Zuleika was special.

'I'm buying a house in France,' I told her. 'I wonder if you'll come and visit me one day.'

'It's not out of the question.'

We only ever spent one night together, in London, on a night so hot we had to leave the windows wide open and pray for a breath of wind. And though it felt strangely beautiful, it felt like a night suspended in time, too, as if it couldn't really happen again. Especially when Zuleika emailed, soon after, to explain that it had been a bit of a mistake, and she now had a regular man on the scene and so would have to chalk our little dalliance up to experience. I scooped up all my feelings in a little pile, and put them back in the drawer marked 'wistful (misc.)'.

And then a few weeks ago, Zuleika emailed again, to say that she would like to come and stay at La Folie after all, from Boxing Day until New Year.

'My batteries need recharging and it would be good to see you,' she wrote.

I breezed to the fridge to pour myself a glass of wine. Though winter glimmered on the horizon, I felt as if spring had just arrived.

# 19

## CHRISTMAS IS COMING

Friday, a week before Christmas. Out scamper the chickens to peck at the frozen remnants of last night's *avoine*. Martha leads, with Mary, Margot, Melissa, Mildred and Meg bringing up the rear. Titus is last out, squatting to squeeze his tail feathers through the pophole. He is looking more like Henry VIII every day.

I pour *aliment complet* into their feed-tin (a grill-pan once used to crisp up chicken kievs in East Dulwich), and smash the ice on their water trough. But there's no water beneath: it's all ice.

After rattling sweet-smelling granules of *luzerne* into a bucket for the sheep, I crunch out to their field. They still run to the old metal feed-trough when I approach, though for the past three weeks I've been pouring their feed into the stout new wooden one I have built. I hope this is habit, rather than an aesthetic decision.

Gaston and Ramekin appear to be more snotty than usual after the cold night, but other than that, everyone seems happy enough. Doris comes and sniffs at my face as I kneel to put hay in their rack. I bless her for the intimacy.

There's still no response to my card on the wall at Champion, advertising Ramekin's brothers, Charlie and the boys. How could anyone not want three such sweet creatures? That's what I'm thinking when two of the strapping lads simultaneously butt Gaston from either flank, and I change my mind.

With a stone, I start hacking at the ice on their water trough, lifting out the shards with my bare hands. I work fast, attempting to stay ahead of the pain, but then the ache is burrowing inside my finger-bones and – growling to myself, which somehow helps – I run indoors to thaw the throbbing under the cold tap.

I drive down to town to buy some bread from the *boulangerie*, only to discover that the beautiful princess doesn't work there any more. But I'm not choosy. I cherish every human contact these days, and have become like the old ladies at the supermarket, who don't want to pack away their shopping at the till too soon, because they're having such a lovely chat with the cashier.

When I return to La Folie, the phone starts ringing as I unlock the door. It's Peter Viola, from the aeroclub.

'I say, are you coming to see *Père Noël* tomorrow?' he asks, his voice as reassuring as hot buttered toast.

'Is *Père Noël* who I think he is?' I reply. 'And, if so, do I have to sit on his knee in an enchanted grotto and tell him I've been good this year?'

'No, no,' chuckles Peter. 'He's flying in to the aeroclub tomorrow afternoon.'

'I'll be there. *Crème brûlée* in the Toquenelle first?'

'One o'clock suit?'

'Perfect. I'll just have to make sure I'm back in time to feed the sheep and play the organ for Mass. *À demain.*'

'They're a bind, these animals, aren't they?' says Peter. 'It's why I've never had a dog.'

186

'True. But commitment is one of those things I feel I need to learn about. So I can't help feeling that the animals are good for me.'

And then the phone rings again, and it's my mother.

'Are you all right?' she asks.

'Yes, I'm fine.'

'It's just that you sound a bit down.' Mothers say this sort of thing, even when you haven't said anything yet.

'No, I'm OK. The sheep are fighting amongst themselves, so I need to do something about the extra rams. But in myself I feel cheerful enough.'

'And what about Christmas? I'm worried about you being on your own. Isn't there someone you could go and visit?'

'I'll be fine. If I'm desperate, yes, I'm sure I can go and knock on someone's door and beg them to take me in. But to be honest, I think it'll be rather jolly; in the bleak midwinter and all that. Of course I'd rather be with all of you. But I can't leave the animals. And my friend Zuleika's coming after Christmas.'

'Oh? I don't remember you mentioning the name before.'

'Perhaps I never did.' And I'm already wishing I hadn't, now.

After I put the phone down, I feel guilty. I should have said more about Zuleika. And about what fun my solitary Christmas will be. It's all very well for me to get a masochistic thrill out of my splendid isolation, but I don't suppose parents ever stop worrying about their children.

Next day, crowds of children are shivering on the apron of the Aéroclub de St Juste, anxiously awaiting the arrival of *Père Noël* from the sky.

Here in the Limousin, Father Christmas travels not in a reindeer-powered sleigh, but in a big red Stearman biplane piloted by an elf called Roger, who moonlights as an Air France captain. I assume *Père Noël* is arriving early to give him time to make his French deliveries before heading across the Channel to squeeze down the chimneys of old England. As Christmas only lasts for one day in France, the pleasure is all in the anticipation.

In Jolibois, almost every *supermarché* shelf has been given over to boxes of chocolates, the streets are strung with white lights, and two hefty Christmas trees have been erected at the top of the Rue du Coq, just far enough apart for vehicles to squeeze through, but close enough together to make an excellent car wash if they were mounted on spindles and motorized.

Further down the street, the railings are camouflaged with pine fronds and shiny gift-wrapped boxes. 'How long before those get nicked or vandalized?' wonders the South London part of my brain. 'But this is Jolibois,' responds the French part, 'where there appear to be fewer people who regard human goodness, beauty and the happiness of others as a personal affront.'

'Are you going home for Christmas?' asks Philippe, the aeroclub's ace mechanic, who has designed and built his own plane out of little more than used toothpicks. I feel strangely proud to be able to say that, no, I'm staying here. We shepherds must wash our socks by night, gather our winter fuel, and so on. There's Midnight Mass to accompany. And Zuleika arrives on Boxing Day.

But I don't tell that to Philippe. Instead, I tell him that this will be the first time in my life that I have not spent Christmas with my family, and I see the event as some sort of masochistic personal test. On Christmas Day, I shall roast myself a fat turkey drumstick, pull a cracker with myself, and remember, too late, that I really don't like mince pies after all. If I can persuade the cat to don a pair of wellies, I'll even have my own panto.

It's only when I start to explain English Christmas traditions that I realize how unlikely they are. The French may share our weakness for indoor pine trees, gaudy decorations and illuminated reindeer, but Philippe begins to eye me as if I'd just head-butted his plane when I tell him the ingredients of a Christmas pudding. Watching his face, I'm reminded of the time I treated Gilles's wife, Josette, to a sniff of Marmite when they dropped round for an *apéro* one night. Smelling it, she burst into tears. It seems that the French don't really *do* sultanas, and suet loses something in translation.

'Just before the pudding is served, we hide old coins in it and then set fire to it,' I explain.

'I'm not surprised you have to pay people to eat that stuff,' wails Philippe. And I haven't even started telling him about bread sauce.

There isn't time, for just now a scarlet blur that must be *Père Noël* comes barrelling past us in a low-level side-slip at full throttle. The roar of the Stearman's great beast of a Pratt & Whitney radial makes my shins tingle. I see a red arm waving; a white beard streaming. From the rear cockpit, Elf Roger coaxes the ancient biplane into a graceful three-point landing and taxis to a halt. *Père Noël* unbuckles his harness, tugs his beard, straightens his scarlet hood, and steps down from the wing like a visiting rock star.

'*Père Noël! Père Noël!*' yell the children, hopping up and down on the apron. I'm equally excited, although it's the presence of an ancient biplane, rather than Father Christmas, that does it for me.

'He really has come,' says a solemn little girl beside me, eyes filled with wonder.

'Yes,' I murmur. 'He really has.'

*

As *Père Noël* is engulfed by the crowd, I hurry back to La Folie to feed the sheep – who blare at me like foghorns in the dusk – and then drive down to Jolibois to play the organ for Mass. It's the last Saturday before Christmas, and the congregation is already droning away at the first hymn, unaccompanied, as I dash into the church and thump up the stairs to the tribune. Lights on. Blowers on. Here goes nothing. The Mass passes in a surge of missed cues and wrong notes. Will I ever learn?

'*Je suis désolé*,' I say, shame-faced, as I slowly descend the stairs at the end, and find the cherubim and seraphim, Henri and Françoise, waiting for me like a pair of guardian angels.

'Are you going to England for Christmas, Michael?' asks dear old Françoise, her peach-face crinkling with gentle concern.

'No, I'm staying here,' I reply.

'With friends or family?'

'Just me and the cat. And the chickens, and the sheep.'

Françoise beams at Henri, and then at me. 'Then why not come to us on Christmas Day? We'll be a bit of a houseful, but if you don't mind a lot of children . . . After all, nobody should be alone on Christmas Day.'

'I'd love to come. Thank you,' I reply, without hesitation. I feel as if I have just wandered into a scene from Dickens. And although I'm pleased for myself, mostly I'm pleased for my mum.

# 20

## THE PLAGUE SHIP

Christmas is coming, the cat is getting fat, and – more to the point – the sheep are sick. Each day they seem a little worse. I'm worried to the point where I can't stop thinking about them. At least five of the eight now have runny noses, and on cold mornings there is a chorus of sniffing and snorting as I trudge out with my bucket of granules to pour into their feed-trough. Proud as I am of its stout timber contruction – culled from *The Smallholder's DIY* – that trough is not going to be much good to me if all my sheep drop down dead tomorrow.

Their mystery malady is not described in *Sheep for Beginners*. Gilles is uncertain about it, too, though he doesn't think it's serious enough to waste money on calling out the vet. But of course I do call out the vet. And I haven't managed to round the animals up before his arrival, so all he can do is peruse them from afar and reassure me that if they can run that fast, they can't be very sick. And he says he won't send me a bill for his trouble.

Whatever the experts say, Gaston – my old and noble chief ram – is not himself. Day after day, while the other sheep are feeding, he stands apart, squashed and motionless, as if he were attempting to balance on a milking-stool. He looks at me with big, sad eyes. I'd love to know what he is trying to tell me.

Having sheep is not what I expected it to be. I thought animals would enhance my life. Whereas they have merely given me a new set of problems. When my charges are happy, I can stand and watch them for hours, basking in their rugged loveliness. Even now, however, I can't wait for the weather to be warm enough to shear them, because I can't imagine what nasties lurk on their skin, hidden beneath those lank woollen dreadlocks. That's bad enough. And when they are feeling wretched, I have that sickening powerlessness that parents must feel when a child is feverish. Personal pain is finite. Imagined suffering is limitless.

This morning the icy rain is lashing down and – before I feed the sheep and take a look at poor old Gaston – I splash round to the chicken house to let the girls out for the day. Huddled on their perches, they look like a bunch of workmen unwilling to leave their cosy hut at the end of tea-break. Only Mildred comes out for a cursory peck at the sodden feed-tray, while the rain falls on her white feathers and – mostly – bounces off. I notice that she has an unusually dirty bum.

'Oh, not you as well, Mildred,' I murmur. Mildred clucks back at me, ever the chattiest of chickens, not unduly bothered about the state of her *derrière*.

Gaston looks worse than ever. Head lowered, he is leaning against the back of the house with an expression of dejection. I walk towards him. There is no sudden jink, no headlong thunder into the distance, sending clods of earth flying with his chiselled hoofs. He attempts to walk away, but his legs will not obey.

Gilles still doesn't think I should waste money on taking him to the vet. 'He's got no teeth, so he can't eat. He'll die soon anyway,' he tells me with a shrug.

To be fair, Gaston has been toothless ever since I bought him. He survives on the expensive granules I feed him each morning, which he snuffles into his mouth with much smacking of his grey-black lips.

I know the old fellow is wasting away. His horns now dwarf his scrawny frame. From a distance, he resembles a television aerial on legs. Or a pouffe with racing handlebars.

But hearing his lungs wheeze and squeal for each breath, I cannot simply let him die. Not like this. As I scoop him into my arms and receive a lungful of his warm rug smell, I recall the first time I picked him up, when Nicholas and I went to collect the sheep from Aubusson. Then I was fearful of the Hades horns. Today he probably couldn't hurt me if he tried. He snorts, and a string of mucus dangles from his nostrils. I wipe it away with my sleeve as we walk to the Espace.

Thank goodness Gilles suggested, all those weeks ago, that I buy Ouessant sheep. Some of the fat beasts I've witnessed in the fields around La Folie would need a tractor to lift them if they were to collapse into dead-weight in a distant pasture.

Gaston eyes me in the rear-view mirrror as I fire up the engine.

'No sex for you today, mate,' I tell him. He doesn't chortle. But I hope he can at least smell something of the comforting whiff of his ewes, left behind in the back of the car.

The vet presses his stethoscope to Gaston's chest and thumps him here and there, one hand on the back of the other. Then he shoves a digital thermometer up Gaston's rectum and the old boy grunts in surprise. I wince for his dignity.

In silence, the vet examines the thermometer. I can see the numbers, but they mean nothing to me.

'*Il est chaud?*' I ask.

'*Très chaud,*' he nods, drawing down the corners of his mouth like a child practising a frown. '*C'est très grave. Il a la pneumonie.*'

'Will he live?'

The vet pauses. 'I don't know.'

'What are his chances?'

'Maybe fifty per cent Maybe it is already too late.' He squints as he fills a syringe, before asking me to hold Gaston as he gives him a jab. 'Will you be able to inject him each day if I give you a syringe?'

'Yes,' I reply, looking away, shrinking at the thought. I am terrified of injections, of needles, of inflicting pain on a defenceless animal. But if it is what Gaston needs . . .

'Here.' He passes me two bottles and a pair of syringes, then hunts for needles, handing me three crackling cellophane packets. 'The injection is intra-muscular, so the needle goes here.' With his third finger he parts the black wool and presses the papery skin that covers Gaston's shoulder. 'You have to push harder than you'd think.'

'Urgghhh.'

The vet smiles. 'It is your first time?'

I nod.

'Then *bon courage.*'

So Gaston and I head back to La Folie, and I wonder if I am about to lose my favourite ram so soon after he has arrived. Not only Gaston, either. The vet has warned me that I must also separate those worst affected from the other sheep. So that means Doris, my most sociable ewe, a plump, gap-toothed madam who faintly reminds me of

Chaucer's Wife of Bath. And it means Ramekin, my back-up ram: Gaston's son and heir, whose crescent horns are still no bigger than the handlebars of a toddler's tricycle.

I clear the barn for Gaston as best I can, organize a small trough of feed and a bucket of water, and then trudge up to the field. The rain is blowing into my eyes, stinging my cheeks, as I climb over the fence. I've brought a bag of stale bread in an attempt to bribe my chosen hostages. Dear old Doris falls for this immediately, bless her, so I grab her and carry her to the barn where Gaston is waiting in the shadows, like a shrunken minotaur in his labyrinth. And then I return for Ramekin, who is much jumpier than the other sheep.

'I'm doing this for your own good,' I tell him, as I make an ineffectual swipe for his legs. And then he makes a mistake, attempting to scamper past me, and I just manage to grab a handful of the wool on one of his haunches. Ramekin is so small that it feels like I've just rounded up a teddy bear. But teddy bears don't bleed. As I pick him up, I notice a trickle of bright blood in the grass. Is *he* dying, too?

In the kitchen, I pick at my supper – a plate of pasta, a glass of red wine – and feel unusually alone. I wish I'd lit the stove today, even though it's at least fourteen degrees indoors. I would never make a real farmer. I don't feel much of a trainee hero, either. Even the white noise of a television – the townie's umbilical cord – would be nice, just to fill some of the gaps that are beginning to appear in my life, gaps that friends used to fill.

If I had my piano here, I'd have some way of keeping myself company. But I can't send for the piano until I have a floor to stand it upon. And I can't lay a floor until the roof has been insulated and covered, the stone walls have been plastered, the breeze-blocks have been rendered, and so on.

So I sit in silence, and tell myself that this – this feeling – is what I came to France to find and face. If, one day, I am to have a wonderful relationship with a woman, I first need to learn to be happy within myself, even when things are tough. And if I am to be a wise old man, I need to live through some difficulties first.

The cat comes and rubs against my legs. I pick her up and hold her on my lap until she settles herself into a circle and begins to purr. Outside, the rain pelts against the windows. And the cat and I stare at each other, and wonder what the hell we are really doing here, marooned in this frozen otherworld.

# 21

## CHRISTMAS EVE

Christmas Eve, and snowflakes are falling silently as I shut the front door behind me and stand on the step for a moment, gazing into the darkness. In the glow from the kitchen lights, I can just make out the lone pine on the edge of the drive, whose tip is a miniature Christmas tree, like the barb on some giant spear. In the distance, to my left, the lamps of Jolibois make a halo in the sky.

Titus and the girls are all safely tucked up in the *poulailler*. Gaston, Doris and Ramekin are in the hay-strewn hospital ward of the barn. This has been one of my longest weeks at La Folie. And there are so many injections to go.

Behind the house lie the ghostly shadows of the other sheep, each curled into a ball like a cat on a duvet, one or two of them still chewing as they ruminate on the day's events. Slept. Ate hay. Drank water (cold enough for headache).

With this snow, the sheep will soon be as white as the hillside. The night is silent as a tomb. It is a proper Christmas night.

In town, an hour before midnight, the church is already buzzing with life.

'*Bonsoir, Michael*,' announces Céline as I walk in, and Fabrice the organist comes shuffling up to shake my hand. He looks relieved to see me; glances nervously at his watch. The little boy I first saw scuttling about in the organ-loft, his mouth no longer caked in chocolate, emerges from behind his father's legs and presents his face to be kissed.

I gallop up the steps to the organ, unlocking the door halfway up with the bronze key that Raphaël has given me. Fabrice follows me up, and we have a final rehearsal, his high, clear voice floating out into the rapidly filling void.

'*Bien*,' he says. '*Bon courage, Michael*.'

'*À toi, aussi*,' I reply.

And then I'm settling into my Bach preludes and fugues, as the waves of happy humanity flood the church, even arriving up in the tribune beside me like water gurgling up a plug-hole from a blocked pipe.

I can't remember when I was last in such a crowd. In London, I was the one in eight million who used to love travelling on the underground at rush-hour, and feeling the press of the bodies, especially in the morning, when people are wearing their freshly scrubbed faces and freshly pressed shirts, and are thinking of all the good things they are going to do today. I used to like watching the women touching up their make-up, making that 'm' in the tiny mirror with their new-glossed lips, wanting to look their best for the boss, or the young man in accounts, or just for themselves, as a defence against the chaos that might otherwise envelop them, the chaos that is always waiting just around the corner to pounce.

I have seen that chaos in the frightened eyes of the sheep

when I have to catch them to inject them. I have known it when I am lying awake at night, listening to the scrabbling frenzy of the creatures just above my head.

I know that the chaos is always there, all around me. I used to be able to see it more clearly as a teenager; was aware of it like a shadow at my back. But London life, with its blanket of distractions, must have desensitized me. And it feels a long way away from me now, amid the goodness and simplicity of Jolibois and La Folie.

Tonight's service feels like a social event as much as a religious one. Gone are the mouse-coloured overcoats of the regular Saturday-evening Mass; gone the souls shuffling in on life-weary limbs, barely raising their eyes to appreciate the stones they know so well. No, tonight there are bright colours and shining faces, lipsticked and rouged, excited to be amongst friends in such a place, on such a night.

I feel excited, too. Few churches in rural France have pipe-organs. And Jolibois is blessed with one that works rather well, largely because Fabrice knows his plumbing and his electrics, and does a lot of the *bricolage* himself. One can often get through an entire Mass without a single note sticking, although the odds are stacked against you for Widor's Toccata.

Most of the stops on the organ are either flutey or woofy, and sound like the shy people you find in the kitchen at drinks parties, or else like the noisy ones whose braying in the other room is what has driven you to seek solace elsewhere. But there are also two thrillingly powerful reeds on the organ – a *trompette* and a *clarion* – which must operate on a ludicrous wind pressure all of their own. I suspect the organ-builder meant them for a much bigger instrument in a much bigger church. Their presence here is the equivalent of fitting a pair of rocket-launchers to a Sopwith Camel. Nothing else on the Jolibois organ will stand up to their farty blasts, which would probably come in quite useful outside the walls of Jericho.

The same organ-builder also included a Tremolo system, to produce a wavering vibrato that will come into its own if the church is ever converted into a cinema. This I never use. The sound it makes reminds me of the flesh-pink bathroom suite at La Folie, which I cannot wait to replace.

The congregation begins to settle, and a hush descends, like when the house-lights go down in a theatre. I put away my Bach and slip into a very slow and quiet improvisation with right hand and pedals, while – with my left hand – I find the music for the first *chant*. Fabrice appears in the pulpit and gives me a little nod. We're off.

I've never known anything like this. There I am, sitting at the organ console, with people pressing all around me, so close that I can smell more than two different perfumes and feel their breath on my neck as they sing. Inchoate mystery of the divine? It feels more like a knees-up down the pub, or the kind of dinner party Marisa and I used to have in East Dulwich, with everyone crowding around the piano after midnight to sing raucous selections from *Grease* and Abba. I may be abroad, a lapsed Anglican in a French Catholic church, but I have rarely felt so at home as I do amongst these smiling people, wrapped up in the drama of the service as if it were a gripping black-and-white film.

And then it's the final hymn – the French version of 'O Come All Ye Faithful' – and in the three-second pause before the last verse, I do something I hadn't planned to do. Pulse racing, I pull out the rocket-launchers – the *trompette* and *clarion* – hold my breath, and launch into the descant.

For a moment, everyone stops singing as the coruscating reeds rend the air, brilliant as war trumpets. Out of the corner of my eye, I am dimly aware of the grey-brown mass of the congregation in the church below turning white, as several hundred faces turn to see what's gone wrong with the organ.

Peering round my music stand, I glance apologetically at Fabrice in the pulpit, who stares back at me, open-mouthed.

And then he breaks into a grin and I can see his lips moving as he starts to sing, frantically waving his arms to encourage the congregation into song.

Organ and congregation are now head to head, two juggernauts racing down both lanes of a deserted high-way, bumpers bashing in an all-out competition to see who can make the most awesome din. It feels like I'm winning, but they're catching up.

Concentrate. With people singing their hearts out all around me, I find myself wanting to wave with one hand, and it's tempting to think that the music will just play itself. Oh, for a pneumatic hoist right now. But here we are, at the penultimate line – I can hear Jason growling *Gloria in excelsis deo* down the phone to me – and then I'm holding the final chord, several seconds longer than necessary, partly because I can't bear to bring to an end the dazzling blaze of sound from the pipes shining above me, and partly because – like someone telling an anecdote that's falling flat at a dinner party – I'm fearful of the silence that will follow. But I needn't have worried. As the notes die away, an excited murmur goes through the church, and I know it is because we have all been part of something that we cannot describe.

Raphaël gives the final blessing, and there is a rustle like the wind in the trees as everyone makes the sign of the

Cross. Then I open a mottled green volume whose cover is stained with twenty-three-year-old Ribena. The book falls open at a page black with notes, and I launch into the music, my left hand stamping out chords, my right hand rippling out semiquavers as if it belonged to an organist far more accomplished than me. I never believed I could do this. And as I stretch my legs two octaves apart for the cataclysmic pedal entry, I can feel the hairs standing up on the back of my neck. I once thought Widor's Toccata must demand some kind of heroic virtuosity to play it. And then I woke up one morning, and found that I could play it myself. It's amazing what the brain gets up to, while our backs are turned.

Much as I dislike being on the receiving end of an injection – the icy swab; the needle held vertical as a lance; the wasp's sting of pain; the lingering resentment – I have discovered that I hate being on the giving end even more.

Tonight it is two a.m. by the time I wander out to the barn, with a bottle of antibiotics in one hand and a sheep syringe in the other. The flimsy needles the vet gave me kept bending when I tried to push them in, so I have bought another Useful Gadget from the smiley blonde lady at Alliance Pastorale. The needle of this thing looks as thick as a child's drinking straw, sliced off at an angle like an italic nib. Ugh. The midnight music has left me on a high, but I am soon brought down to earth as I enter the barn and see three pairs of eyes peering at me from the darkness.

The sheep run in circles around me as I stand in the middle of the dark barn, for the silent injections clearly hurt. Gaston is very weak, but Doris charges into the old metal manger with a clang that makes me wince, a few seconds before Ramekin knocks over a stack of my surplus

fence-posts, ready-tipped with tar for the day when I summon up the energy to enclose another field.

Once I have caught each animal, I grit my teeth, grip its
flanks between my knees, and slide the italic nib as gently
as possible into the leathery skin. Doris, bless her, barely
flinches. Gaston is the worst because he feels so scrawny;
I fumble to find a scrap of flesh to inject on his bony
shoulders. Then I am pressing the needle into the charred
parchment of his skin, and he staggers as it goes in. Day
after day, I gaze at him, and try to decide whether he's
getting better or worse. At least the wheezing has stopped.
But it's hard to tell whether his strength is returning.

Even in his weakened state, Ramekin is impossible to
catch. In the end, I just stick my leg out and he runs
straight into it. I inject him as he lies passive at my feet.
For a moment I think I've killed him, he's so still. But
when I take my hands away, he leaps up and scampers
away in a blur of shiny hooves. I sigh, but not with relief.
For there is another slick of bright blood in the imprint of
his muzzle in the straw.

# 22

## CHRISTMAS DAY

Christmas Day. The sleet is blowing sideways, and I am staggering up a French hillside, trying to catch Doris in the dark. Too soon for dusk, it feels as if someone has turned down the brightness on my life. The blizzard flings itself into my eyes. Lunch with Henri and Françoise, the cherubim and seraphim, amid the cosy bustle of their extended family, already feels like a distant memory, though I only left their house an hour ago.

I drove back to La Folie feeling guilty about the three sheep imprisoned in the dark barn. But as I rattled up to the house, my headlights picked out six green jewels shining in the gloom. And the jewels blinked. The door of the barn stood open. Gaston and Ramekin, still weak, were soon caught. Doris is another matter.

Onward I trudge, struggling to keep up with my patient. Doris is just ahead of me now, ears pricked, head held high as she keeps a watchful eye on her gaoler.

At home in Surrey, my family will be sipping their coffee and port, still wearing the paper crowns that fell out of their crackers. I can see them chatting in the twinkling glow of the tree-lights, surrounded with crumpled wrapping paper, shiny hardbacks, and strange kitchen utensils that will soon find their way to the very back of the drawer.

Mum will be saying that she thinks the Queen looked a little older this year. Dad, rosy-cheeked, will be pretending he's not really having a snooze. And my brothers will be attempting to play with their presents, which is not easy when you've just been given yet another set of paint-brushes and an electric wok.

Later, my mum will phone and tell me that she's heard from my sister and her children in San Francisco, and I will tell her what a lovely Christmas Day I've had.

'Please, Doris,' I murmur. I can see the sleet turning to mahogany as it soaks into her wool.

I'm only a yard away now. Just one dive . . . 'Yaaaargh!'

Doris blinks, sidesteps, and I crash into the mud.

We repeat this procedure many times over the next half-hour.

Doris trots. I sprint.

I dive. Doris jinks.

And I fall flat on my face in the freezing mud. Happy Christmas.

Each time, Doris stops, turns round and gazes at me as she might gaze at a broken fence-post. You'd think she might have the common decency just to give herself up. God knows, I'm trying to help the girl.

By now, I am cold and soaked and desperate. I want to be inside. And then I remember that the stove is unlit, and there's no wood left to burn until I have sawn and split more logs in the barn.

'One option,' says a voice in my head, 'might be to stop feeling sorry for yourself and to make a bit more effort.'

I want Doris to be well. I want to be anywhere but here, alone inside this bleak moment in darkest Abroad.

'Come on!' I yell into the snowy abyss.

And it's not Doris I'm calling. It's myself.

# 23

## CIRCE

Zuleika has landed. And it isn't long before the local inhabitants – that's me – begin to feel the strain of the invasion.

La Folie, so big and yet so small, is still waiting to be renovated. Sure, I have built gates and nesting boxes; feed-troughs and fences. I have installed a shower in the bathroom and made other puny domestic improvements. But the yawning void of the summer sitting-room and the whole of the *maison des amis* are still waiting for me to press the *maçons* and *menuisiers* into committing to a definite date for starting work. In the meantime, the liveable part of the house is no bigger than a pocket sub-marine. This may be fine for one man and his cat. But it's not with several people staying, especially when one of them is Zuleika.

I thought Zuleika was going to be coming alone. And then, in an email, she casually mentioned something about 'my current squeeze', so I asked if she'd like to bring someone with her. She said yes, please; she'd bring her gay flatmate, Billy. And my brother Steven, a sculptor, and his

Romanian wife Lumi have decided to come, too. So we shall be five for New Year. It has not occurred to me that such a decompression from the depths of my hermitic retreat could give me the bends as I rise to the surface.

But the real problem is that Zuleika is a paid-up Big Smoke person, allergic to mud, fresh air and – as I shall soon discover – me. She needs her own space, too. A lot of it. God knows why I ever thought a few days at La Folie might be good for her.

Marisa said La Folie felt like sanctuary; Simon called it A Perfect Place. Two of my flying pals from Rochester who came in August were so bored that they spent most of the daytime in bed. Bemused French visitors describe it as *le bout du monde*, the end of the world. One childhood friend who stayed was so flummoxed by the lack of distractions that she spent a whole weekend yelling and swearing at me, and then couldn't understand why I dropped the teapot when she suggested a second visit. My dad has told me things here that he never told me back home in England. And Zuleika?

Zuleika's stay starts so well. I manage to turn up at Limoges airport on time in the Espace, and we seem to have a million things to say to each other as we drive back to La Folie. Next morning, we go to the market at St Juste, though it's hardly the weather for being outside. The wash of sunlight that filters through the milky clouds fails to melt the sugar-frosting on the fields. But we need provisions, and Zuleika saves me from buying unwanted *fromage* from a cheese lady who has inveigled me into trying a piece – I'm so bad at saying *non* – and a gnarled old gent in a black beret advises her not to purchase any of the huge black radishes in the market.

'I warn you, *Madame*, they can stick in your throat and kill you.'

This is all very charming, and satisfies Zuleika's craving for French Experiences.

Steven and Lumi arrive, and Zuleika – wanting solitude, or a stronger signal on her mobile – decides to walk down to Jolibois in the icy rain. I've rather lost track of the days, what with the sick sheep and the visitors, and forget to tell her that, as it's Monday, all the shops will be shut. She returns looking like a cartoon cat that has been locked in a cold-store. If we touch her, I fear she'll shatter into a thousand pieces.

And from here on in, things begin to go *poire*-shaped. Zuleika's flatmate, Billy, arrives, bringing me teabags and lemon-butter biscuits from Fortnum's. For Zuleika, he brings a personality transplant. Her gentleness and warmth vanish, and now she's all glossy brilliance and irony and a thousand miles away. Her double-act with Billy functions as an extended private joke.

There were meant to be five of us at La Folie for the *nouvel an*. But with all Zuleika's personalities on display, there are at least twelve people sitting down to dinner. And eight of them *vant to be alone*.

The storm-clouds gather. Zuleika has stopped speaking to me, and appears to be trapped in a small black mood to which only Billy has access. Unused to either mucking in or muddling along, both of them look cold and miserable in their black designer clothes, and only perk up when their mobiles bleep with another text message from the outside world. I presume they're texting Air-Sea Rescue at Culdrose, in an attempt to get themselves winched out of here.

'This place feels like the Big Brother house,' I hear Zuleika murmur to Billy, 'only without the comfy chairs.'

Everybody is trapped, and it must be my fault. I've raced down to the supermarket umpteen times, provided lashings of wine, kept the stove burning with enough logs to immolate several martyrs, driven people wherever they want to go, offered them the use of either car, and it isn't enough. The trouble is that, once you come in and shut the door behind you, there are no distractions here. There is no telly; no place to hide.

I had imagined that my guests would take pleasure in helping out with some of the outdoor tasks around La Folie, but it turns out that they're much happier feeling bored indoors than staggering out into the blizzard to chop wood or collect eggs or help me inject the sheep.

'I'll do my best to help, Mike, if it's absolutely vital,' says Steven, shivering beside the stove.

'Has Michael always been this gung-ho?' I hear Billy ask, in an appalled stage-whisper.

'He's always had a thing about self-improvement, especially for other people,' laughs Steven, who sounds as if he knows I'm listening. 'When *Star Wars* first came out, and our whole family went to see it in Bogotá, he brought his school notes along to give us a lecture on Napoleon in the queue outside the cinema. And then he tested us, to make sure we'd been listening.'

I smile at the memory of this me from another universe; I wish I had his childlike certainty to help me now.

Indoors or outdoors, it's too cold and miserable for my guests, and all the charming local restaurants I promised them are closed. The air in the submarine is rapidly running out. So I carry on as usual, by myself. Only it's worse than usual, because the sheep appear to have deteriorated. Tonight I found bright splotches of blood in the feed-trough.

I am used to feeling alone, but not *this* alone.

'Are we still connected?' I ask my friend, as she sits in another country by the stove. Even the cat has decided it prefers Zuleika to me. At this rate, I'll soon be talking to the goldfish.

'Yes, we are,' she lies.

Outside in the gathering dusk, I can see Daphne and Ella at the water-trough, dipping their soft muzzles to drink. But the water has turned to ice.

# 24

## JANUARY: THE WILD BULL OF CRETE

La Folie is empty again, and I am struggling to return to my familiar rhythms. I had hoped that having a house full of guests would recharge my batteries, but instead they appear to have been drained.

And then, one fateful morning in the barn, there is a violent change. Gaston stands motionless in his pen as I feel my way through the darkness. He doesn't move as I come closer to examine him. Instead, he lowers his weary head, as though too weak to support it any longer.

And that's when he charges me.

Luckily the little rascal doesn't have room to get up much speed. But it doesn't half get your attention when thirty pounds of flying Ouessant ram crash headlong into your unsuspecting thigh in the dark. It's like being karate-kicked by a Chelsea pensioner.

I clench my fist. I yell. I punch the air. Not because I'm hurt, but because I'm so happy. For I know what this means. It means that the randy old patriarch is on the mend. Gaston is back. It makes me want to hug him. And then he lowers his head for another charge.

Under the circumstances, I opt to skip the hug. I can take his temperature tomorrow morning. Instead, I half run and half dance out into the frosty sunlight. For this promises to be a happy new year, after all.

Peter Viola phones, and suggests a New Year flight. So things are looking up all round.

At the aeroclub, a small crowd has gathered to drink coffee and discuss flying. They watch with fascination as we zip ourselves into the Arctic survival suits that Peter pulls out of his locker.

'Only *les Anglais* are crazy enough to go flying in this weather,' growls grouchy old Marcel, sucking on a cigarillo. Peter winks at me as we wheel his microlight out of its hangar.

'*C'est vrai*,' Peter calls back to Marcel, grinning with delight. 'And only *les Français* are crazy enough not to.'

We soar over the Monts de Blond in the Thruster, which feels like a motorbike with wings, only noisier and draughtier.

'This is the life,' yells Peter over the distorted intercom. I give him a thumbs-up and we grin at each other. I can't wait to have the Luscombe here at St Juste. But first I still need a thumbs-up from the committee, before I can be granted a space in the hangar. And in the meantime, the weeks and months drift by.

A British couple lands soon after us, in a battered old 1940s Auster they've flown down from Fontenay-le-Comte.

'God, it feels good to blow away the cobwebs, after the New Year we've had,' says the pilot, Gary, jumping down from the cockpit. He's a big man, in a voluminous sheepskin flying-jacket. I can see why he needs such a big plane.

'Why, what went wrong?' I ask.

'Oh, you know. Friends to stay,' he groans. 'What's so funny about that?'

'Sorry,' I say, converting my smile into a frown. 'It's not. I'm Michael, by the way. How was the flight?'

'Couldn't see a damn thing, really,' he says. 'Thought we might wind up in Spain, there was so much cloud. And then it cleared, and here we are.'

'I love these old things,' murmurs Peter, gazing appreciatively at the Auster, and addressing no one in particular. 'I had one myself once; wish I'd never sold it.'

'So New Year was a bit of a trial?' I ask, turning to Gary's wife, Liz, all blond highlights and tailored tweeds, who is checking the Auster's undercarriage. A pilot herself, she looks as if she'd be more at home at the controls of a Citation than an Auster.

'It was absolutely awful,' she says, ducking out from under the wing. 'We had a houseful of grumpy Londoners, who complained because the house is only half renovated.'

'And you couldn't go outside because of the weather?'

'Exactly.' She nods, the word trailing off as she gazes at me.

'And all the wonderful little restaurants you promised them, the ones with ten-euro menus, were shut?' I continue, feeling a warm glow creeping up my spine.

'How did you guess?' asks Gary, squinting at me with interest.

'I was there.'

'And when we *did* finally find an expensive place for New Year's Eve,' continues Liz, 'it wasn't terribly good.'

'Well, at least *you* found somewhere.'

'Yes, and everyone got terrible food poisoning.'

'Ah, thank you.'

'I beg your pardon?' asks Liz, bemused.

'Sorry. I mean, *poor* you.'

'How was your New Year, then?' she asks.

'Not half as bad as I thought.'

Each day seems to dawn more icily than the last. Yet today the sky is so clear and blue and gilded with early-morning sun, the temperature could be another ten degrees colder and I wouldn't mind. Gone is the squelch underfoot of the past few days. Now the ground crunches like walking on muesli. With the dreary zinc patina of sleet and snow scraped away, the world looks refreshed: raw as a gleaming snake that's just shrugged off its worn-out skin. I can breathe freely at last.

Gazing out of my bedroom window at the frosty beauty of La Folie – at the white trees and the perfect sky – I feel renewed. Frustrating as it is to waste this perfect flying weather, the world is still beautiful, I remind myself.

I have just put a saucepan of water on the stove to boil myself an egg when I remember that I took a dozen eggs to Fred and Émilie yesterday. So the fridge is bare. I wander out to the chicken house, and find a freshly laid one just sitting there, ready for my breakfast. The sight of its smooth, pale perfection, nestling in the straw, makes me smile. In the nesting box on the other side, Martha is in the process of laying another, with Melissa queueing next in line. They often prefer to queue rather than use the 'wrong' side. Gilles says that the eggs are better left for a couple of days before eating them. '*Sinon, ils sont toxiques,*' he warns, wagging his sawn-off finger at me. But today's is still warm when I slide it into the trembling water.

Nevertheless, it is not a boiled egg that has made today such a good day. The good news is that Gaston is officially better. Out in the barn, I've shoved the thermometer up his bum, just like the vet did, carefully avoiding eye-contact out of respect for the old boy's dignity, and because I don't want him to charge me again. His temperature is back to normal. Still a bit off-colour, perhaps, and still a bit runny in the nostril department. But he has a future after all, and the wheezing and snorting have passed. There is not a trace of blood from Ramekin's nose when I grab him for his last injection. And I could swear that Doris smiles a brave smile at me as she submits to the final needle.

Sheep smell wonderful, especially when you know they're feeling better; when you know you won't have to give them any more injections for a long time. And there's no doubt about it this time: Doris definitely gives me her gap-toothed, gummy smile as I gently hoist her over the fence, and Ramekin bounces with lamb-like delight as I stand him next to his dad in the frosted grass.

The other sheep come trotting over to greet the returning heroes and listen to their tales of war and woe. They are a flock again, and hustle back up the field to their favourite tree, like happy teenagers who have rediscovered their old friends at the start of a new school term.

Seeing them all together reminds me that I urgently need to find a home for my surplus rams. It won't be long before they are all fighting again. And lambing – if it should happen – may be only a couple of months away. The moment will come when I must capture three of Ramekin's young brothers – Charlie, and the two sweet-faced thugs – and take them on a journey from which they will not return. But for now I just watch their silent communion, and give thanks.

# 25

## PHAETHON

With the sheep fully recovered, I can start thinking about the house again, and about persuading some local *ouvriers* to start doing heroic things on my behalf.

Today, after a mercy dash to the *boulangerie*, I am off to buy kitchen units in Limoges. Never mind that the kitchen in the *maison des amis* is a figment of my imagination, and still needs a floor, walls and a staircase to the next level. I never was very good at getting my priorities right.

Usually, when driving anywhere, I take the Espace Mouton-Mover and brim with local pride. I still feel such a beacon of Englishness in le Pug Rouge that I need only fly a Union Jack from the aerial and fill the boot with a dozen crates of Stella to complete the picture. The jovial comments from the locals about an English invasion don't help, however warmly they are meant. But *gazole* is so much cheaper than *super* in France that on longer trips I crouch down in le Pug and do without the friendly waves of passers-by. I really should transfer the little car on to a French *immatriculation*.

The road out of Jolibois splits into two lanes as it curves up and around a steep hill. Seeing a lorry ahead of me, I put my foot down as I pass the *Risque de Verglas* sign. There's no danger of skidding, because it hasn't been raining that hard. Absolutely no danger at all.

I'm level with the lorry's tail-gate when the steering begins to wobble.

Ace driver that I am, I ease off the accelerator and work on controlling the wobble.

And the wobble gets a whole lot worse.

*Mon Dieu.* Seconds divide themselves into tenths, and then the tenths subdivide into hundredths.

Now I'm swerving left, right, left . . . oh, my giddy aunt . . . and the world is flying sideways as the car takes me on my most expensive fairground ride ever.

Somehow I manage to miss the lorry, largely because the car is now spinning backwards up the hill at sixty miles per hour on the wrong side of the road, yet somehow in slow motion.

*This is going to hurt.*

In the split-second before the impact, I feel more embarrassed than afraid.

Considering that I hit the ditch/bank combo side-on at about fifty, the crash is almost disappointing. I open my eyes to find that I am not playing a harp on a cloud after all, and – apart from the poor old Pug – the only thing I've broken is the *baguette de campagne* that was on the dashboard before me. My shoulder's sore, too, and the engine is making horrible gurgling noises, so I switch it off and push what's left of the car off the road and into the ditch. There's no hiding that English number-plate.

I pull out my mobile. But I can't think of anyone to phone.

What happens next is deeply touching and, I suspect,

deeply French. Every driver who passes slows down, not to gawp, but to ask if I need help. Weather-beaten dudes sucking on Gitanes; stately women with plum-coloured hair; even a couple of very pretty young things whose offers of assistance tempt me to reply that, *bien sûr*, I am at death's door, but that if they would just come and gently stroke my forehead, it might perhaps ease my passing into the hereafter.

Then a Merc swishes up, closely followed by the rattle of a battered 2CV. A wiry businessman and a swarthy *paysan* approach me: Don Quixote and Sancho Panza, right on cue.

'Are you all right?' they enquire, as we all gaze at my ex-*voiture* and discuss the scale of the damage to my ego.

'You're the third person who's done that here this month,' says Don Quixote gravely. 'We must phone the police.'

'*Un moment, s'il vous plaît,*' I entreat. My hands appear to be shaking. Do I really want to get the *gendarmes* involved?

'You haven't been drinking?' hiccups Sancho. No, I haven't been drinking. But a month ago I was fined forty euros for not carrying a spare brake-light bulb. And I still don't have a red emergency triangle in my car. So the guillotine beckons. Obviously I can't tell this to the Don or Sancho, in case they decide to make a citizen's arrest.

Too late. Within a couple of minutes, two huge moustaches emerge from a police car just down the hill. They must have been hiding round the corner, waiting for me to crash. My heart thumps as the moustaches – preceded at some distance by two impressive bellies – approach.

I needn't have worried. Gentlemanly and solicitous, the police are mostly interested in getting the traffic moving.

So one of them parks his manly bulk slap-bang in the middle of the road and forces everyone to drive around him. A few minutes later, we are all shaking hands and promising to keep in touch, before the recovery man takes me and what's left of my car to the Peugeot garage in town.

'*Elle est morte*,' says the grey-haired garage-owner sadly when I ask what he thinks. At first I don't want to believe him, because he is wearing a brown anorak. But secretly I know he's right.

And so I sit in my broken little car, gathering up my belongings – a few dusty cassettes, a foot-pump from Halford's and a lacerated *baguette* – as I take in the familiar reek of diesel fuel and boiled sweets for one last time. '*Au revoir*,' I murmur, giving the dashboard a final pat.

A few days afterwards, the blue-and-yellow Jolibois road commandos re-route *la route* in the wake of my stupidity. So I can now claim to have made such an impact in France that I have changed the very direction of society.

# 26

## ICARUS

Weather shocking. Horizontal rain; heavy branches ripped and smashed on the drive. Everything brown and dank and muddied; every footstep a squelch.

In London, I once worked in an air-conditioned office where there were no windows at all. We relied on phone calls from the outside world to discover whether the sun was shining, or whether the onset of a new Ice Age had followed the morning rush-hour. Here at La Folie, I have the opposite problem. Right now, the great outdoors is very much indoors.

Even the chickens are struggling. They look confused and bedraggled, unable to understand what's happening as they stand out in the rain, getting soaked. The Rastafarians lean under the eaves behind the house, looking equally morose, and applying rather more intelligence to the problem.

At the bottom of the drive, the river has burst its banks, flooding the road. The celebrated gothic bridge that features in all the postcard views of Jolibois looks as if it's paddling. The way the waters are rushing and gushing, a sheep could easily get swept away down there. I still can't quite believe that – if Gilles is right – I am going to have my own lambs before long. He says that Doris, Daphne and Ella look thoroughly pregnant. If so, their lambs had better be born with webbed feet.

By lighting the stove this morning, I have broken my own rule about minimum temperatures. But just as humidity makes a hot day seem hotter, so dankness chills the bones. And at least I am in the cat's good books for a change. She has been looking at me askance ever since I put her on the diet food, because she's become such a heffalump since the colder weather began and her mouse supply dried up.

For my six o'clock think, I am confined to the dark kitchen. I sit at the little wooden table where I first sat with Zumbach and Émilie, all those months ago. This weather is shrinking my world. If I could just escape for a while in my aeroplane, if I could just roar skywards, and turn and swoop and dive and climb in the empty air, I could perhaps release myself from some of the avoir-dupois that is chained to my shoulders, weighing me down. Viewed from the glittering freedom of three thousand feet, problems become insignificant, unless your cockpit has begun to fill with smoke.

Water people love to dive deep into the ocean, or skim across its surface in a yacht. Earth people are drawn to mountains and caves. Fire people want nothing more than the heat of the sun on their skin. I am learning to work with the earth. But the sky is where I want to be. If I must come back in another life, let me be a bird or a thundercloud.

# 27

## JUDAS ISCARIOT

Next morning at La Folie, quite without warning, a dirty white lorry splashes up the drive in the darkness. I peer down out of my bedroom window, and see that the back of the lorry is groaning with gleaming scaffolding.

*Mon Dieu.* I have grown so used to living in my small submarine that I almost forgot that I was planning to renovate La Folie.

But now, if I'm not much mistaken, the masons have arrived.

Three dusty handshakes, and then they are marching their scaffolding bars into the yawning cavity of the summer sitting-room, their hobnail boots crunching on the concrete floor. I fumble for the lights – naked bulbs dangling from a spaghetti of exposed wires – and watch, fascinated, as the shadows of medieval yeomen carrying lances dance up the walls. And then I am rushing around, too, hauling boxes of books and dusty sheet music out of their way, apologizing for the state of my building-site.

'*C'est pas grave,*' they growl, tipping their caps. '*Pas de problème.*'

Probably they want me to leave them to it, for they have the air of well-briefed commandos carrying out a raid. But I can't help wishing I could join in. In addition to wanting to be Queen Victoria's train-driver, a Spitfire pilot and a cinema organist, I've decided I want to be a stonemason, too.

There is an honesty written in these men's faces, and a brutal strength about the way they attack their labour, that makes me stand and gawp in wonder. I didn't know that men still worked like this any more. They don't even have a cement-mixer to mix the wagon-loads of mortar that they will soon be pressing into the joints. It's all done with shovels in a flat trough.

So begins a period in which the masons' lorry sends the chickens flying just before eight each morning, and the sound of hammers clattering on stone begins to echo through the house. Outside, winter may have La Folie firmly in its watery grip, but inside the house, things are at last beginning to grow and develop in a kind of indoor version of spring. And as the house begins to flower, I feel myself expanding, too.

Action inspires action. Ideas beget ideas. I'm glad to have company; to have noise in the house, over and above the scuttling of rodents and the creaking of rotting beams. It gives me the feeling that I'm doing something, even when I'm doing nothing. I can't help feeling personally responsible for all that crashing and banging next door. So when the masons head off for their two-hour lunch-break, I have a similar break myself, to reward myself for all our hard work.

I take new pleasure, too, in donning my grubby jacket and filling the feed-bucket for the sheep in the morning, smashing the ice on the water troughs, or hauling out another armload of fence-posts, now that the workmen –

Serge and his silent son, along with the burly Gérard (who has no teeth, but a toddler's gummy smile) – are here to set an example. I'm so much less lazy when someone is watching me, witnessing my idleness. So, for once in my life, I find myself able to look workmen in the eye. The secret, I've discovered, is to be shouldering a sledge-hammer at the time.

The men take no English tea-breaks; never stop for a fag. The bashing and clanging stops at noon, restarts some time before two and continues until just before six. When I wander into the war-zone at the end of the day, it has always been immaculately swept, with my motley belongings piled beneath a dust-sheet. I am ashamed to say that this is the tidiest room in the house.

Along with Gilles, Serge is my new hero. He has the rugged features of some ancient warrior, and walks with a slight limp following a fall, years ago, from a high ladder. Probably during the siege of Poitiers, is my guess. After he has done a tough day's work at La Folie, Serge labours elsewhere, he says, until eight o'clock at night, to feed his three children. Yet etched into his handsome, dust-veneered face, he has the smile-lines of a man who is unfailingly cheerful, and responds to every unforeseen snag – such as me changing my mind about the style and colour of the pointing for the umpteenth time – with a shrug and that most blessed phrase in the *ouvrier*'s vocabulary: '*Pas de problème.*'

Serge is an inspiration. His is the gentleness of a man who is truly strong.

'I'm just taking some of my sheep to market,' I tell him one morning, as nonchalantly as possible. I feel myself joining a grand tradition of young chaps – from Jack and his Beanstalk downwards – who have set out on just such a sunny morning as this, taking their sheep to market.

Admittedly, Jack was taking Lucy the Cow, whereas I'm taking Charlie and the sweet-faced thugs.

I shall be sorry to say goodbye to these three strapping brothers. But poor old Gaston has his work cut out, defending his wenches from them. I can't believe the ewes are still on heat, when Gilles is convinced that they are already pregnant – but nobody has told that to my trio of priapic lads. There is a serious risk of in-breeding. So it's urgent that I find them a new home, today.

Gilles has told me that I should find several Ouessant-buyers at the market in les Hérolles. I picture a well-heeled Dutch couple buying them, as lawn-mowers for the grass behind their signal box. (It's not only *les Anglais* who are buying up rural France, although the Dutch appear to be unusually specific in their tastes. All the local Dutch people I've come across live beside the railway line, presumably because it's the closest thing they can find to a canal.)

The market at les Hérolles happens only once a month, so I am determined not to miss this opportunity. After weeks of rain, there's not a cloud in the sky as I head off in the Espace, taking my sheep to market, their three brown heads and six perky ears just visible in the rear-view mirror.

I tell myself that I will not – must not – take my chaps back to Jolibois, come what may. I even have the thought that I could stop and quietly lift them into someone else's field, in the first known case of sheep rustling in reverse.

And then I arrive at les Hérolles, a tiny village that hosts its huge market on the twenty-ninth of every month. There are people selling cheap raincoats, and honey in plastic pots, and chickens packed into crates as tightly as oranges. But I can't see any sheep. My three are still standing patiently in the boot of the Espace, watching the world go by.

At last I find the animal market with its fifty-odd steel pens spread over an area the size of a football pitch. They're all empty.

'*C'est fini, Monsieur,*' explains a stooped old man, with a slow blink and a shrug. It's ten a.m. And the livestock market ended an hour ago. 'But look – there's a *marchandeur, Monsieur.* Perhaps *he* will buy your three little sheep.'

I follow his bony, trembling finger to where a stocky man in wellies is standing. He reminds me of Peter Lorre after a rough night on a trawler.

'*Des Ouessants?*' Peter Lorre raises his bushy eyebrows, and his eyes light up like the bumpers on a pinball table. Yet his voice only makes me think of vinegar gurgling down a sink. 'Where are they?'

I jab my thumb at the Espace, and attempt to look like I've done this before. All I need is a different face, different accent, twenty years' experience and a beard, and the illusion would be complete. But the fact that he knows about Ouessants is encouraging: he must have someone in mind – a Dutch couple with an overgrown garden beside a railway, perhaps – to whom he can sell them on. He wouldn't care about the breed if he just wanted to eat them, because Ouessants are too small and valuable for that.

'How much do you want for them?' he rasps, as he squeezes the flesh on their backs with a hand like a claw. Why should he care how fat they are, when their value lies in their sweet natures, scarcity and aesthetic appeal?

'*Cent euros pour les trois,*' I say: a hundred for the lot.

Lorre spits on the ground.

'I'll give you thirty,' he croaks, his face setting like quick-drying cement. With the market ended, he knows he's got me over a barrel.

'I can't do it for thirty. Each is worth at least eighty euros.'

'Not any more, they're not. It's not like the old days, you know.'

'*Donc, pour soixante-dix . . .*'

He shakes his head.

'*Cinquante?*' I murmur, embarrassed. A small crowd has gathered to watch the market's final transaction.

'I'll give you thirty,' he snarls, '*et c'est tout.*'

On my way down here, I would happily have given my three rams away. All I really wanted was a good home for them. But I *can't* sell them like this for ten euros each. It's an insult to Charlie and the boys.

'*Tant pis.*' He shrugs, turning to go. 'We'll not fall out over it.' And then he delivers a low blow. 'They're not tagged,' he hisses. 'You'd better watch out for the *gendarmes* over there . . . because they'll have you, just like that.' He grabs his bicep and jerks his forearm upwards, glancing at the policemen. For a moment, I think he's about to shop me.

I gaze at my young charges. They stare back at me doubtfully. In this noisy, alien environment, I'm the closest thing to a friend they've got.

I grit my teeth. 'All right, I'll take thirty,' I murmur, wishing I could grab the words back as soon as I have said them, and feeling his rough palm shaking mine. Something in me doesn't want to sell my sheep to this man. But the deal is sealed.

'Then put them in the lorry,' he says.

The tail-gate of the lorry is raised, and my heart sinks. Pressed against the far end are a dozen grey sheep – each at least three times the size of Charlie – collapsed like bloated junkies in the fetid straw. Compared with my bright-eyed Ouessants, they have the blank stares of the condemned.

I set my first ram down on the floor of the lorry, and am relieved to see him trot instinctively into the ovine melee. Something doesn't feel right, but I can't put my finger on it.

The door is opened again, and I lay the second ram inside. And now there's just little Charlie, so much smaller than his two brothers. I gather him into my arms, and feel his poor heart beating wildly with alarm. Then he's in the lorry, too, and I can't seem to tear myself away. Charlie peers back at me, confused.

'*Je suis un peu triste . . .*' I explain to the kind-looking man who is holding the door open, waiting for me to move.

'*Ah, oui*, you are sad.' He nods with an understanding that takes me by surprise.

And then Peter Lorre is unfolding his cheque-book, and I tell him that no, the money must be '*en espèces*'. I'm expecting him to refuse, but he makes a big show of putting away the cheque-book and grumpily unfolding three notes from an envelope in his pocket. There's no going back now. The mob is watching. Yet there's still something I need to know.

'What are you going to do with my sheep, *Monsieur*?' I ask.

'I'm going to look after them,' he says cheerily. I feel a great weight lift from my shoulders, a boulder that has been weighing there for weeks as I have worried about the future of my sheep. 'And then,' he hisses, leering as he slices his hand violently across his throat, 'I'm going to *eat* them.'

I nod, feeling my knees wobble beneath me. I want to change my mind, to find another way. But it's too late now. The deal is done.

And then I just want to get away from there, hurtling back to Jolibois with the road blurring ahead of me, and thirty pieces of silver jangling in my pocket.

# 28

## FEBRUARY: DREAMING IN FRENCH

Winter creeps onward at La Folie. Day after day, Serge and the masons appear, and their hammering ransacks the silence. The trees are still bare, but the sheep grow shaggier by the week. I cannot wait for the day when Gilles will come and shear their wool, two years in the tangling.

On the phone, my mother often asks me if I am dreaming in French yet, in the same tone that she asks me if the bathroom in the *maison des amis* is ever going to be finished. Mum proudly remembers dreaming in French when she was propping up the suspended-ceiling business in Paris in the 1950s, and this is therefore the family yardstick by which to judge whether or not I am fully Frenchified.

Though I cannot yet claim such a qualification, my French must be improving, because the locals have stopped making polite comments about it. Indeed, now that my linguistic manglings are no longer a talking point, I begin to suspect that the phrase I used to hear – *Ah, vous parlez bien le français!* – really means 'Your French is charmingly hopeless, but well done for trying.' Alarmingly, most of *les Anglais* don't.

I want to hide when I hear people in the paper-shop demanding cigarettes in English, with not so much as a *s'il vous plaît* to acknowledge that we are in someone else's country. And then there's the English woman trying to buy meat in Champion, yelling 'Mince! MINCE! *MINCE!*' at the bemused assistant, in a misguided quest for *steak haché* that sounds more like she's barking instructions at a Butlin's drag act.

Though my own vocabulary is patchy – and my accent is heavily influenced by Inspector Clouseau – I am quite strong on useful things such as ovine intestinal conditions, bathroom fittings and Things To Shout Whilst Playing Tennis. Thus *Allez, allez!* is how one encourages an octogenarian doubles partner to hobble after a lob, *Gourmand!* means 'Why did I go for that blasted volley?' and *Bien servi* is what you mutter when you've just been aced by a twelve-year-old.

My favourite new word is *les perce-neige* – snowdrops – because, bless them, these perfect flowers have finally arrived at La Folie, bowing their heads at each van and lorry that rattles up the drive. I have never in my life felt excited about a flower, but I almost gasped at the sight of these, their innocent beauty gathered into dazzling clumps like children at a first communion. Flowers, I begin to see, are not simply pretty things that grow. They are part of some huge clock, too; harbingers of a different season; a promise of better times to come. Spring cannot now be far away.

'Do you really think they can understand you?' asks Serge the mason, leaning on his shovel. He has just caught me chatting to the chickens. As you do. Indeed, you'd be surprised how much there is to say to a chicken, when you live alone and don't have a telly. But what Serge clearly finds hilarious is that these are French chickens, yet I'm attempting to parley with them in English.

With all due respect to Serge, it's easy to underestimate how much English the local chickens understand. And that goes for the local people, too, as I discover in another excruciating scene at the local *supermarché*. I'm just queuing to get my tomatoes weighed in Champion when I hear a voice like an Essex chainsaw coming from the frozen-food section.

'OI! TAKE YOUR FRIGGIN' EYES OFF 'ER!' I turn to see a vast, red-faced woman in a velour tracksuit, gesticulating wildly at me. She looks like Les Dawson's evil twin. 'You just can't keep yer eyes off every friggin' French tart in a tight skirt, can yer?'

*Mon Dieu.* For a second I consider ducking behind the organic cabbages. But it's not me she's berating in that foghorn voice. It's the little bald chap just ahead of me. I know it's him, because his shiny pate suddenly flushes pink and turns from gloss to matt, like a cooked prawn.

'Er . . . ta, luv,' he mumbles to the pretty girl doing the weighing, before grabbing his carrots and slinking back to Momma. I can see from the storm-clouds in the girl's eyes that she knows exactly what Momma said.

'*Désolé*,' I whisper.

'*C'est pas grave*,' she murmurs, as she sticks a label on my tomatoes.

But, in truth, I think it is.

# 29

## THE AMAZONS

The demise of le Pug Rouge has reminded me that I still have to replace that smashed headlamp on the Espace. I ordered and collected a new one weeks ago, from the Renault garage behind Champion, and somehow forgot to fit it. And today, yet another attempt to sit down and make a start on *The Labours of Jack Larry* has made me feel that I really should be outside enjoying the Sunday-morning sunshine, practising my car maintenance.

I have just extracted the shattered carcass of the old headlamp when I manage to slice my finger on the jagged glass. *Merde*. Blood splashes on to the floor of the winter sitting-room as I hurry to the sink. I run the wound under the tap. I wrap it in kitchen paper. I elevate the bleeding part. And the bleeding continues. It occurs to me that I have never cut myself this badly before.

Now any sensible country person would, I'm sure, just spit on the wound, wrap it in a cobweb, and quietly wait for it to stop bleeding.

But I am not a sensible country person. No, as an ex-townie with a strain of blokish hypochondria that verges on Munchausen's, I'm ashamed to say that I catch myself wondering if I am going to bleed to death.

That's if the tetanus doesn't get me first.

I sometimes wonder how long it would take someone to find me, if I were to have a serious accident at La Folie. The nearest inhabited house, where Gilles and Josette live, is more than half a mile away, and – when Serge and the workmen are not here – the only daily human contact I have is with the postman. I first thought about this on the day I went into the *cellier* at the back of the *maison des amis* to get some things out of the freezer, shut the door behind me, and heard the door-handle clatter on to the floor outside.

I haven't quite reached the stage where I think about it every time I eat a bony fish (the cat has yet to learn the Heimlich Manoeuvre) or climb a ladder to seek out the thundering critters in the roof (the cat draws a line at anything bigger than a rat). But I always carry my mobile phone when I'm working with the chainsaw in the barn, and I make a point of rushing out to greet the postman every time he drives up to the house in his yellow van. I like to think he'd begin to wonder, if I stopped emerging for my '*Bonjour Monsieur, merci, et bonne journée*' routine of a morning.

Drip, drip, drip. I had not thought the old man had so much blood in him. I can't possibly drive, not with all this blood splashing everywhere. It occurs to me that I could phone the *pompiers*. But I can't look up their number without Macbething the yellow pages. And even I am prepared to admit that a fire-engine might be just a little *de trop* under the circumstances.

I am just thinking about all this when – with a roar of rotors – a helicopter ambulance comes thwott-thwott-thwotting low over the house, like a genie from a lamp, low enough for me to see that there is a stretcher strapped to one of its skids.

Well, I'll be — I know the French healthcare system has a good reputation, but this is amazing. Over here, chaps.

The helicopter doesn't stop. It swoops down into the valley, so steeply that I wonder if it has an engine problem. And then it is hidden by the trees, and I go back to examining my finger. The bleeding has stopped. A transfusion will not, I think, be required.

At nightfall, I drive down to Gilles's house, to tell him about the helicopter, and ask him what he thinks it was all about.

Gilles comes to the door looking pallid, devoid of his usual twinkle. Even the Byronic wave in his hair appears to have gone flat. He murmurs a greeting and weakly shakes my hand.

'It's Josette,' he tells me in a low voice.

'Is she sick?'

'I was in the tractor, hammering in fence-posts, and she was directing me,' he says, staring at the ground.

I put my hand to my mouth. I've seen how that pneumatic sledgehammer works, slamming the heavy wooden posts into the earth.

'No, no. I didn't hit her. But I lowered the front-loader of the tractor without thinking, and . . .' He grimaces, wrings his hands. 'And she must have been underneath.'

'So she's . . . she's . . . ?'

'Not dead. But they think she may have broken her back. I've just come from the hospital in Limoges. It's a terrible thing to do that to anyone. But to your wife . . .'

Gilles appears to be lost in his own thoughts. Then he points to my bandaged finger.

'Did you hurt yourself?' he asks.

I shake my head, too ashamed for words.

A couple of nights later, I make my first appearance at the French evening class in town. Ten English invaders sit nervously twiddling their pencils, perched on the tiny chairs of Jolibois Primary.

Behind me sit Dave and Celia, who are busy setting up a photographic business – or were, until Dave fell off the back of a lorry and bashed his knee. Over there is Cackling Madge, who resembles a china ornament loosely wrapped in brown paper, and has presumably chosen France because she's a sixty-a-day gal and fags are cheaper over here. Up at the front sits Ralph the celebrated artist, one part Frankie Howerd to two parts Oscar Wilde, who has come to Jolibois to paint in tranquillity, darling, along with his wife, Olga, who claims to be writing a novel but I think may be spying for the Russians.

Simon and Nigel sport V-necked sweaters and identical goatees. Though they don't talk to anyone, I suspect they've bought a modern *pavillon* and do something sinister in interior design. And then there's Somerset Stan, who is always talking about chopping down hawthorn hedges (or 'artharn adges' as he calls them), alongside his sweet, rather fragile wife, Helen, who whispers that 'Although I look older, I am actually younger than him.'

Our teacher is Nicole, a heroically patient and infectiously giggly lady who used to teach English to French children, and now teaches French to English adults. She is trying to explain the subjunctive to us, but Celia and Cackling Madge seem far more interested in discussing the shortcomings of French paint, Olga the spy is asleep and Somerset Stan wails that he only wants to know a bit of slang for ordering timber at the local builders' merchants. Then Ralph the artist performs a hilarious mime of someone drowning slowly in a vat of treacle, and Olga wakes with a start.

'What, Ralphie? What?' she cries in a bleary panic, and we all fall about laughing, including Nicole.

Back at La Folie, there are three messages blinking on the answerphone. The first is from Gilles, and I wince when I hear his tone of voice, which is still low and grim. But Josette is on the mend. I listen to the message twice, to make sure I have properly understood. Yes: the doctors say she has broken no bones in her back, though she will need months of physio.

The next message is from Ralph and Olga, my new friends from French class, inviting me to dinner next week.

'I promise it won't be too English, darling,' says Ralph. 'There'll be some civilized French people for you, too.'

The third is from Céline who works in the *boulangerie* and does the flowers in church, to say that she and her husband Luc would love to come to supper on Sunday. So my first-ever all-French dinner party is approaching.

On Saturday, shortly after suffering a catastophic defeat on behalf of the Jolibois Men's over-35s second tennis team, I am sourcing ingredients for Nigel Slater's fish pie in Champion when a terrifying vision appears before me. A pair of Siamese twins, conjoined at the head, is having an epileptic fit beside the *haricots blancs*. All I can make out is four staggering legs and a mass of straggly black-and-blond hair. The creature is clutching its head in its hands as it bumps into shelves, writhing in agony. All around me, people are staring, open-mouthed, trolleys pointing at the hideous scene.

And then the sound of two distinct, pipe-scouring screams rends the air and the vision flips into sharp focus.

It's a cat-fight. And it's very, very nasty. I'm relieved to see that, this time at least, *les Anglais* are not involved. Two women – both in their thirties – appear to be trying to kill each other by the time-honoured method of yanking out great clumps of each other's hair. The fresh milk always runs out early at Champion, so perhaps they're both after the last carton of *demi-écrémé*.

To my considerable surprise, I find that I have instinctively grabbed one of the women – a shrieking bundle of black hair – and am holding her arms in an attempt to stop her pummelling the other's face. '*Arrête! Arrête!*' I growl. This turns out to be a very bad idea, as it merely allows her blonde nemesis to land several free shots. Oops. Sorry, *Madame*.

For the next few seconds, the scene is a blur. I try and work myself between the two wild animals, but each has some sort of Vulcan death-grip on the other. Attempting to prise them apart is like trying to rip the beard off a mountaineer.

'*Salope!*' screams the blonde fury.

'I have my own husband,' screams her adversary. 'I don't need yours.'

Then another man leaps in to help, grabbing the blonde woman from behind, and together we attempt to stop the carnage. I hear the ugly *thwock* of heads knocking together, glimpse a blur of white knuckles clenching shaggy fistfuls of black hair, am dimly aware that a crowd has gathered to watch. Ah, another peaceful day in Jolibois. For a second the other man and I make eye-contact, and I can see we're both thinking the same thing: *Mon Dieu*, these women are strong!

'*Laisse, laisse,*' I say gently to the blonde woman, attempting to prise open her fists. Let go of all that hair. Her rage is so powerful. And now she, too, catches my gaze and stares at me with a mixture of confusion and anger. Here she is, having a perfectly normal cat-fight in the middle of her local supermarket, and she's got some English bloke in tennis whites quietly telling her what to do. I can see her brain spinning like the wheels of a fruit-machine as we lock pupils in the heart of the maelstrom.

Then she head-butts the woman I'm holding. Something warm spatters my hand.

There's another flurry of shouting and flailing limbs, and then we are pulling them apart. The spectators disperse on tiptoe, and the frenetic corrida fades back into a humdrum supermarket. I follow the black-haired woman as she staggers away into the Italian cheese section.

'*Madame*,' I say softly. 'Are you all right?'

'*Oui, ça va*,' she grunts, still trembling with adrenaline. Blood streams from her nose. Four gashes stripe her cheek. I want to help her, to offer a little human warmth, but I can see that she needs to be alone with the mozzarella. I feel pretty shaky myself, so I go and stare at crème caramels for a while.

My wrists ache, and I'm sickened at the sight of some-one else's blood on my skin and clothing. As I walk back past the scene of the fight, I see the white floor-tiles are covered with clumps of black hair. A doughnut of grannies is still standing there, leaning on their trolleys, excitedly gossiping about what they've just seen.

'*Merci, Monsieur*,' whispers the store security guard as he passes me.

'*Pas de problème*,' I reply, without thinking.

I want to get out of here, so I make for the check-out. But – uh-oh - there's the blonde woman, waiting to pay for her shopping, with a sheepish-looking husband in tow. I slip round the back of the pasta and rice and head for check-out number one, right at the other end of the line. I'm suddenly not feeling very brave at all.

Cooking is usually therapeutic, but tonight, for my first all-French dinner party at La Folie, the pressure is on. Besides Céline who does the flowers and her husband Luc the *pâtissier*, there will be Fabrice the organist and his wife Marie, who works in a hardware shop in town. The good thing about inviting people over is that it makes me tidy the house. I can't do much about the mountain of builders' rubble out the front. But at least I feel moved to scoop out the grey candyfloss of spiders' webs from between the oak beams and wipe the latest rodent gore from the kitchen floor. I thought rodents were meant to hibernate in winter. Don't tell me: the cat is taking them in their sleep.

'This place feels like the end of the world,' mutters Céline. Everyone has arrived at once, and Luc presents me with one of his very own *tartes aux poires* from the shop.

'*Excusez-moi que c'est un bordel,*' I say, attempting to shepherd everyone through to the kitchen for drinks. This is a phrase I've heard Serge use when things are a little untidy. Céline looks a bit stunned, but says nothing. It's only later that I discover that I've just apologized for the state of my brothel.

At first, I find their silence unnerving. Even by the standards of the silences I've weathered at Gilles and Josette's, this one is an abyss. Being the host, I make a few conversational sallies, but am soon beaten back by the monosyllabic brick-wall with which I am confronted.

Even the cat, embarrassed, clatters out of the cat-flap. I'd follow her, if I could fit. And then a realization dawns on me, like a saucepan falling on my head. Back when I first met Céline arranging the flowers in the church, she told me that Fabrice was her son-in-law. So that makes Marie their daughter. No wonder there's no small talk. This isn't a dinner party, it's *Ask the Family*.

'*Donc . . . qui voudrait une boisson?*' I ask, rubbing my hands, to a barrage of shrugs and raised eyebrows. '*Il y a du Ricard, du pineau . . .*' Father and son-in-law choose Ricard; mother and daughter point at the pineau. I begin to wonder if they're playing the Gibson Game on me. This is a cruel sport we used to play at school, when teachers were kind enough to invite a group of us over for tea. The aim was not to say a single word, even when spoken to, with the winner being the very last person to speak. Right now, I feel like I'm up against the French premier league.

Marie wins by miles, with a score of fifty-eight minutes. In the meantime, with a drink in my hand, I feel emboldened to make my confession.

'I hope you don't mind,' I say cheerfully, 'but I haven't made a starter.'

Four pairs of eyes widen. Yesterday's cat-fight quite scuppered my mental shopping-list. And today is Sunday. I was so busy making my Nigel Slater fish pie – something appropriately *anglais*, without quite slipping into *rosbif* territory – that I missed the shops. I'm waiting for them to laugh and say '*pas de problème*'. Even a muttered '*c'est pas grave*' would be nice. But the silence only deepens. Céline and Marie exchange glances in a 'chin up, old girl' kind of way. Fabrice's mouth falls open as if he were a fish on a slab. I feel like a character in an HM Bateman cartoon: The Man Who Failed to Cook a Starter for his French Guests.

Stunned by their response, I now make an even graver mistake. I decide to rustle something up from the manky detritus at the back of the fridge. By jove, I'll show these Frenchies how to cook.

Unfortunately, the fridge contains half a packet of out-of-date *lardons*, the shrunken scrapings from Friday night's teriyaki turkey, a wilted lettuce, some sheep antibiotics and three eggs. Right, no problem: one warm egg-and-bacon salad with teriyaki trimmings coming up.

I can tell immediately that this is the first time my guests have been faced with green egg hash with black shrapnel on the side. For one awful moment, I think that Marie is about to burst into tears. It's fair to say that my creation tastes quite a lot worse than it sounds, and makes me wonder if I should have added the sheep antibiotics after all. But no matter: there's still my *pièce de résistance*, the fish pie, to come.

'And what do you call this?' asks Luc, who has become quite chatty after a couple of glasses of wine.

'Fish slush,' I reply. Monumentally overcooked during the Startergate crisis, Slater's inspiration has metamorphosed into a noxious grey sludge.

'*C'est vraiment . . . différent,*' gulps Luc, his chattiness evaporating.

I am about to apologize for the fish pie, and then remember not to. I have at least given my guests the satisfaction of confirming their worst fears about English cooking. And besides, I can tell from their laughter that they are finally beginning to enjoy themselves – perhaps because it's time for *le fromage*, and they've finally found something they can eat.

'*That's* a pretty cheeseboard,' exclaims Céline. 'Where did you get it?'

'Thank you,' I reply. 'I made it myself, when I was at school.'

'Ah, so does it bring back memories?'

'*Oui, de temps en temps.*'

We talk about Jolibois, and the English invasion.

'It would be all right if they would learn to speak just a little French,' says Céline.

'Ah, but we're no better,' remonstrates Luc. 'Because we can't speak English.'

'But we're in France,' I laugh. 'You shouldn't have to speak English here.'

'I bet you haven't found it difficult to integrate, Michael,' he says, 'because you speak such good French.'

'Music helps,' I reply, looking at Fabrice. I decide not to try to explain that I am still sitting out my six-month trial period with the locals. 'And then there's the tennis club. And even the Mushroom Society.'

This produces much mirth, as none of them have ever heard of the Mushroom Society. To be fair, my membership of it has not been an unmitigated success. I joined after I went on one of their mushrooming walks, and was carried away by the saprophytic enthusiasms of the ladies who ran it. I thought I might make friends with fellow foodies whilst learning how to sniff out a *trompette de la mort* at fifty paces. But it turns out that wild mushrooms only do their thing in France for a few weeks in the autumn. How is a fellow supposed to know that?

For the rest of the year, the Société Mycologique busies itself with the production of a thick bi-monthly newsletter which, in attempting to put the fun into fungi, only manages to put the *non* into *champignons*. It seriously makes me want to hide from the postman. I am now wondering if the Snail Society might be more my *tasse de thé*.

'How long are you going to stay in France, Michael?' asks Céline. 'Don't you miss England?'

'Maybe he misses the food,' giggles Luc, nudging Fabrice in the ribs.

'I miss certain people,' I reply, 'and I miss not having a piano.'

'*Ah, mais oui,*' nods Fabrice, trilling with his fingers on the dining table.

'Is it true that you have an aeroplane?' continues Céline.

'Er, yes. A very little old aeroplane,' I tell her hesitantly. 'Nothing special. And yes, I miss that, too. So I'm going back to England soon, to go flying. Just for a weekend. But in answer to your question about how long I plan to stay in France: I simply don't know. I suppose it depends on whether I meet someone. A woman to live with, I mean.'

Everyone considers this in silence, as I remove their cheese plates, still heavy with fish slush.

'So do you think French food is better than English food?' asks Fabrice finally, as Luc begins to slice up the flaky, syrupy *tarte aux poires* that he has baked that afternoon. The other three have never been abroad, but Fabrice is a man of the world, having once spent a fortnight in Stoke-on-Trent when he was training to be an engineer. He says the best things about English food were toffees and Newcastle Brown Ale.

'Right now, Fabrice,' I reply, tucking into the warm, sweet *tarte* that reminds me of sinking into a comfy bed at the end of a long hard day, 'I think it's the best in the world.'

Next morning, the washing-up piled beside the sink looks so daunting that I almost think I might set about writing the opening chapter of *The Labours of Jack Larry*. And this reminds me that now would be a perfect time to start work on the *potager*. Before Josette's accident, Gilles told me that he'd come and plough the would-be vegetable patch for me, once I'd removed the old fence and nuked the *mauvaises herbes* with something he called Rrrrrondop. He also told me to buy some spuds to plant.

Very soon, too, I will have to build a new fence, as Frère Sébastien advised, or else Titus and the Egg Squad will make short work of all the prize tomatoes and beans and basil that I am planning to grow.

My confidence is hard to justify, for by nature I am a serial plant-killer, incapable of keeping anything green alive, if we discount the furry bits on the cheese at the back of the fridge. At Windlesham, I was the one child who failed to make his mustard seeds sprout on the damp blotting paper. At Sherborne, I snuffed out numerous spider plants (parched) and cacti (drowned). Later, in East Dulwich, I planted many splendid shrubs, to no avail. All dead, dead, dead.

Undaunted, I remove the decayed old fence from around what must once have been a very splendid *potager*. I buy a hundred metres of green chain-link *grillage* from the lovely ladies at Alliance Pastorale ('*Another* fence, *Monsieur?*'), forty stout wooden fence-posts and a small book called *Potager: Cultiver de Beaux Légumes au Naturel*. Then I napalm the *mauvaises herbes* with Rrrrrondop, just like Gilles said. And I wait. The thistles and nettles and brambles and Triffids first wilt and then slowly brown, like leeks in a pan. I should have done this with the brambles on my archaeological dig; the one where I found the Massey-Ferguson and the rotting cart.

Ten days later, Gilles comes and ploughs and harrows with his mighty engine-of-war. Josette is still in pain, but mobile, he tells me. I dig and rake. And how proud I feel of my freshly made vegetable bed, which really looks good enough to lie down and go to sleep in. It's not yet time for planting. But if I were a potato, I should be extremely happy to do my sprouting there.

# 30

## THE AUGEAN STABLES

Just as each country has its own terrifying delicacies, so they have their own fearsome mythological beasts, too. The Irish have their Bogles. The Scots have their Kelpies. The Danes have their trolls. And the French have their *fosses septiques*.

Zumbach told me it would be all right to leave emptying mine until the autumn, but somehow it slipped my mind. Now, however, I am beginning to catch a whiff of ancient Rome on still evenings, and I know that it is time for me to make my heroic venture into the underworld. Especially as I am off to Blighty to fly my plane next week, and do not wish to return to find La Folie inundated beneath several years' worth of liquid ordure.

I have no idea what it looks like, but I do know where the *fosse septique* is located. The beast is surrounded by a ring of pine trees in a small depression several yards away from the house, like an altar in the centre of a druidic circle. I have scratched at the grass there, and come upon smooth concrete: I have touched the very surface of the gates of hell.

Straight after breakfast, I stride out to it with a rusty old scythe I have found at the back of the barn. Martha comes to spectate as, gritting my teeth, I hack away at the earth and scrub that covers one of the monster's lids. There are three of these: one large and two small, arranged like the eye and nostrils of Polyphemus. Kneeling beside the eye, I reach across to the far side of the concrete disc, and attempt to lift it.

Nothing. So I jam my fingers under the lip closest to me, shut my eyes, grit my teeth, clench everything, and heave.

The earth moves. I am half expecting to be enveloped in a pestilent mist; to hear the distant groaning of a thousand penitents. There is none of that. But I do catch a glimpse of something dark, gleaming and evil. I breathe the stench of darkness. And as I gingerly lower the hell-hole cover, I can already feel the hoofs of the Four Horsemen of the Apocalypse clattering up the road from Limoges. Every time I flush the loo now, I say a little prayer.

So today a brave man is coming to empty the beast. I have chosen a company called le Petit Vidangeur, after spotting one of their pocket-sized lorries in town and deciding that there's a sporting chance it might be able to squeeze its way up the drive.

*Le patron* sends his biggest lorry. I hear it labour and then judder to a halt, stuck on the drive's final hairpin.

A few minutes later, there comes a knock at the door.

'*Monsieur*,' says a harassed-looking man in blue overalls. 'May I use your phone?'

From the shouting on the other end of the line, I can tell that reinforcements are not on the way. The man in blue overalls puts down the receiver, shakes both fists at the ceiling and strides out of the front door, muttering under his breath as he disappears back down the drive.

Watching him go, I ponder the mysteries of French sanitation. I started to have my doubts when Céline and her family came to dinner. They all stayed until almost midnight, yet no one showed the slightest inclination to use the facilities. They simply held on. And Marie seemed positively shocked when I asked her if she wanted to visit *la salle d'eau*. I'm not sure, but I think she may have thought I was asking if she'd like to take a shower.

Ten minutes after his vanishing act, the man in blue overalls is back. He knocks at the front door, with a haunted look about him.

'Do you have a spade, *Monsieur*?' he says, wringing his hands.

After we have dug out his lorry and are nicely covered in mud, there is another phone call to *le patron*. This time, when the man in blue overalls stomps out, he looks on the verge of tears.

Sweating and swearing around the distant lorry, he begins to bolt section after section of additional piping on to its unwound hose, thick as one of Serge's forearms. Blue sections, brown sections, sections that look as if they were unearthed at Pompeii. Each section is ten feet long, and must be about as heavy as one of my sheep.

At last the Heath-Robinson hose reaches the Pit of Hell. And with a hissing of pistons, and a squelching noise like the sound of a fat child being dragged from a swamp, the *vidange* begins.

I can breathe again. It has taken this heroic fellow two hours to do a job that should have taken twenty minutes. *Le patron* has told him to charge extra, because of the time it took. But that's *le patron*'s problem. I write out a cheque for the amount I was originally quoted. And then

I pay the difference, in cash, to the man in blue overalls. God knows, he's earned it.

I begin to understand why, on the roadside in France, one will frequently see a chap proudly pointing his *petit zizi* at the hedge, in a happy display of *liberté*. There's little *égalité*, so far as I can tell, since women are deprived of this small pleasure. But there's often *fraternité*, in the sense that the Frenchman likes nothing more than to line up alongside his comrades in looking upon the hedge, gazing out across the sunlit fields as he joins in a communal tinkle. Safer by half to use the great outdoors than to risk the wrath of the dreaded *fosse septique*.

# 31

## URBAN PASTORAL

My trip to London is only for a long weekend. I am not running away, but I do want to remind myself what it is that I have left behind. I need to shake out the cobwebs from my flying, so that the Luscombe and I are not still feeling rusty when we are on short final for Le Touquet or Chartres. And I am more than usually desperate to climb back into the cockpit of a Tiger Moth, too.

Once again, I am late getting away from La Folie. I've never been one of life's early birds, but today's close shave looks as if it will be more exciting than most. When I should be on the road to Limoges airport, I'm still feeding stale bread to the Rastafarians and counselling the cat on how to deal with an obsessive-compulsive rooster. Gilles has offered to take charge of everyone while I'm away. He doesn't think any lambs will be born for a few weeks yet. I'm still finding it hard to believe that the toothless Gaston can have impregnated Doris, Daphne and Ella. But Gilles is convinced that something will happen in the end.

At the airport at last, I'm trying to find a space in a car-park jam-packed with Brit-registered Fiestas and

Cavaliers. Parking is free, so cars are abandoned here for months on end while their owners sit in Chingford and dream of being able to snatch another weekend at their little place in Chateauponsac. Today there's not a single space left, so I have to invent one. If I cannot be Queen Victoria's train-driver or a Spitfire pilot or a cinema organist or a stonemason, I might come back as a cowboy car-clamper in my next life. One could make a jolly good living out of all the Brits at Limoges.

I race for the airport building, my suitcase bumping behind me as I rush for the big white marquee that is the temporary terminal. Back in the 1970s, they never dreamed of all *les Anglais* who would one day be flocking to the Limousin.

The Ryanair check-in closes thirty-five minutes before departure, and the flight from Stansted has already arrived. A contraflow of happy English passengers is squinting out into the frosty sunlight, looking for their friends. I can see why the locals talk of an invasion.

'Golly, you said it would be rustic, Jill,' trills a lady beside me, 'but I didn't expect the airport to be just a tent!' Well, yes. We're temporarily under canvas because the old terminal is having to be extended to cope with the new influx. Now if you don't mind moving your trolley, Madam . . .

And then I'm at the check-in with three minutes to spare. Ahead of me, an English couple is being stung for their overweight baggage.

''Kin 'ell, Shaz, the luggage is going to cost us more than the ticket,' wails a shaven-headed walrus in a scarlet tracksuit with three livid white stripes that run from neck to ankle.

Shaz, no stranger to the tea-trolley, looks blank. 'I'm

not leaving the jam, Del,' she says, widening her stance like a Sumo preparing to engage.

Del sighs, and opens his wallet to pay for the most expensive jam in the world.

I can't talk. My own hand luggage is stuffed with *Oeufs Frais des Poules Contentes de La Folie*, which I'm worried may be fried by the X-ray machine.

'Hey, Michael, you're cutting it fine, aren't you?' chuckles the young man behind the check-in desk. At first I can't place him, but he reminds me: I was practising the organ in the church before Christmas, while he and Fabrice were setting up the gaudy illuminations around the crib.

'*Deux minutes? Pas de problème*,' I reply, as the last-call-for-boarding announcement comes over the tannoy.

I know this announcement is a fib, because I can see all the passengers squeezed into the airless, chairless holding-pen on the other side of passport control. So I ask the glamorous blonde lady behind the bar for a *café allongé* and wait for the latecomers to hit the check-in.

Watching them is a grim sport, and I do it not out of *schadenfreude* but because it gives me an obscure sense of catharsis: pity at their plight, fear that it will be me next time round. Thirty-four minutes before the plane is due to take off, the latecomers arrive at the desk, puffing with relief when they see the queue for the X-ray machine, and then gasping when they're told that they're too late to check in.

'But look, they haven't even started boarding yet!' pleads a leather-faced gent in a pink fleece and a Panama hat that's two sizes too small for him.

'I'm very sorry, Sir. Ze check-in is closed,' says the young man apologetically. This is cut-and-dried airline policy, and may explain why their punctuality figures are so good.

I've seen men yelling till they're blue in the face, their wives ululating, their children sobbing into their teddy bears, and it hasn't made a *soupçon* of difference. Ze check-in is closed.

You can head into town to catch the train to Paris, or else you can re-book for tomorrow's flight. Either way, you've had it. I used to think that watching this painful little drama would persuade me to arrive a little earlier if ever I were travelling myself. It clearly hasn't worked.

On board the plane, all the safety announcements are made in English alone. I sip a cup of watery tea and, on Peter Viola's recommendation, read *Nous Deux* magazine. This is full of tacky photo love-stories which, he assures me, are far better than Flaubert or Balzac for learning the kind of colloquial French that people actually speak.

And then I'm in a taxi crossing London Bridge, and I can see the cabbie peering at me in the rear-view mirror. I don't want to chat, I want to look at London. But he wants to talk, especially when I explain that I moved to France to learn to be brave and live closer to nature.

'Blimey, you could do the same thing on a nudist beach,' he says, roaring with laughter. 'Especially at this time of year.'

'Maybe you're right,' I reply, pretending to take him seriously.

'What do you miss about London then, guv?' he says. 'Bet everything's better in France, innit?'

I gaze at the soaring buildings, and at the huge advertisements for watches and perfumes and recruitment companies that I've never really noticed before. I'm struck by the brilliance of the lighting that blazes into the sky.

And everyone looks so *young*. I'm used to deserted streets, with maybe an old boy on the corner who'll give me a friendly wave. Here, I see people hugging and kissing in groups. Three Japanese girls snapping each other in their perfect outfits. Skateboarders loafing in baggy beige. An Asian couple in matching specs, pushing a pram. City workers spilling on to pavements, joshing, pint glasses in hand. The ghosts of friends I've left behind.

'All this is what I miss,' I tell him. 'I just miss all these people.'

At Rochester airport next morning, I'm glad to find there's nobody about. Alone in one of the silent hangars which, sixty years ago, housed Stirling bombers, I run my fingers along the Luscombe's smooth leading edges, picturing the air blasting against them at three thousand feet and a hundred miles an hour.

With its curves and 1940s elegance, I like to think that the Luscombe carries some hint of a genetic link to the Spitfires and Hurricanes of my childhood dreams. But it is no warbird. With its high wing and fixed undercarriage, it looks more like a proto-Cessna. Mine is a jaunty butter-cup yellow, with white wings and tail, and a white stripe down the side. I can't wait to hear what grouchy Marcel and the old boys at the flying club at St Juste will have to say about it.

I rock the ailerons, listening to the gentle rasp of the pulleys inside the wings. Unscrewing the fuel cap, I dip my fingers into the tank. I cannot feel any liquid, but the tips glisten when I draw them out. So I did leave the tank full, after all. Good. Less room for condensation and corrosion that way.

Footsteps crunching behind me break the spell. It's Nigel, one of the yellow-jacketed ground-staff, watching me from behind the tinted lenses of his spectacles. My heart sinks. Nigel is never happy unless he is thoroughly miserable.

'Well, well, well,' says Nigel in a nasal sing-song. 'Here's trouble.'

'Hello, Nigel. Can we get Zulu-Alpha out, please?'

'Frogs kicked you out, have they?' he whines.

'Just a few days off for good behaviour.'

'Oh, right. Sunny all the time, is it? Girls, girls, girls?'

'Beautiful girls, Nigel. Girls everywhere. I have to beat them off.'

'Bastard,' he says. 'And then he expects us to move his plane for him. Bastard.' He is silent for a few moments. 'Is it true they don't wear any knickers?'

'I honestly couldn't tell you, Nigel. Sheep are more my thing these days.'

Nigel finds this so amusing that he hugs his sides and crosses his legs and starts hopping up and down with pleasure.

'Sheep! Sheep! Well, you said it, mate, you said it.' And then he forgets that he was supposed to be being sulky and recalcitrant, and starts heaving planes around, making a space for the Luscombe, without even thinking about it. 'Sheep!'

While I wait, I head into the airport café to grab a bite of lunch, hoping to see some familiar faces. At least the lovely Nathalie is still there: a proper French lady cooking proper French food.

'*Ah, Michael, ça va?*' she says, heaping a steaming portion of *boeuf bourguignon* on to a plate for me, as I queue at the serving-hatch. '*Ça te plaît, d'habiter en France?*'

'*Tout à fait. Je l'aime bien.*'

'Cor, blimey,' says one of Nigel's yellow-jacketed colleagues, in the queue just behind me. 'Doesn't anybody

speak English around here any more? It's like bloomin'
*Allo, Allo.*'

After I've eaten, Nathalie comes and sits with me,
pulling hard on a cigarette, eager to hear news of her
homeland. She looks just the same as I remember: blonde
and soft and ever so slightly worn around the edges, like
a well-loved paperback. She rolls her eyes at how much
my French has improved since I was last here. For her,
thoroughly established in her English adventure, just a
few months have passed. For me, several lifetimes.

'I'll be back,' I promise her. 'I still have to come and
pick up my plane.'

Nigel has pushed the Luscombe into the watery sunshine by the time I emerge from the café. After a thorough
pre-flight, I prepare to fire her up. Parking-brake on. Stick
tied back. Wheels chocked. Fuel on. Throttle closed. Give
the prop six swings, then three squirts of prime, then
another six swings, then crack the throttle and – bingo –
she starts first time. Always works like that, when no
one's watching.

But today there's a problem. With the engine clattering
away happily enough, the oil pressure is reading zero. I
tap the needle. It's not budging and – after waiting for
another five seconds – I shut down the engine. I don't
want it shaking itself to pieces. A few minutes later, I try
another start. Still no oil pressure, damn it. So I shan't be
flying anywhere today.

I check my watch. There's still time to drive to the Tiger
Club at Headcorn.

'Oh, gawd. Here comes trouble,' groans Terry, the duty
manager, when I wander into the shabby Portakabin that
serves as a clubhouse. 'Frogs kicked you out, have they?'

'No, just a few days' home-leave for good behaviour,' I

laugh, wondering if Terry and Nigel may be twins separated at birth. Or perhaps they are simply graduates of the same school of sparkling repartee. There is a split-second hiatus as I click my transmitter back on to the frequency marked EBB (English Blokish Banter). I happen to know that Terry is a teddy bear beneath his gruff exterior, but it's tactful to play along with his miserable-old-bugger act.

'So you've decided to come and annoy me,' he continues.

'I missed you, Terry. Found I couldn't live without you.'

'Oh, yes? Missed my ugly face, did you?'

'Your charming personality, mostly.'

'Liar.'

'Any chance of my taking one of the Moths up for half an hour or so?'

'That depends if you're planning to crash it or not.' Terry gives me a long hard stare. I grin back, expecting him to crack, but he doesn't. 'Anyway, where's your Luscombe?' he asks. 'Crashed that, have you?' Sometimes even teddy bears have their off-days.

It's good, climbing into a Tiger Moth. It makes me feel as if I am preparing for the future, buried somewhere in the past. It's not just that Pa flew Tiger Moths in the 1930s. Or that, as a child of seven, this was the first plane in which I ever flew. Learning to fly the aircraft has always been a first step en route to flying a Spitfire. And everything about the plane just feels and smells so right, with its majestic curves, its primitive instruments that look as if they were hauled up off the *Titanic*, and the old magenta-and-silver de Havilland colour scheme. I suppose it all felt new-fangled and sporty when Pa used to fly these things.

They say G-ACDC is the oldest Tiger Moth still flying, although it has been crashed and rebuilt so many times that the only truly original part remaining may be the fire-proof data-plate. I climb on to the wing-root, then down into the wooden cockpit, feeling the hefty rudder pedals under my feet as I do up my straps. Then I don my leather helmet and goggles, too, enveloping myself in the muffled sensations of this otherworld.

A few minutes later, I am taxi-ing across Headcorn's bumpy grass, weaving left and right because it's impossible to see anything over the nose. At last, lined up between the white runway markers, I open the throttle.

The vibration of my leather helmet slapping against my eardrums is deafening. For a second, we veer sharply to the right. Alarmed, I counter the torque with left rudder, and then both feet are jiggling and dancing on the pedals as G-ACDC gathers speed. The tail comes up first and – blimey, that was quick – we are airborne.

The climb attitude is steep, the noise ferocious – I can feel it all the way up my spine – and everything is shaking from the clattering of the Gypsy Major that's hauling me skywards. Much as I adore my Luscombe with its little 65hp Continental, there is something raw and pure and ancient about climbing at full power in a heavy plane with a dirty great beast of an inefficient engine roaring it into the sky.

And then it's getting colder as I climb above the scattered clouds, wanting to gain enough height to try some spins. Spinning still frightens me, ever so slightly, but it thrills me, too. Putting a plane into a spin, on purpose, is not unlike looking down the barrel of a loaded rifle.

At three and a half thousand feet, I lock the anti-stall slats, haul back on the stick, kick in some hard right rudder, and watch fields and trees filling and whirling in my vision like green linens in a tumble-dryer.

How extraordinary, I think to myself, that this is still possible in the twenty-first century: to rent an ancient biplane – the oldest of its type still flying – and set it spinning vertically towards the earth in a sunlit sky above the fields of Kent. Levelling off, I unclip my radio mask and take a lungful of the icy air. When first I learned to fly, five years ago, I was disappointed to discover that – because flying is scientific and technical and subject to all sorts of laws – the one thing it could never be was romantic. But today, as I swoop and dive, and feel the cold blast of the wind above the clouds, and listen to the ancient Gypsy Major still grinding out its galloping horse-power, I feel as never before the intense romanticism of flight.

Next I cruise towards Dover and out over the glittering water, just far enough to allow me to make a graceful arc back over the White Cliffs. I feel a familiar pang as I do so, a pang I have never fully understood. A longing for something I never knew. I miss England, even though I am right here, flying over the top of it.

I wish there were someone with me now, wish there were a leather-helmeted head in the front cockpit, a gloved hand offering a thumbs-up in the rushing slipstream.

If I could place anyone there now, crouched in that cockpit, grinning at the clouds and the blurred needles of the ancient instruments, who would it be? Clara Delaville, who stole my childhood heart? Zuleika, chasing her grandpa's ghost? For a moment I wish it could be my grandfather, Pa, dreaming of his perfect omelette even as he banks us in a steep turn over the White Cliffs, with the ball perfectly centred and the speed pegged at sixty-five.

And then I realize that it would be none of these. It would be me as a little boy in short trousers and tortoiseshell National Health specs, infatuated with aero-planes, dazzled by the very idea of ever growing up, let alone learning to fly.

Michael, aged seven, reaches behind him from the front cockpit, and I shove my arm out into the slipstream to grasp his tiny hand.

'This is so cool,' crackles a high-pitched voice from somewhere far away.

## 32

## BEGINNINGS AND ENDINGS

Filled up with flying, and having arranged for the Luscombe's oil pump to be examined, I return to France. At the start of my adventure, the man in the paper-shop warned me that it would take six months before the locals began to accept me. And, lo and behold, almost six months to the day after my arrival, the ice is beginning to thaw. Not that people weren't friendly from the start; they were. But – with obvious exceptions, such as Gilles and Jérôme – they were friendly-at-a-distance; more wary than warm. Now they are beginning to invite me over for *un apéro* or for dinner, and to call out to me in the street. I am beginning to feel at home.

I am beginning to recognize, too, that the routine of life at La Folie is a rare blessing: the cat coming to claw at my head in order to wake me for feeding duty; the chickens streaming out from the chicken house, one by one, with Titus always bringing up the rear, struggling to squeeze his mighty tail-feathers through the pop-hole door; the sheep galloping down the hill to greet me, gazing warily at me as they munch their *luzerne*. Chopping wood, cleaning the chimney, stoking the stove.

Repetition and routines begin to seem important; the more boring and strenuous the better. I am a dilettante by nature, all too easily seduced by the next shiny excitement that comes along. And the more I think about what may be involved in becoming a hero, the more some element of repeated grind – of Sisyphus pushing his rock up a hill, day after day – forms part of the picture.

My contemporary heroes are not drawn from the beautiful brilliants; from the footballers or tennis players or rugby men gifted with unnatural magic in their boots or wrists. No, they are the grunting sufferers: the Olympic rower, incarcerated yet again in a windowless room, hauling out repeated agony on his screaming ergometer; the middle-distance runner, training her body to the point of injury and past it, crawling over broken glass to a distant horizon way beyond my own threshold of imaginable pain; the round-the-world sailor, straining night after night to push her boat through lonely ice-storms, utterly alone. My dad, who may have been carried aloft on the shoulders of his peers for a single moment of pure sporting glory at the age of eighteen, kicking a rugby ball that no one else dared kick between two uprights, but who then spent forty years trudging daily into an office to do a job he didn't enjoy, because he had a family to support.

And me? While my puny repetitions are structured on a daily basis, I am beginning to glimpse a wider landscape; beginning to sense for myself how nature plays out her invisible patterns and repetitions on a far grander scale than human beings – even those standing on the shoulders of giants – can ever hope to match. The stars wheel above me in the heavens. The universe stretches out around me, towards infinity.

The next day finds me standing on a French hillside, at five o'clock on a Tuesday afternoon, counting small black sheep. I know there should be five of them. But I have counted twice. And the discrepancy can mean only one thing. Oh. My. God.

Without fireworks or brass bands; without bunting strung from every roof; without even any obvious signs of gestation, it has happened.

My first lamb has been born.

Watching this knock-kneed, hop-skippety creature bouncing around its mother, Daphne, I can hardly believe it is such a recent arrival on the planet. The tiny creature looks so ready for life.

Following the advice in *Sheep for Beginners* – my copy dog-eared with reading and re-reading – I pick up the lamb and walk backwards with it towards the sheep shelter, holding out the damp, fragile form so that Daphne can see it and smell it. She trots after us, yelling furiously, while the rest of the sheep fan out in a fighter escort, baying with angry solidarity.

And now a moment of panic. I have laid the lamb in the straw inside the shelter, but Daphne stops a few yards away, making a hell of a racket, unwilling to enter what is clearly a trap. Instead she turns and begins to walk away. The lamb bleats weakly – more 'wwrrr' than 'baaa' – and, for a second, Daphne stops, head poised, listening. Then she continues to walk away.

I grab the lamb again; carry it towards its trembling mother. This time, Daphne's maternal impulses prove stronger than her instinct for personal safety, and she follows her child into the prison where I have placed it. The door clangs shut. And I race off to telephone Gilles.

I don't know if my newborn lamb is a boy or a girl. I've had a good look at its bits and pieces, but I'm not entirely sure what I'm looking for. There's definitely a little bibbly thing dangling between the hind legs, but Ceilidh the guinea-pig-eating dachshund had one of those, and she was a neutered female. Hence the need for Gilles, although I'm also hoping for his reassurance that the lamb is in good health. It looks a bit wobbly to me, and I'm not sure that it has eaten, or even if Daphne's teats are both fully operational.

'*C'est un petit mâle*,' says Gilles gently, examining the lamb. He's wearing his familiar grey jumper, a mass of loose threads, which has been mended and darned so many times that the original garment must have ceased to exist. He hasn't brushed his hair. Josette, walking stiffly beside him in her matching wellies, looks better than I was expecting, though I can see her concentrating hard to manage her pain. She makes all the right sort of cooing noises about how *mignon* the little fellow is, even though she must have seen several thousand newborn lambs before. Then her husband expresses a squirt of milk from each of Daphne's teats to demonstrate that all is well.

'See how one is smaller than the other?' he asks. 'That's because the lamb has already fed from one side.'

So we leave mother and child to their own devices and, as we do, I am thrilled to see the lamb butt its tiny head beneath Daphne's undercarriage for a mouthful of milk from her fuller teat, and its tail begin to whirr like a propeller. I am going to call him Camillo, the name of one of my favourite Shakespearean characters. This may be because the first time I saw *The Winter's Tale*, starring Survival-Kit Toby at Windlesham, Camillo's costume had been made out of our old sitting-room curtains, donated by my mother the previous year.

Everything is going to be OK.

But Gilles looks quite ill when I tell him what I've done

on the potato front for the *potager*. He did tell me to buy some seed potatoes to plant. And those twenty-five-kilo sacks from Gamm Vert seemed like such a bargain. So I bought two. We stand beneath the warm afternoon sun, looking at my sacks of spuds, and then at the would-be *potager*, and then back at the spuds.

'*C'est beaucoup*,' he says, scratching his head in a look-what-the-funny-Englishman-has-gone-and-done-now kind of way.

'But Gilles, we English do eat a lot more potatoes than the French,' I plead, unwilling to admit that I thought that if you planted one small new potato in the spring, it would become one big old potato in the autumn.

'Even so, when you come to dig them up, you may find that seven hundred kilos of potatoes is rather a lot for one person.'

A week later, I have three jet-black lambs, their pure new wool not yet bleached to chestnut by the sun. Camillo has a white stripe on top of his head, like a badger. Claudette is a perfect, skittish little madam. Of the three, Emil is very much the runt of the litter and my absolute favourite. The poor chap began life as a girl, until Gilles came and took a look at him and pointed out that he has a couple of extra bits attached. I still haven't got the hang of this.

'Emily has turned out to be Emil,' I tell my mother on the phone.

'Oh, you *can't* have!' she gasps.

'Not a meal, Mum. *Emil*.'

But as I wander out to feed the sheep in the late-afternoon sun, I can see immediately that something is not right. Seven Rastafarians come galloping to greet me. And one lies, curled up, asleep in the grass. It is little Emil. I race over to him.

He is not sleeping. A panicked eye gazes up at me. His knock-kneed limbs twitch. Emil is panting like a steam train, his stomach pulsing, a froth of beaded bubbles at his mouth.

As gently as I can, I scoop him up into my arms. I have always wanted to hold a lamb like this. I know there is only one reason I can do so now. Emil and I gaze at each other, both equally afraid. *Please stay alive.*

Emil's mother, Doris, thunders after me, bleating wildly, as I carry off her precious charge.

Spinning the Espace around, I smash the passenger-side indicator on the bumper of Serge's van. No time to inspect the damage now.

'*C'est un agneau, un cas urgent,*' I rasp at the bored lady in the vet's surgery. 'Can somebody please help me?'

Hearing the tremor in my voice, she leaps into action. 'In there,' she says, peering into the box cradled in my arms. 'Oh, what a beautiful black lamb.'

'*C'est grave,*' says Pascal the vet, the moment he begins to examine Emil.

'So what can you do?'

'*C'est très grave,*' he repeats. We look into each other's eyes. 'All right,' he shrugs. 'I'll see what I can do.'

With the second injection in his neck, Emil goes into spasm. It looks as if he is trying to gallop headlong into the air. I lay my hand softly on his flank and he subsides, still panting.

'If he's still alive in the morning, inject him with this,' says Pascal solemnly. 'If not, you must bring him in for an autopsy.'

In a daze, I carry Emil back to the Espace. He is still breathing fast, but seems more peaceful now. I start the car, and – as we move off – reach out a hand to lay it on his chest.

Oh please, no.

I switch off the ignition and sit in silence for a moment. For the second and last time, I scoop up the warm body in my arms, cradling the lolling head, gazing at the gleaming Bakelite hooves, stroking the soft wool on his lifeless back. He feels so almost alive. I try to close his eyelids, but Emil continues to stare at me with that same frightened, please-help-me expression.

Pascal looks up in surprise as Lear returns with Cordelia in a cardboard box.

'I'm so sorry,' I manage to say, 'but I think he is already dead.'

'Ah, I see,' says Pascal, with such gentleness that I have to grit my teeth against the tears that I can feel stupidly welling up inside me. 'Take him into the back, then. We will do the autopsy now.'

So I stand in the doorway as Pascal cuts open my little Emil, who this morning was bouncing around his field. 'It's pleuropericardia,' he says, showing me the colourless liquid trickling in the cavity around Emil's gleaming heart. 'There is really nothing you could have done. But you must now inject the other little ones against it.'

And then I am back at La Folie, and sit gazing across the valley as the last rays of winter sun light up the little chapel on the hill. But what was once a peaceful scene is now a place of torture. For behind me, Doris is tearing around the sheep-field, yelling at me and at the sky, in anguish for her lost lamb. For Emil, who must be out there, somewhere, if only she will call him long and loud enough.

# 33

## APRIL: THE LONE PINE

The Luscombe's oil pump is fixed, but the aircraft remains marooned at Rochester while I wait for a space to become available in the half-empty hangar at St Juste. Finally, I reach the top of the waiting list. And the aeroclub committee decides to change the rules.

They tear up the waiting list.

I don't think this is because I am *anglais*. Peter Viola has a place in one of the hangars, after all. What matters is that I am grounded until further notice.

Things are not looking too hot on the piano front, either, because I still don't have a floor in the summer sitting-room. I can't have a floor until the walls are finished, and Jou-Jou the stonemason says the walls are made of the wrong kind of stone. He cannot find a product that will stick to the particular ash-based breeze-blocks that Zumbach used when he began to renovate La Folie. At least, not one that he can guarantee for ten years, as dictated by the law and the prophets.

Ridiculous as it seems, I am beginning to pine for that piano, as I might pine for a person. As I do pine for a person. The eminent psychiatrist was right: for someone to share my life here.

Someone like Clara Delaville, but who is a grown-up, not a ghost-child.

Someone like Zuleika, but who is not impossible.

Someone like Amy, the girl in the powder-blue dress, but with whom my soul truly connects.

I don't know what I want, it occurs to me, as I sit on the terrace for my six o'clock stiff Pastis and a handful of *pistaches*, and have my nightly think.

The trees on the other side of the valley have grown so thick and lush that the view has changed in three dimensions. I failed to notice the end of winter, and I appear to have missed the beginning of spring. I was expecting a crash of thunder; a swallow; a sign from the heavens. Once again, I remind myself that I promised to notice the changing of the seasons, here in France; to appreciate that metamorphosis which was invisible to me in London. But I find that the seasons move as imperceptibly as a glacier carving out a valley, or the hour-hand of a clock. Time's passing passes me by.

The landscape draws closer as nature advances upon La Folie, like Birnam Wood advancing upon Dunsinane. I cannot see far into the distance. Yet I sense that I am beginning to see what is close to me more clearly than ever.

I contemplate the lone pine, which appears unchanging, and yet which I know is invisibly growing, too. I sip my Pastis, and wish I could play some Chopin, right now. The Fantasie-Impromptu, whose melody keeps leaping into my head. If I had my piano here, I might release some of the yearning I feel. Certain harmonic and melodic progressions have a way, like the best architecture, Persian rugs and ingredients in a perfect soup, of ordering the universe in a way that makes love, goodness and human sympathy seem not merely possible but inevitable.

So here I am, in front of my piano. I can picture the keyboard's white and black gleam; the burnished strings stretching away from me, reflected in the polished lacquer of the open lid.

In my head, the first thing I play is a simple chord, with both hands. The weight of the notes is like the give of the sand beneath my feet as I walk along a beach with someone for whom I have always longed. We are in E-flat major; my favourite key, the key of all that's good in the world. Every key evokes a different mood: A major for summer pleasures, G-flat major for heartfelt longing, C minor for sadness you can describe, C-sharp minor for sadness you can't, G major for a trusted friend, B minor if they should ever let you down.

E-flat major is the sound of my mum's lasagne, the sound of the twilight on a clear summer's day, the sound of the Espace when it starts and I'm not expecting it to, because I'm late for playing the organ for Mass. It is the key of Chopin's most beautiful nocturnes and waltzes, three-quarters of Mozart's horn concertos, of 'Spread A Little Happiness' and 'Someone To Watch Over Me'.

An octave in the left hand. The right hand, playing the first inversion in that tenor range where the piano sings most plangently.

Play both hands together, and we are at home, there are lights in all the windows, two dogs sleeping in front of the fire, and I have somehow invented myself a gorgeous wife who is, even as the notes die, mixing me the perfect gin-and-tonic.

That's how it feels to play an E-flat-major chord, when you don't have a piano.

I have begun to scan the piano advertisements in the

local free-sheets. Perhaps I could buy a cheap second-hand upright, and tuck it into the corner of the winter sitting-room as a stop-gap.

Clutching at other straws, I recently spotted an advertisement in the local paper for an orchestra that is seeking a pianist, and rang to offer my services. Never mind that I wouldn't be able to practise. The Club Philharmonique de Limoges sounded like a first-rate ensemble brimming with young players – demure harpists, sultry oboists, sexy cellists and so on – just waiting to make sweet music with a pianist from the land of Elgar and the Wurzels.

A second after I had expressed my keenness to join, I asked the conductor how many players were in his symphony orchestra.

'*Nous avons un bugle et un accordéon,*' said Monsieur André, sounding a bit like a doctor listing symptoms. '*Une flûte, une clarinette et quatre violons.*' If this was symphonic, then so was my chicken house. And what Monsieur André failed to mention was that the average age of his players was seventy-seven.

This is, nevertheless, all part of the adventure. And afternoon rehearsals are lightened by our cheery English bassist, Jack – a retired engineer from the RAF – who likes to yell 'Cuppa tea'd be nice!' after each piece we murder, be it '*Le Petit Village*' or the Hallelujah Chorus. The incongruity of this, in a room where nobody else speaks a word of English, makes me laugh every time. And then, at the next rehearsal, a lady with a tea-urn appears – paid for out of Monsieur André's own pocket – and both members of the English rhythm section fall silent.

The Club Philharmonique makes a unique sound, to judge from the stricken faces of those who hear us. Actually, that's an exaggeration. There is so little music-making in the Limousin that several people are weirdly appreciative of our aural devastation.

This week, at my first concert with the group in Limoges, I am aghast to spy poor Henri and Françoise, the cherubim and seraphim, amid the collateral damage that we call an audience. Especially since it emerges after the concert that one of the wind players had his music in the wrong order, and played exactly one piece behind everyone else throughout the performance. It says a lot for our abilities that no one noticed.

'Are you all right?' I ask Henri and Françoise, as we leave the hall. The blessed couple do look slightly pale.

'*Mais oui!* We didn't run away,' chortles Françoise, her peach-skin face wrinkling into a happy smile. 'You'd have to play much worse for us to do that.'

# 34

## MAY: THE GOLDEN FLEECE

Gilles is waiting for me when I return to La Folie after the concert, leaning against his van in the evening sunshine.

'*Ça va, Michael?*' he asks, wrinkling his nose in classic Gilles fashion.

'*Oui.*' I nod, surprised. 'Is everything all right? Josette still on the mend?'

'Oh, she's all right,' he says. 'She complains a bit, but what can I expect?'

I usher him inside for a drink.

Gilles is shearing two hundred of his sheep next week, and asks if I'd be willing to help. My heart leaps. Sheep-shearing. Yes, this is the kind of rugged peasant activity for which I came to France, and I'm thrilled also to have an opportunity to make my contribution to rural French life in general, and Gilles in particular. The man does such a lot for me, and it's so hard to think what I can do for him. Giving is always more comfortable than receiving. I once saw sheep-shearing on *Blue Peter*, and it looked rather complicated. But I've studied the pictures in my sheep-husbandry book, and there can't be all that much to it.

'*À la tienne, Gilles*,' I say happily, as he clinks his glass of bitter Salers Gentiane against my Pastis.

At the aeroclub, there has been much whispering in dark corners. Peter Viola keeps me posted about developments regarding the possibility of finding a space for the Luscombe in the half-empty hangar. But things are not looking good.

There is no room at the inn. My aeroplane is going to languish for ever at Rochester, costing me three-hundred quid a month for the privilege of never flying it and merely having the occasional love-in with Nigel.

'You shouldn't have taken a place for granted,' snaps Michel, the new club president, as we stand on the apron watching a Robin DR400 do endless circuits, the squeak of its tyres on the runway reaching us a split second after the little puff of smoke as the wheels make contact.

'I suppose it just looks to me as if there's plenty of room in there,' I reply, gesturing into the half-empty hangar, newly built.

'There are rules. And the rules must be obeyed,' says Michel sternly.

The countryside looks less lovely than usual as I drive back to Jolibois. Grey sky, grey cows, grey grass. In time, I will learn that Michel's attitude reflects a fundamental difference between French and English ways of thinking. In England, we don't have very many rules, and bend them to make exceptions or special cases. In France, there are thousands of rules, and exceptions are not permitted. This is why there are so many committee meetings: to change the rules in order to admit the exceptions without breaking the rules.

I cannot fault the kindness of the people I have met. But every so often, I do find their willingness to hide behind statutes and sub-clauses and *réglementations* in triplicate ever so slightly frustrating. I am beginning to think that I may be forced to sell my aircraft, as I sold Charlie and the boys.

Three days later, I am summoned to Michel's office at the aeroclub, and learn that the committee has changed the rules. A place in the spanking new hangar is finally mine.

Buoyed up with my good news, tail wagging, ready for action, I don my grubby blue workman's overalls, and head off in the Espace for Gilles's shearing barn. I wish Serge were here, because I'd like to be able casually to mention to him that I'm just off to shear some sheep, as we manly peasant farmers are wont to do when the mood takes us. But the workmen have downed tools for the time being, as the question of what render will stick to Zumbach's ash-block walls continues to stymie progress.

It's a ten-minute drive to the hamlet where we are to shear the sheep, and today is one of those glittering spring mornings when the fields just seem to be smiling back at me as I drive past them, the dew beginning to steam in the sun, the sheep munching on their lush new grass with the urgency of children attacking a box of chocolates. I have no radio in the Espace, so I sing to myself instead.

At the barn, I'm surprised to find that there are already five men pacing around inside. Gilles introduces me.

'*Salut, Michael*,' he says. And then I hear him explaining to the men that although I'm *anglais*, I'm OK.

'*Bonjour, Messieurs*,' I chirrup, my nostrils smarting at the ammoniac fug that comes of keeping a hundred sheep penned in a small barn overnight. There are some gruff replies, and I shake hands with each man in turn.

I wonder what all these chaps are going to do with

themselves while Gilles and I shear sheep. But after a few seconds of muttering and nodding, our jobs are allocated and a very French pecking-order of machismo is established.

At the top are the shearers themselves: an ultra-cool Paul Newman type, and a fleshy, red-faced ox who's already sweating heavily in the heat of the sheep-filled barn. Both wear tight jeans, with low-slung shearing belts strapped around their hips, like weight-lifters. Then there's Robert, an old shepherd with a mighty crook and a face as craggy as the Pyrenees, whose job it is to hook each sheep by the hind leg and drag it on to the shearing mat. Next, Gilles and another man – who looks more of an outsider in his gold-rimmed bifocals and scarlet jumper – take turns to wrestle the animal over on to its bottom, ready for its cut, set and blow-dry. And then there's me. My job is . . . well, my job is to collect the wool.

The shearers pull the starter-cords of their well-oiled Lister machines, and the angry buzzing begins. I experiment with various techniques for collecting wool in a manly fashion. I even attempt to channel my inner Frenchman, who would surely find a way to do it with *élan*, *panache*, *savoir-faire* and all those other French concepts for which there is no English word. But everything happens so fast, and it's not easy to look dignified when you're scrabbling around on your knees, desperately trying to scrape up all the greasy fragments of poo-matted fleece from under the feet of two sweaty sheep-shearers, before the *mouton*-wrestlers manhandle their next victim into the barber's chair.

Every so often, my job also involves climbing a ladder up to the mountainous wool-sack, hopping in, and then jumping up and down on the shorn fleeces. I try to imagine how a cowboy would behave on a trampoline, and end up feeling more like a clown on a bouncy castle. I remind myself that I am here to make a contribution, come what may.

Once the ewes are shorn, it's time for the rams. Each one of these mighty brutes is the size of five of my Rastafarians, and the first one struggles like a tackled rugby-leaguer when Robert hooks its leg. The man in the scarlet jumper backs away nervously, and – spying my chance – I make a heroically rash bid to establish my credentials. I grab the flailing beast with both hands; attempt to drag it forward on to the shearing-mat. But it won't budge. I might as well be trying to move an oak tree. Except that this particular oak tree has decided to go into reverse.

I glance up to see that the other men have stopped to watch, grinning like a bunch of rugby forwards interrupting a scrum to gaze at a streaker. Cool Hand Luke has even lit a cigarette. Oh Lord. I dig my heels in, take a tighter grip on the ram, and shove with all my might. This is for England. Thankfully, the animal picks up my desperation and begins to stagger forward, more out of politeness than anything else.

Chuckling, Gilles takes over from me. '*Bien fait, Michael*,' he says kindly. And I resume my wool-gathering duties with new ardour as the last few rams line up for their crew-cuts.

'How many sheep do you have?' I ask the man in the scarlet jumper, as – happy and weary – we wander back through the sunlit fields to Gilles's house for lunch.

'Only three,' he says sheepishly. So I have found a fellow townie-in-mufti. '*Et toi?*'

'Eight,' I reply, trying to sound nonchalant about my vast flock. We stop to admire Gilles's newly shorn rams, munching contentedly in the sunshine beside us. '*C'est bien d'avoir des moutons, non?*'

He nods and smiles, the sunlight glinting off his glasses as he squints at me. We lean on the fence and breathe in the warm, fragrant air. Somewhere in the distance, a church bell chimes. And for this moment, for one Frenchman and one Englishman somewhere in the middle of France, all is right with the world.

# 35

## PEGASUS

Dinner with Ralph the artist and Olga the spy, at their plush old townhouse in the heart of Jolibois, is a cheery affair. After the leaks and creaks of La Folie, I feel like some shivering, threadbare nephew invited to dine at the home of an indulgent uncle, where every room is warm, and the doors fit properly, and the windows keep out the cold.

'Here's a knocking indeed,' bellows Ralph, his vast frame filling the doorway as he welcomes me into a brightly lit hall, which appears to double as a studio. 'Come in, my boy. How wonderful to see you.'

The walls are covered with effusively colourful paintings of people eating and talking, which comes as no surprise in the light of Ralph's own expansive girth and talent for surreal anecdotage.

'Oh, don't look at them, don't look at them,' he wails, covering his eyes with his hands.

'But why not?' I ask, admiring a painting of three chefs working in a gleamingly detailed restaurant kitchen.

'Because they're all *awful*. Don't be polite, my boy; I

can take it.' His booming voice echoes upwards through the house. 'I know they're terrible.'

'On the contrary, I think they're jolly good.' I'm worried he's about to burst into tears. 'Why are you so hard on yourself, Ralph?'

'Because of Rembrandt. Ah, my poor, dear Rembrandt.' He places his hand on his heart and points to a corner of the room that is piled with a riot of paints and brushes. Sellotaped to the wall are a number of faded postcards of Rembrandt self-portraits, their corners curling with age. 'I keep them there, to remind me of what I shall never be able to do,' he intones.

'Do you think that's a good idea?' I ask. 'To judge yourself against Rembrandt?'

'I can't help it,' he groans, gazing at the postcards as if in a trance, and then shaking himself back into the present. 'But enough of my shortcomings. How are the sheep? And the chickens? Have you started writing that book yet? You must come upstairs and meet everyone. You'll be all right, because your French is so good, you beastly swot.'

Olga the spy is standing at the top of the stairs, looking voluptuously maternal in a green velvet dress. She smiles at me, twinkling like a character from Beatrix Potter, when I present her with a box of eggs from Martha and the girls.

'How lovely,' she says, showing me into a cosy drawing-room where two men and two women, all in their forties or fifties, are lounged on sofas and sipping sherry from antique glasses. 'This is Michael, who lives with sheep and chickens,' she explains in French, as she introduces me to a handsome, well-pressed man called Yves-Pascal, whom she describes as the local *notaire*, and his wife, Ariane, a tall, sternly beautiful woman with a dancer's build and posture.

'Ah, so you are the Englishman who bought La Folie?' says Yves-Pascal, peering at me quizzically. 'I'd have handled the sale myself, but I was on holiday at the time. You'll have dealt with my partner, Jacques'

'You're not to start talking shop now, *chéri*,' mutters Ariane.

'No, no, but I know the house, and I remember the sale,' says Yves-Pascal. 'It was the Polish ecologist who sold it to you, wasn't it? I saw the house years ago, before he started working on it. It was an awful ruin, and you couldn't believe anyone could live there. But his wife had fallen in love with it, and insisted he buy it for her. And then . . . it all ended so sadly.'

Ralph bundles back into the room, pours me a sherry, and flops himself down into a heavy indentation in one of the sofas. 'Ah, this is the life,' he roars in English. 'And now we can all get *pished*.'

It turns out that he and Olga used to live in a cottage next door to Gilles's shearing-barn, in the hamlet where we sheared his sheep last week. So they know Gilles and Josette, at least by sight.

'What we could never work out,' says Ralph, 'was who he was shouting at. Because he always seemed to yell at his dogs, his sheep, and that poor, dear woman in exactly the same way. It used to quite make my eyes water.'

'Was that why you wanted to move?' I ask, deciding that this is probably not the time to mention Josette's accident.

'No, we just wanted to feel more in the thick of things, if things in Jolibois can ever be said to be thick,' he replies gloomily. 'Just try saying that after a bottle of Armagnac.' This thought seems to cheer him up. 'But what about you, my boy? Where would *you* live, if you won the lottery? Where would you go, if you could live *anywhere*?'

I think about this for a moment. 'Truthfully, I'm there already, Ralph. I can't think of anywhere I would rather live than La Folie.'

'Well, that's . . . that's marvellous,' he says, draining his sherry glass and gazing at Olga, who is deep in conversation with Ariane. 'Shall we eat?'

Over the next few weeks, I book up several flights to England to collect my plane. I keep a close eye on the weather forecasts for both south-east England and northern France. And the news is never good. If it's fine here, it's wet there. On the rare occasions when it's fine there, the storm clouds gather over France.

And then, finally, the clouds part to leave a perfect blue sky, and the weather map of Europe is covered with yellow discs, as if a dozen individual suns were expected in the heavens this week.

So this is it. I am about to fly myself across the Channel to France, in an aeroplane almost sixty years old. It won't be quite as quick as the outbound jaunt on Ryanair, but nor was Odysseus's journey home from Troy. Scheduled flights have no place in a heroic quest. And besides, the sedateness of travel is part of the pleasure of flying old aircraft; it simply doesn't work to be in a hurry.

I shall need to stop at least twice en route to refuel: once at Le Touquet, to clear customs, and once at Chartres, which looks to be roughly the mid-point of my final leg to St Juste.

At La Folie, I've left Gilles in charge of the animals, with strict instructions not to over-feed the cat. At Rochester, the little yellow Luscombe gleams in the Kent sunshine as I make my final checks. I've filed a flight-plan for my first leg to Le Touquet, made fourteen trips to the gents, said goodbye to Nathalie in the café, and packed my stripy pyjamas behind the seat.

'Wheels chocked, brakes on.' I talk myself through the start-up procedure, reminding myself to slow down.

'Fuel on. Throttle closed. Magnetos off.' I pull the propeller through a few blades, then walk back to the cockpit to give her three squirts of fuel with the manual primer. 'Sucking in.' Pull through another six blades.

'Throttle set. Contact!' I give the prop a hefty swing, and the engine coughs into life. Dashing round to the cockpit, I check the instruments and ease the throttle open until the engine is steady at a thousand revs. Thankfully, the oil pressure looks good, so I don the regulation life jacket and hang an emergency transmitter round my neck before removing the chocks, hauling myself up into the cockpit and strapping myself in.

Nigel and the rest of the ground-staff make a big show of sniffling into their hankies as I taxi out across Rochester's apron for the last time, presumably because I haven't had time to buy them leaving presents. *C'est l'humour anglais*, I think to myself. I shan't miss the insults they hurled at me every time I had the temerity to ask if it would be too much trouble for them to fish out my plane from the crowded hangar. But I shall miss flying over Kent and Sussex, and all the towns and villages I have come to know so well from the sky: Headcorn, Canterbury, Tenterden, Goodwood. I shall miss flying over Windlesham, too, skidding high over the tennis courts and the carpentry shed and the chapel, and the child-ghosts of Clara Delaville, Amelia Blunt, Norman Handley and the rest.

It is time to let all that go, for my flight-path lies in another country today.

Soon I am climbing up, up into the ether, and out across the Channel. Clouds are gathering, but I can see a wide break in the clag over the French coast, as if a pair of diaphanous white curtains have been drawn back for my arrival. Beneath me, the oil-tankers drag endless wakes behind them. I glance back for a final look at the White Cliffs of Dover. France, here we come.

I'm disappointed to find that the huge break in the clouds over the French coast has become rather a small hole by the time I get there. Disappointed, and somewhat alarmed. This does not bode well. Spiralling down through the hole in the clouds, I'm further put out to discover that the base of the weather is no more than nine hundred feet off the deck. Dry-mouthed, and scanning my instruments every five seconds, I track cautiously along the coast. Down and to my left, I can see the ruins of the old German gun emplacements, surrounded by the pock-marks of a sixty-year-old artillery bombardment, and then I'm skirting the huge cranes on the wharf at Boulogne. But there's little pleasure in flying in this patchy soup. After waiting so long to make today's flight, I now can't wait to be back on terra firma.

At last le Touquet appears, its grey runways just visible against the grey landscape. At least, I *hope* it's le Touquet. When I land and clamber down from my cramped cockpit, the man in the fuel lorry speaks to me in French. Phew. So at least I haven't ended up in Holland. From here at Le Touquet, I still have over four hundred miles to fly, but the clag is lifting and the weather to the south sounds flyable, even if you wouldn't quite choose it for your daughter's wedding.

After a hurried mushroom omelette that is too pale and dank to have enraptured Pa, I climb into the sky once more. But halfway to Chartres, the weather deteriorates. The twin spires of the cathedral loom out of the mist like a drawing behind tracing paper, and a light rain begins to smash itself on to the perspex of the windshield in front of me. This is not good. After landing, I have to taxi to the fuel-bowser with my face pressed close to the windscreen in an attempt to see through the rain.

Inside the clubhouse, a gaggle of bored-looking pilots regard me with half-hearted curiosity. They seem astonished to hear that I have crossed the Channel, today of all days. The club's internet connection is down, and so – with the help of a fresh-faced young pilot who braves the rain to stand and photograph my plane – the only weather forecast I can get is a recorded one on the telephone. The outlook is not inspiring, but it sounds as if it should be flyable. My new photographer friend phones ahead to a pal in Blois, who kindly offers me a space in his hangar if I cannot make it to St Juste by tonight and need to divert there.

While I'm waiting for the sky to brighten, I follow the young photographer into the hangar where his own vintage aircraft is stored: a noble-looking Fairchild Argus in RAF camouflage and markings, squatting purposefully on its huge undercarriage.

I tell him that I know a bloke called Harry who flies the same type in England.

'*Ah, oui, je connais Arry.*' He laughs. It's a small world, when you fly vintage aeroplanes.

But it feels like a very big world when you're droning over unfamiliar French countryside at 1,200 feet, hoping that Blois will appear out of the gloom. I feel like I'm swimming through an ocean of dirty washing-up water, with a frothy scum of clouds on the water's surface above. Every slight blip and variation in the engine's steady clatter makes me grip the stick a little tighter and shift uneasily in my straps.

Please, I really don't want an engine failure now.

Luscombes will glide rather well, even after the engine stops, so there's always a good chance of landing safely in a field, especially in the middle of the countryside. But at such low altitude and in such conditions, I do not fancy trying my luck. The sooner I land, the bettter.

When Blois materializes on the nose, it's obvious from the silence on the radio that everyone has given up in disgust and gone home. The place is deserted.

And then, just as I am circling for my final approach, I spy a couple of hunched figures in anoraks gazing up at me. People! They look as if they are watching the final scene in *Close Encounters*, the bit when the aliens finally descend.

As I taxi over to them, one of the anoraks makes a sign for me to stop the prop, as if he were a *marchandeur* explaining to me what he is planning to do with my sheep. I attempt to signal that I don't want to stop the engine, because it is so difficult to re-start when it's hot. But his semaphore is more insistent than mine, and I back down. I stop the engine, its jagged roar replaced now by the tin-drumming of rain on the Luscombe's aluminium skin.

Unfortunately, Blois is a large airport, and the hangar space arranged by my new friend at Chartres is almost a mile away, on the far perimeter.

'Just start her up and taxi over there,' shrugs one of the men. 'We'll drive round and help you get her inside, and then give you a lift to a hotel.' This is typical French kindness. But the rain is getting heavier, and they have clearly never tried to re-start a hot Continental with no impulse magneto. Every swing of the propeller takes as much effort as splitting a log. Twenty minutes later, my khaki flying-suit black with rain, I must have chopped a full winter's supply before the beast finally grumbles into life.

So follow three days holed up as an accidental tourist in

Blois, staying in one of those self-sluicing lunar-landscape hotels that I swore I'd never re-visit, waiting for the rain gods to relent. And then I am once again hammering through clear blue skies to St Juste, on the last leg of my journey. I am beginning to think it might have been quicker to walk.

My route takes me over the top of La Folie and – though I can't spot my Rastafarians from 2,500 feet – it's good to see that the place is still standing and that I remembered to bring the washing in before I left.

We're home at last, and a small welcoming party is waiting to greet the Luscombe.

'I raced out of the café as soon as I heard the sound of your engine,' says Peter Viola, strands of his white hair flying in the breeze, as I clamber down from the Luscombe and resist the temptation to kiss the tarmac. 'I *knew* it was you.'

'What a pretty aeroplane,' says Jacques, the flying schoolteacher, beaming with pleasure as he strokes the fuselage. 'Is it a Cessna?'

I smile, and shake my head.

'How was the trip?' growls wily old Marcel. 'Did it take long?'

'A little longer than Ryanair,' I murmur, wishing with all my heart that I knew the French for 'Piece of cake, old boy.'

As far as I can tell, the main difference between flying in France and flying in Britain is that here in France pilots drink too much coffee whilst waiting for the midday sun to cool, whereas in Blighty they drink too much tea whilst waiting for the clouds to lift. There's also the niggling worry of over-flying a French nuclear power-station, for which the fine is said to be forty-two thousand euros – or roughly what it costs to scramble two Mirage jets to come and shoot you down. And then of course there are the radio calls.

Here I am, practising my landings, a day after my arrival at St Juste. I'm comfortably trimmed at a thousand feet, announcing over the r/t that I am *vent-derrière pour une touche* ('downwind for a touch-and-go'), when I hear sniggering in my headset. I know that snigger. It's the flying schoolteacher, Jacques. He must be buzzing around up here, too. I wonder what I've said *this* time.

As I enter the aeroclub, I can tell from the way people are smirking and hopping from foot to foot that my latest gaffe has already been gleefully shared.

'*Ne t'inquiète pas, Michael*,' chuckles Jacques, patting me on the shoulder. 'We love your English humour.' He gently explains that what I *should* have said is that I was '*vent-arrière pour un touche*'. I kick myself, because I knew this perfectly well. And instead, what I have just told everyone from here to Brive is that I am feeling the effects of a surfeit of baked beans, and hoping for a fondle. But no matter: the Luscombe is finally hangared in France, and another stage of my adventure is complete.

## 36

## THE MOWER AGAINST GARDENS

La Folie is unusually silent just now. The house has still not fallen down, although that may be because it is so full of the scaffolding that Jou-Jou's team of masons erected before disappearing without trace several weeks ago.

I was going to scramble up the abandoned scaffolding myself, to paint the towering ceiling of the summer sitting-room. Anything, to bring the arrival of my piano a little closer, and to avoid having to sit down and face not starting my unstartable book. But then Jou-Jou, just as he was leaving, made me promise to tie myself on to the scaffolding, in case I should slip and fall. And I suddenly realized that I had urgent digging to do in the vegetable patch.

The renovations may have squealed to a halt like a train on wet rails but, for the moment, the animals of La Folie are doing very nicely, thank you. Claudette and Camillo are happily springing round their field, and – now that the wall-to-wall mud is beginning to dry outside – the chickens are enjoying being able to dig blissful dust-baths for themselves beneath the lone pine, noisily ruffling their feathers and showering themselves with claw-scratchings of dry earth.

The first time I saw a chicken having a dust-bath, I thought it must be dead. That contorted mass of feathers looked like something that had been run over, with wings and legs spread-eagled in all directions. And then I thought it was having an epileptic fit, from the way it shuddered and shook. Now I know that it is simply approaching chicken nirvana.

The vegetable patch does make me cringe. If this were East Dulwich, I could at least call it an urban wilderness, and Southwark Council would presumably give me a grant and an ecology medal. But this is the Limousin, where every self-respecting *paysan* has his own *potager*, and mine is a disgrace. The postman glares at it witheringly every time he comes to deliver another catalogue of pork bargains from Netto.

On the upside, everything in the *potager* is thriving. On the downside, this means that I now have a prize crop of weeds, creepers and Triffids. There is not a single spud or *légume* to be had.

'*Ah, mais c'est trop grand,*' remonstrates Ariane, Yves-Pascal's sternly beautiful wife, when she and the well-pressed *notaire* rumble up to La Folie for an aperitif. 'Large *potagers* always fail.' Now she tells me.

Gilles needn't have worried about my having too many potatoes. My two twenty-five-kilo sacks are still in the barn, now looking like a pair of giant hairnets sprouting an orgy of excited green spaghetti. I never got around to planting them, because – with perfect male logic – I didn't want to plant one potato until I had time to plant them all.

And then there is the jungle, advancing upon me once more. Even in the field that Gilles ransacked for

me with his mighty engine-of-war, all those months
ago.

'It's time you mowed that field, Michael,' he told me,
with unusual sternness, last time he was here.

# 37

## JUNE: THE ANCIENT MARINER

Summer has launched an early assault upon La Folie, spear-headed by an air force of angry flies. I'm not sure if this is because the cat has left so many rodent cadavers to fester behind the wood-burning stove, or because the sheep are grazing too close to the house.

Newly shorn by the heroic Gilles, the Rastafarians have gone from being a bunch of Bob Marley wannabes to smart Sammy Davis Jnr lookalikes in one swift trim. I wanted to shear them myself – 'Leave some for me, Gilles,' I begged him, as he buzzed away with the Lister – but thirty seconds of attempting to scalp Daphne was enough to persuade me that I'm not yet ready to go into the hairdressing business. I was too worried about digging the throbbing, jagged teeth of the Lister into her trembling black skin.

'It's easier to start on large, fat sheep,' said Gilles consolingly. 'On your Ouessants, all the angles and corners are too tight. And they haven't sweated enough to smoothe the shears.'

The sheep may not be sweating, but I am. The thermometer is pushing thirty degrees, the ground outside is cracking up, and the cat lies cooling her belly on the soothing stone of the kitchen floor. I'd join her myself, but I haven't washed that floor for longer than I care to admit.

Despite the heat, there are encouraging signs of progress at La Folie. Claude, the pit-bull from the tennis club, turns out to be a fast-and-furious electrician, and has visited to rub his bald head and to *oh-là-là* at the *Charlot* electrics of La Folie. If his wiring is anything like as good as his forehand, I should have illuminations in the *maison des amis* before Doomsday – which is roughly when I am expecting Monsieur Étang, the overworked plumber, to return. And today, though there is still the small question of how to dress the breeze-block walls, forty square metres of prime oak flooring has arrived for the summer sitting-room. I huff and puff to stack the tight bundles of planks beneath the scaffolding, while the cheery walnut who has delivered it watches me with amusement.

'*Il fait chaud, oui?*' I gasp, stopping to catch my breath.

'Hot? You can say that again,' he says, beginning to whistle while I work. A tiny man with wisps of grey hair clinging to his shiny brown head, he looks as if he would be more at home in a coconut shy than a timber-yard. 'You should ask the *mairie* to give you a sign for this place,' he says. 'It's impossible to find.'

'But I *like* the fact that it's a little hidden,' I pant from behind a stack of oak.

'Hidden? You can say that again. It's the end of the world. And look at the state of the drive!'

'Ah, yes. I need to have that cut back.'

'Cut back? You can say that again.' The whistling resumes. 'Incidentally, if you don't mind my asking, how are you going to lay the floor with all that scaffolding there?'

I give him my best French shrug, adding the regulation *boff* for emphasis. That scaffolding gives me confidence, because it makes me think that one day the masons will return. They couldn't just have dumped it here, could they?

A chance meeting with Jou-Jou, at the Café de Mortemart, reveals that the search for a suitable *produit* for the walls of the summer sitting-room is turning into a grail quest of Arthurian proportions.

How weary he looks today. His shock of hair, which I suspect may not have been combed since the Stone Age, is greyer than I remembered, and there are new lines and wrinkles etched into his square face. His wrist is supported in a makeshift sling, and he rubs it constantly with his other hand.

'I fell off a ladder,' he tells me, grimacing at the injured wrist. I can see that his hand is swollen and bruised; yellow, green and purple.

'Does it hurt?'

He nods. 'This hot weather helps. But when it's cold and wet, it's terrible.'

It makes me feel guilty that he is still having to worry about my walls. As he sips his coffee and tells me his tale of all the advice and counter-advice, the suggestions and counter-suggestions that he has received on the subject of a *produit* for the summer sitting-room, he makes me think of the Ancient Mariner with an albatross strapped around his neck, compelled to tell his tale to every third person who will listen. All Jou-Jou needs is a long straggly beard and a glint in his eye, and the illusion would be complete.

An idea occurs to me. I wouldn't dream of mentioning it to Jou-Jou, were we standing in the summer sitting-room, gazing up at the work in progress. But here we are on neutral territory, and I find myself thinking the unthinkable; saying the unsayable. I wonder, aloud, how Jou-Jou would feel about my finding someone else – someone English and unusually large, perhaps – to do the work of rendering the walls?

Jou-Jou's tired eyes flash and he seems to grow two inches taller. For a moment I think he's going to hit me, or hug me, or both. He puts down his coffee cup with a clatter, reaches behind him, and – as the other people in the café sit open-mouthed – unstraps the albatross dangling from his neck in one triumphant movement.

Jou-Jou beams. 'I'll even let you keep the scaffolding for a few more weeks,' he says. It's lucky he doesn't know how heavy Douglas the giant is, or he might have second thoughts.

On the radio in the café, I can hear a slushy French love song being played, heavy with sentimentality and schmaltz. But to me, right now, it might as well be a Chopin nocturne. For the piano – my piano – has just come another semitone closer to France.

I would be quite happy with the shameful lack of progress I've made in renovating La Folie, if Marisa and I – in our East Dulwich days – hadn't watched so many inspiring documentaries about young couples turning piles of rubble in the Ardèche into gleaming palaces, in roughly the time it has taken me to persuade Monsieur Laveille the joiner to give me a quote.

While these televised paragons convert disused pumping stations into stately homes with their bare hands, what have I done? I have converted a small stone pigsty into a chicken house. It's not much, but I'm proud of it.

Having Douglas the giant as my near-neighbour hasn't helped. An ex-rugby international with a black-belt in DIY, Douglas has single-handedly restored an entire farmhouse while I was down at Monsieur Bricolage trying to decide what colour to paint my shutters. I realize that if I, too, could only learn to be as rugged and skilful at plumbing and plastering as Douglas, then my life would be simpler, if sweatier.

As anyone who has ever attempted to renovate a house will know, the root of the problem is contingency. The oak floor cannot be laid until the Velux windows have been installed. The windows cannot be fitted until the scaffolding has been moved, and that won't be until after the walls are painted, which can only happen once the rendering has been done.

But now that I have stopped judging myself against Douglas, and decided to employ him instead, my life has improved considerably. Today is a good day, for today we are mixing cement. Well, *I* am mixing the cement as if I were a proper builder, and Douglas is using it to render the walls of the summer sitting-room.

Douglas, fortunately, is a proper plasterer. He's also that rare thing: an English tradesman who has managed to get all the legal stuff sorted at the *chambre des métiers*. So he's actually legit (which is more than can be said for me, in my new role as a plasterer's mate). This is my justification for breaking my own rule of only employing French *ouvriers*. Too many other tasks hang on this one being completed.

So here I am, shovelling great globs of gritty Angel Delight into a bucket and hauling it thirty feet up the ladder to Douglas, who says he feels a bit like Michelangelo, working amid the soaring roof-timbers.

'Muck up!' he yells at me, every quarter of an hour.

'Here you go, boss,' I pant, as I heave the leaden bucket of cement sludge up to him.

'What do you call that, then?' he sneers, peering at my handiwork.

'That's muck, that is, boss.'

'No, it's not. It's *soup*.'

'Right. Sorry, boss.'

So I pour the soup back in the mixer and start adding more cement. And I am just thinking that this is the strangest relationship with a paid tradesman I have ever had, when suddenly there is a grinding of gears behind me, and – like a *deus ex machina* – Monsieur Étang, the plumber, turns up.

My first thought is that I have been overdoing the Pastis. I have been ringing Étang for several weeks, to ask him when he is thinking of doing the work for which we agreed a quote way back in December. So to come face-to-face with a vision of the man, right here on my doorstep, is an unsettling experience.

'What did his parents feed him as a baby?' asks Étang, gazing up in awe at Douglas atop the scaffolding. I see what he means. It is a vision that conjures images of King Kong clinging to the Empire State Building.

But Étang has rattled up the drive, bless him, just to tell me that it will be some time next year before he has time to install my new bathroom. Despite the heat, he is sporting a yellow anorak/sou'wester combo which strikes me as not the best possible advert for his working practices.

'*Mais* Monsieur Étang, you gave me the quote last December,' I say.

'*Ah oui, je sais*,' he groans, close to tears. 'But I've got customers who have been waiting since 2002.' The poor chap glances nervously over his yellow shoulder, as if half expecting to see a phalanx of Jolibois women waving their bath taps at him. It must be terrifying to be in such demand. And if ever I have children, I shall be sure to put them down for Étang at birth.

# 38

## ARIADNE

Six o'clock, and the cat and I are sitting on the terrace, gazing at the shrinking view. The trees seem to grow taller and greener every day.

As I sip my Pastis, it occurs to me that I really wasn't prepared, when I first moved to France, for how much there would be to do. I assumed life would be magically less stressful than in London. I feared I might be bored. I thought I would spend most of my time sitting on a hill top, meditating on how to be a hero. But it's difficult to be a hero when life keeps getting in the way. It's not just the renovations, the wood-cutting, the trips to the bank for yet more wads of euros, and the trips to the *supermarché* for yet more restorative doses of Pastis. Add a bunch of sheep and chickens into the equation, an encroaching jungle, the pressures of an overgrown vegetable patch, the need to earn an honest crust and somehow to heat the place, and I have enough fun activities to distract me from ever noticing that I don't have a telly to distract me. I've barely even had time to go flying since I ferried the Luscombe down here.

The phone rings, and it's Simon, in East Dulwich.

'We were just talking about you, and wondering how you're getting on,' he says. 'Found a sexy *copine* yet?'

'Not yet,' I reply. 'And any woman who sets foot in this place is sure to run away as soon as she sees the state of it.'

'You should get a dishy Portuguese cleaning lady, like Colin Firth does in *Love Actually*,' he says, chortling to himself.

'Mm. Yes. Maybe.' The truth is that cleaning ladies are so hard to find here in Jolibois that I would happily settle for someone who won't kick the cat. I can't be fussing about youth and beauty, too.

Well, all right, I *have* replied to one ad in the window of the *tabac*, placed by a lady who was looking for cleaning work. But it was pure chance that she turned out to be a breathy-voiced nineteen-year-old called Marie-Sophie. And our chat turned out to be one of the shortest phone conversations ever.

'Would the work be declared or undeclared, *Monsieur*?' she asked.

'Undeclared,' I assured her, thinking that she would obviously want to be paid in cash. I could hear her having a heated discussion with someone else in the background.

'And is it for a family with children, *Monsieur*?'

'Just me,' I replied cheerfully. 'I live alone.'

There was more growling in the background, and her father came on the line to grill me about my intentions. Too late, I discovered that cleaning ladies in rural France prefer to be paid with social-security cheques, all fully declared, rather than with ready cash. And that men who live alone in Jolibois are a cause for considerable suspicion and alarm. *Papa* hung up on me.

The subject of cleaning ladies comes up the next

evening, at the home of Yves-Pascal and Ariane, the well-pressed *notaire* and his wife. They have invited me over for dinner, and usher me into a beautiful salon that seems to belong to a different universe to La Folie, or Gilles's old mill house, or the other rustic houses into which I have been welcomed for a glass of red wine or a simple supper, their interiors heavy with brown oak furniture and faded floral wallpaper.

*Chez* Yves-Pascal, diaphanous white curtains hang like clouds between floor-to-ceiling windows that flood the room with a fragrant light, scented and filtered by the flowers and shrubs in the garden outside. There are velvet sofas and armchairs which seem to sigh with contentment as you sink into them – a luxury I have not permitted myself at La Folie, but which I appreciate now, unaware that what I am appreciating is really an English touch, not a French one.

The whole room envelops me in its civilized elegance, turning me into a boorish simpleton in my clompy shoes and mud-stained shirt. Especially when two poised young women – the daughters, I assume, both petite and *charmante* and somewhere in their early twenties – appear carrying trays of canapés. I know I'm staring, but I don't seem to be able to help myself.

Grey-eyed Yolande has an airy, bohemian air about her, coupled with a stillness that makes me think that she is noticing things – a glance, a remark, a tiny hiatus – in alarming detail. Her skin, stretched tight over her cheek-bones, reminds me of unglazed porcelain, while the speed of her chatter betrays years spent in Paris. I am struck all the more by the sparkle of Sandrine, her younger sister; warmer and less mysterious than her sister, yet with something of the quicksilver evasiveness of a bead of mercury in a puzzle. Her dark eyes fix upon me for a second and then wander elsewhere, in search of a more interesting subject.

Ariane comes sweeping into the room from the kitchen.

'*Donc, vous habitez à La Folie?*' she says, picking up the conversation we had at Ralph and Olga's, and frowning at the two trays of canapés on the glass-topped table in front of the fireplace.

'What's wrong, *Maman?*' asks Sandrine quickly. The two sisters glance at each other.

'*Rien,*' says Ariane, turning both trays through ninety degrees, so that they sit sideways rather than lengthways on the table.

'*Oui,*' I say, shifting to perch on the edge of my seat. '*C'est La Folie. Et je l'aime bien.*'

'*Quoi? Ah, La Folie.* Yes, it's a wild, old place, isn't it? Yves-Pascal said there was an ecologist there before you. Romanian, I think?'

'Polish, actually. And he did have a singular attitude to nature, which was simply to leave it to its own devices.'

'*Quelle horreur,*' drawls Ariane with a shudder. Behind her, Yves-Pascal has appeared, cradling a bottle with unusual care. 'And now you live there all by yourself? How do you manage?'

'The winter was tough at times,' I reply, watching as Yves-Pascal pours vintage *pineau* into five crystal glasses, the golden liquid making *blup-blup-blup* sounds as it gurgles from the bottle. 'And I'm fighting a losing battle against the spiders and the flies and the rising piles of paper. I don't suppose you can recommend a good cleaning lady, can you?'

'Ah!' interrupts Yves-Pascal, the lines on his face dancing with a smile that is somewhere between a beatific grin and a grimace.

'Marie-Claude!' shrieks Sandrine, giggling. 'Oh, *Maman*, you can't.'

'Yes, she can,' mutters her sister.

'Ah, Marie-Claude,' echoes her father, clasping his hands and letting out the kind of sigh that would not disgrace a dying Romantic poet.

'I might be able to,' says Ariane, glaring at them both and inviting me to help myself from one of the trays of canapés: a smart-casual arrangement of pink radishes, each neatly trimmed to leave just a tiny flash of green stalk attached, with a bowl of buttery dip beside them, several folded napkins, a fork and a silver teaspoon. I hesitate, my hand paralysed in mid-air.

'Um . . .'

'It's all right, just use your fingers,' says Ariane kindly.

'I dread doing something in an English way, and finding that it is deeply offensive to the French.'

'Oh, don't worry about that,' chuckles Ariane. 'I'm Belgian myself.'

'*Santé*,' says Yves-Pascal, with sing-song cheeriness, and we all clink glasses. 'Marie-Claude!' he whispers, winking at me.

Dinner passes in a happy blur, not because I have drunk too much, but because I am dizzied by all this care and sparkle after months of mud and rain and sheep and soot.

We have moved from the dinner table back to the pillowed chairs that sigh when you sit on them, and are now indulging in the very un-Jolibois practice of inhaling some sort of molasses-infused vapour from a smouldering narghile; a bong, in other words, that Yves-Pascal has brought back from one of his trips to Turkey.

The ornate ceramic urn sits gently smouldering, while we pass its silver mouthpiece, attached via a length of embroidered hose, between us. I was expecting the taste to be acrid and alarming. But the sensation turns out to be more like inhaling a warm cloud of peppermint tea.

'So why did you choose to live *here* of all places, Michael?' asks Ariane, puffing on the bong. 'Why Jolibois?'

I wander back in time, through the smoke, to attempt to recall why it was. I know I wanted to be far enough south to have better weather, but close enough to England to see my parents. I remember scouting out aerodromes in the pouring rain, and being immediately drawn to this place that combined medieval higgledy-piggledy with supermarkets and a cinema. I recall that I saw the gleaming pipes of the church organ as a good omen, along with the neatly brushed clay courts at the tennis club and the ten-euro lunch I wolfed down at le Cheval Blanc, when I was still in shock at the fact that I really was going to buy my very own house in France.

This is all Ariane wants to know, but I'm just getting into my stride, and I need to tell her all the other good things about living here: about the way everyone shakes hands at the slightest provocation; that there are squawking chickens for sale outside the smart *coiffeur*; that people murmur '*Messieurs, Dames*' when they join the queue at the bank; that other drivers don't hoot me if I'm a nanosecond slow to notice that the traffic lights have changed, and the only time they flash me is to warn that there's *un flic* with a speed-gun just around the next corner.

It feels as if people trust each other here. Outside the clothes shop, closed for lunch, a rack of ladies' blouses is left to bake in the sunshine. Jou-Jou the mason doesn't expect to be paid a *centime* until the job is done. Children, when introduced, still present their faces to adults to be kissed.

There are surreal pleasures, too, such as the night when an old couple who have pulled in at le Moulin Vaugelade, just down the road from Gilles's house, insist upon giving me forty bananas after I help jump-start their car. What are they doing with all those bananas, by moonlight? Where are they taking them?

'But all this,' says Ariane, sounding as if she wishes she never asked, 'it's just because we're in the countryside. It would be the same in rural England.'

I wonder. My parents now live in Somerset, and I went to school in Dorset. I have some picture of rural English life. And it is not the same: not worse, not better, but different. There, in Somerset, my father was upset to have his tractor-mower stolen by skilful thieves. Here, Douglas the giant left his front door open, just over the hill from La Folie, and returned to find that someone had half-inched his daughter's cello. Life is not perfect. *Et in Arcadia ego*.

Fast jets roar low overhead in Jolibois, just as they do in Castle Cary. The difference here is that the cafés are still populated with the time-worn *tricolore* of wrinkled *paysans* in blue overalls, swigging their red wine before rumbling off in their white Citroën vans. There in the south-west of England, I see young men in the pubs, the collars of their pink polo shirts turned up, their silver Freelanders waiting outside as they sip their pints of IPA. Cattle farmers have diversified into buffalo, wild boar, bison and ostrich. The local pig farm has been converted into a candle factory.

Here in the Limousin, it's still sheep and cattle all the way, and let's tighten our belts another notch, *chérie*, to mark each passing year.

I think about all this as one of Ariane's beautiful daughters passes me the wand of the narghile, and I take another puff.

'You're right, Ariane,' I tell her. 'This could be rural England. But it would be an England of fifty years ago. Living here makes me feel nostalgic for an England I never knew.'

'That's so sad,' she says. And we all sit in silence, gazing at the wisps of smoke drifting from the top of the narghile.

'Marie-Claude,' whispers Yves-Pascal beside me, giving me a hearty nudge in the ribs.

Next morning, I am woken by an unusual sound. Something is wrong. Titus is singing his heart out on top of the rubble dump. *Cocorico! Cocorico!* Why isn't he in the chicken house, clamouring to be let out? I couldn't have left the door open all night, could I?

Yes, I could.

I start counting my chickens: look, there's Martha, there's Margot, Melissa's in her usual place on the window-sill with Titus, and there are Mary and Meg under the Espace. Mildred must be in her nesting box, squeezing out an egg.

But Mildred's not there.

Nor is she in the barn, the workshop or under the pine trees by the *fosse septique*. Unlike Martha, she hasn't worked out how to use the cat-flap, so she's not hiding under the kitchen table, either.

It's too soon to be alarmed. Mildred will turn up. I know she will.

After lunch, there's still no sign of her. I fire up the brushcutter, and start cutting a swathe through my jungle in search of the runaway. I've just refuelled for another session when my heart leaps. For there, in the long grass, is a white feather.

Two paces further on, and there's another feather. Then

another. And another. The regular spacing is odd. Was Mildred dropping them as she journeyed to find her way home, like Theseus with Ariadne's ball of wool? Or to help me to rescue her? What's unusual, too, is that these are the soft, downy feathers that sit close to her skin, not the stiff quills of her wings and back. In a game of strip poker, a lady doesn't surrender her underwear first.

Holding my breath, I follow the innocent trail. Feather follows feather until, turning a corner, I breathe a heavy sigh.

There is no blood. But there, amid the green bracken, lies a tell-tale avalanche of white. Someone has burst open a feather pillow beneath the trees.

I can't help wishing it were one of the others. Mildred was such a chatty soul, with a frank opinion on every subject, and a forceful cluck that always felt as if she were thwacking me with her handbag. The poor dear started life at La Folie at the very top of the chicken pecking order, but what with all her hang-ups and neuroses, gradually found herself demoted. Two parts Margaret Thatcher to one part Joyce Grenfell, Mildred was the sort of girl you notice before anyone else, and hope she doesn't notice you.

And now she's gone, and the place feels empty without her. It's stupid, I know, but every chicken counts when you live alone. I still think she's going to come waddling round the corner, clucking about how Titus never does the washing-up. And I expect her to come rushing to greet me when I rattle up the drive in the Espace, playing her suicidally literal game of Chicken.

The other birds seem confused, and have made me understand the word 'crestfallen' in a whole new light. Titus, bless him, has bravely taken to perching on Mildred's spot nearest the door of the chicken house. So if the fox returns, he will now have to reckon with Titus first. Titus may be very stupid, but I find his bravery deeply moving. And wish I had a little more of the same quality myself.

First Emil, and now Mildred. Creatures I barely knew, and yet whose deaths have hit me harder than I would have believed. I've come to France to learn to be tough, and what I'm discovering is that I'm less tough than I ever imagined.

## 39

## WHERE THE WILD THINGS ARE

A week later, I am sitting at the kitchen table, sipping scalding coffee from one of Zumbach's earthenware cups, enjoying the silence of the early afternoon. I am meant to be editing a CV for Gilles's son, the silent thundercloud from Châteaudun, but mostly I am thinking about poor Mildred. Suddenly I hear a commotion upstairs. Clitter-clat go the mighty claws across the bedroom floor, just above my head. The cat must be taunting its latest victim.

But no: the cat is sitting on my lap. And she has heard it too. Ears flattened (her), heart pounding (me), we leap up to investigate.

Nothing. The air is so still that I can hear the sheep tearing at the grass outside. The cat stares up at the roof beams, clearly thinking in terms of vampire bats. With a child's foreboding, I check under the bed. Still nothing.

Recently, I decided that I should learn to co-exist with the invisible scuttlers in my roof-space. They were here first, and if I were to regard them as benign sitting-tenants, I might sleep better at night. Why can't we all just get along?

But in the mornings, when I trudge out to feed the sheep, I have started to find clumps of yellow *laine de verre* – glass-wool insulation – in the scrub around the house. The critters – whoever and whatever they are – are renovating my roof, sans planning permission. This means war.

My bedroom is a small box with an open space above its ceiling, enclosed by a low parapet. This space is the place, I have no doubt, Where the Wild Things Are.

I toy with the idea of donning my wolf suit and climbing up there to investigate but, after considering this for a split second, opt to volunteer the cat instead. Something about that shadowy space unnerves me, as if there might be some sleeping evil up there. If so, I have no wish to wake it from its slumber.

Standing on tiptoe, I can push the wide-eyed volunteer just far enough up the wall for her to scramble over the parapet and on to the ceiling. I hear her padding like a cat-burglar across the tongue and groove, as I wait for the wild rumpus to start.

Above me, the cat has stopped to sniff something. My skin prickles and my heart leaps as a stray image jumps inside my brain: a rusty man-trap on a heavy iron chain.

'Eva, don't move a muscle,' I hiss. The cat peers down at me, spooked by my tone, pupils dilated with the excitement of this real-live game of Murder in the Dark. 'Don't you dare move,' I repeat over my shoulder, as I race to fetch the ladder.

Up I climb, and close my eyes with relief as I register that the rusty trap is not set, after all. To be certain, I lob the end of its chain towards the jagged jaws.

The thing snaps shut with a force that could shatter a man's arm as if it were a stale baguette. Unperturbed, the cat slinks into the shadows, while I wonder if it's too early for a Pastis.

Wars, unfortunately, have a habit of escalating. That very night, as I lie in bed, the critters unleash their elite storm-trooper brigade just above my head.

*Buh-dumm. Buh-dumm. Buh-dumm.* Oh golly. What the hell is that thing? It sounds about the size of a small grizzly. *And it's only got two legs.* My mind races through the obvious possibilities: King Kong? Rumpelstiltzkin? Mrs Rochester?

*Buh-dumm. Buh-dumm. Buh-dumm.* It's stopped. I hold my breath, listening. And not four feet from where I am lying in bed, staring up into the inky darkness, there comes an eerie sound. Someone is drumming on the floor. It sounds almost as if he's peeing through the ceiling at me.

*Nom de Dieu!* He *is* peeing through the ceiling at me.

'Right, that's it, Georges,' I say out loud. 'This time you've gone too far.'

I name him Georges on the spur of the moment, because I'd hate to think of someone I don't know peeing through my bedroom ceiling.

Next day, I drop in on Gilles for *un apéro* and ask him what he reckons.

'I think it's a *fouine*,' he says, stroking his beard. 'And you must do something about it, or it'll have the tiles off your roof. You should call in *la chasse*.'

'But won't the horses have trouble getting up the stairs?'

Gilles pulls a business card from a board criss-crossed with faded ribbons. 'Phone this man.'

I put the card in my shirt pocket as I rise to go.

When I get home, I look up *fouine* in my French dictionary: a stone marten.

Then I look up stone marten in my English dictionary: 'Hunts rats and mice.'

Oh, great. So I've got a whole food chain up there. Yet something stops me phoning the number on the card. I feel I should give diplomacy – and Georges – one last chance. One day, I will learn to stop giving my animals names.

It soon emerges, however, that Georges's dirty protest through the ceiling was not an escalation of violence, but a parting shot. The smell of the cat must have been enough for him to decide to move out. And I only wish I could explain to the cat what a heroic victory she has won.

# 40

## LES ANGLAIS

Raphaël le Prêtre has invited me for supper after the
Saturday-evening Mass. I'm expecting him to ask if I'd
mind playing the organ a little more quietly during the
*chants*. Instead, as we tuck into our steaming bowlfuls of
beetroot soup, the conversation turns to Jolibois and its
future. And Raphaël says something that makes me stop,
spoon suspended in mid-air, and wonder if I've misheard
him.

'This place is dying, and you're our last hope,' he
declares, with a dramatic wag of his finger.

Now I like to think that my contributions to the
Jolibois men's over-35s 2nd tennis team will one day
include the occasional victory amongst my defeats. But
isn't Raphaël going just a bit far? I mean, it's all very well
to cast me as the Clint of Jolibois, but I still have a lot of
work to do on my backhand, and I don't have a poncho.

'*Je ne suis pas sûr . . .*' I begin.

'You have wealth and education,' he says, waving his
hand.

'*Er, tu crois . . .*'

'You have youth,' he continues.

'*C'est gentil.*'

'You have children.'

'*Non, je n'ai . . .*' I'm about to explain that I don't have any children, and then – as the centime drops – I blush the colour of the soup we're slurping. Raphaël is not talking about me at all. He's talking about *les Anglais en général*.

It's surprising – and encouraging – to find a Frenchman casting the arrival of *les Anglais* here in Jolibois in such a positive light: as a force for good, rather than for ill. When I trundled down from the organ loft after Mass last week, the cherubic Henri's wife, seraphic Françoise, was saying that she thinks *les Anglais* are beneficial for the region, too, because we tend to renovate so beautifully all the old houses that the French never wanted to buy in the first place. And, as the man in the paper-shop tells me, at least we're not Parisians.

Well, *allez les Rosbifs*!

Next day, a squirrel flashes into a tree as I bump back up the drive to La Folie, and I stop to take a closer look.

I know, I know. It's only a squirrel.

But that isn't a grey squirrel. It's a red one, and the first one I've seen at La Folie, its eyes glittering, its auburn coat shining in the dappled sunlight as it sits on a branch and twitches its whiskers at me. I'm struck by how much smaller it looks than its grey cousins, and how it appears more like a creature complete in itself; less like a rat with a bushy tail.

I haven't seen a red squirrel since I was a child. And I'm surprised to find myself suddenly longing for flapjacks in front of *Jackanory*; for Spangles and Jammy Dodgers, and for kicking through fallen leaves with my Clarks Commandos on the way to school. I feel like I've just spotted someone who died long ago, like my first English teacher, Mr Gould, who would read us Tennyson on a Saturday morning with tears trickling down his cheeks.

I think I must have been spending too much time alone.

'*C'est normal*,' shrugs Gilles, when I tell him about the squirrel. For red squirrels are indeed still common in France. How can a man know that something is special, until it is lost?

I find myself hoping that I and my fellow Brits here are not like the grey squirrels introduced into Britain from America in the nineteenth century, forcing the indigenous red squirrel into retreat. I don't want to discover that I have unwittingly become part of some eco-cultural catastrope.

The French have always been much bigger on this sort of thing than we are in Britain. They have their Académie Française to safeguard the lingo. Radio stations are expected to include a fixed proportion of French music in their Anglo-dominated playlists. Each little town, Jolibois included, has its *jours du patrimoine*, when significant events in local history are celebrated. Not for the tourists, but the locals.

All this makes me wonder if there is a way of living here, for those of us who have bought property in France, that will not stamp out the local culture in the way that it has already been all but crushed by the Brits in the Dordogne. Far better if France were to rub off on us than we on it.

I like the fact that *émail* remains – as far as the locals here are concerned – the ancient craft of enamelling, and even the telephone is regarded with suspicion. When I phone Monsieur Laveille about his quote for the oak floor in the summer sitting-room, he insists on driving over to speak to me in person. Presumably his horse-drawn cart is in for a service, or he'd have turned up in that.

In England, I try not to phone people at meal times. There's always the danger they might choke on their Pot Noodle at their desk. Here in France, it's quite the opposite. Everyone goes home for lunch, so meal times are the time to catch people, and the small ads for tractors in the window of the *tabac* invariably advise 'H.R.' (*heures repas*).

Even the *ouvriers* who possess mobile phones never switch them on, claiming that '*il n'y a pas de signal ici*'. Mind you, from what I've heard, there may be a selective mobile-phone signal which works fine for arranging amorous liaisons, just not so well for fielding enquiries from clients.

I have noticed, too, that the local *ouvriers* have no desire to work slavishly just to amass a fat pile of *fric* in the bank. They earn what is needful to live, and *ça suffit*. In England, this might look like laziness. Here, it looks like contentment.

A few days later, Ariane, the *notaire*'s wife, phones.

'Are you all right, Michael?' she asks.

'Yes, why?' I'm wondering if they've all come down with typhus after puffing on whatever was in that narghile a fortnight ago.

'I think I've found you a cleaning lady. She should be giving you a call later in the week.'

And so I come face to face with the famous Marie-Claude: a pocket battleship with sharp eyes and sharper teeth, who can't be much older than me, yet who exudes a powerful aura of maturity and superiority. Trim, neat and wearing very little make-up, she would be rather attractive if she weren't so scary. She certainly doesn't spare my feelings when it comes to describing what she thinks of the state of La Folie. I explain that I feel ashamed about the mess, and am most awfully relieved that she's come to help sort me out, but she still looks at me as if she's caught me throwing pebbles at puppies.

'Was this place *habitable* when you bought it?' she demands, gazing around her as witheringly as a scout-mistress interrupting a pillow fight. Because even if it was, she intimates, it certainly isn't now. Remembering an urgent appointment, the cat slinks out of the cat-flap.

'*Er, oui*, but there was – there is – still a lot of work to do,' I stammer, wondering if I could squeeze through the cat-flap, too.

'*Dis donc*,' she mutters.

Ariane warned me on the phone that Marie-Claude was '*très timide*' and nervous about working for an Englishman. I honestly think the wrong one has turned up. 'Jolibois Cleaning Lady Kidnapped by Aliens' will be the headline in tomorrow's *Le Populaire*. And I'll be the next to go.

Admittedly, La Folie does look a little as if Hurricane Jean-Pierre has just hit. My filing system consists of various piles of paper strewn all over the floor, and I still haven't found the right sort of cupboard at the *dépôt vente* for things like clarinets, aircraft batteries and tennis racquets.

'So you haven't bought *une bombe*?' enquires Marie-Claude, becoming even less *timide* by the minute. I guess she has finally decided the house is so irredeemably dirty, it would be best just to blow it to bits.

'*Une bombe? Pourquoi?*'

'*Pour les araignées*,' she whispers, gesturing at the ceiling. Ah, of course: an aerosol to kill the spiders. And she's whispering because the spiders may overhear. What if they use their spidery powers on us before we can nuke them with *la bombe*?

'But I like spiders,' I explain. 'They kill flies.'

'In that case,' asks Marie-Claude flatly, 'would you like me to leave all of those?' She indicates the soot-blackened candyfloss of spiderwebs between the beams, which makes the winter sitting-room resemble a cross between Miss Havisham's mouldering boudoir and a coal bunker.

'*Ah, er, non*,' I concede, cringing anew. '*Vous avez raison*. I'll buy a bomb for the spiders.'

Marie-Claude and I soon discover that we feel differently about all sorts of animals. I tell her how excited I am about the red squirrel on the drive, and she shrugs and says she hopes the hunters will kill it. Similarly, when Martha and the rest of the Egg Squad wander into the kitchen for a chat, they are soon sent into a clucking retreat with a whack from Marie-Claude's broom.

'Ouch,' I cluck.

'I've just hoovered up a mouse,' she says, when I return from apologizing to the chickens on her behalf.

I begin to apologize for the mouse. It's true that I do quite often come across the desiccated bodies of the cat's cast-offs, several weeks after even the flies have lost interest in them.

'*Mais, non!*' declares Marie-Claude, her eyes shining with triumph. 'This one was alive.'

'And now it's in *there*?' I ask, aghast, pointing at the vacuum cleaner.

She nods, brandishing her feather duster as proudly as if she were a big-game hunter leaning on an elephant gun. I can just see her in a pith-helmet and baggy shorts.

I grab the vacuum cleaner and take it outside. I have become inured to the cat's kills, and will happily continue eating my supper when she is throwing a half-dead mouse around the kitchen. But I still don't like the idea of hoovering a mouse to death.

The bag is clogged with dust and hair. I give it a shake,

and listen. Nothing twitches within. But at last, as I peer in through the hole with the help of a torch, I spy a shape like a grey truffle, and hook it out with my fingers. The poor creature is entirely enbalmed in dust – even its eye-balls are caked with the stuff – and I can see its lungs fluttering as it fights for breath. I picture it inhaling the howling, poisonous gale, and shudder at the thought. Then I dunk it fast, once, in a bucket of water. Now at least I hope it can see. I lay it in the undergrowth and wish it *bon courage*.

'Was it still alive?' asks Marie-Claude.

'Yes, it survived.'

'Ah,' she murmurs, raising her pencilled-in eyebrows and wiping her unadorned hands on her tunic. I can't tell if she's disappointed. But I shall be sure not to leave her alone with the cat when next Tuesday comes around.

A few days later, I'm hurling empties into the bottle bank beside the river when a shiny silver car draws up.

'*Excusez-moi, Monsieur?*' says the attractive woman passenger, fluttering her eyelashes at me with a desperation that is distinctly un-French. 'Er, Chapterie?'

I glance across at the driver, a shiny-faced Toby-jug of a man in dark glasses. He shrugs and mangles a smile. English, too, no doubt.

The woman holds out a scrap of paper with an address on it. And then, in her bravest schoolgirl French, she asks me if I know where it is.

'I don't know that house,' I reply in French, touched by her willingness to make an effort, and not wanting to snub her like a Paris waiter. '*Mais pour Chapterie, vous prenez le deuxième pont, et puis continuez tout droit.*'

She looks blank. He looks even blanker.

'*Le deuxième pont*,' I repeat, searching their faces for a

glimmer of comprehension. And then, in English: 'For Chapterie, take the second bridge, and then it's straight on till morning.'

'Oh, you're English!' she says, breathless with happiness, as if I were clad in full Zulu garb with a spear to her throat and she had just noticed an 'I love Marmite' tattoo on my ankle.

I smile and tug my forelock.

'We're house-hunting!' she adds, as if I hadn't guessed. Although, to be fair, they *are* a little on the young side.

'That's a good restaurant, by the way,' I say, pointing at another name she has scrawled on her piece of paper.

'Oh, it's the hotel where we're staying. Is it far?'

I fish a map of Haute-Vienne out of the Espace. 'You should get one of these,' I say.

'Yes, we've realized that,' she laughs. 'But it's Sunday, and everything's shut. Isn't it funny?'

Ah, the English abroad. In some ways we're so charming in our enthusiasm for adventure, and our willingness to explore other cultures. And yet we're flooding so inexorably into rural France that it's hard not to feel for the locals, stranded on the beach as the Anglo-Saxon tide comes in. I know I'm part of the problem, and wish I could be part of the solution.

Later, I drop in at the aeroclub. For some while, I have been planning to take my aeroplane higher than I have ever flown it before. Partly this is just for the hell of it, and partly because I want to fly the Luscombe over the Pyrenees to Spain. Before I do, I need to know how the fifty-year-old engine is likely to perform at altitude, rather than have it spoil my day by spluttering to a halt just when I'm overflying a jagged Pyrenee. But today the puffy clouds studding the sky turn into a steely overcast, so I restrict myself to practising some touch-and-goes.

Afterwards, I take the Espace to the garage at Carrefour, just across the way from the Toquenelle café, where Peter Viola and I drank those first coffees together, all those months ago. The kiosk is shut, but you can still buy fuel if you have the right kind of card. The smartly dressed English couple in front of me don't. They peer at the screen, puzzling over which button to press to *valider* their transaction, while the queue lengthens behind them.

'*C'est là*,' I explain, gently pointing out the green button embossed with a 'V'. This has been worn to a shine by tens of thousands of French digits, like the toe of the Virgin in the church just up the road.

Hubby presses it and I lead him, in French, through the next few stages: pump number, type of fuel, and so on. After a few seconds' delay, a rejection message flashes up and the card pops out. He's about to reinsert it when I explain – still in French – that it is the wrong type of card and will not work.

'*Ah, oui, oui*,' he nods, pretending to understand, and pointlessly shoving the card back into the machine. So I tell him again, in English this time.

'Look, it's the wrong kind of card. You need one with a pin number.'

'Oh, you're English, thank God!' he exclaims, as if I'd just relieved him at Mafeking. And I remember something Marie-Claude told me this week, when we were cleaning the windows of the summer sitting-room together.

'You can immediately spot English people in a shop,' she said, 'because they'll be the only ones who are talking very loudly. Is that because they want everyone to know they're English?'

It's true: I've never heard a French person speaking noisily in a shop, except for that time when I got sprayed with blood in the cat-fight at Champion. But I don't believe the English yell to draw attention to ourselves. No, it simply hasn't occurred to some people that they do not live in a private, sound-proofed bubble.

'So what the hell are we are going to do?' snorts the man at the petrol station, glaring at the wicked French machine.

'You'll have to find a manned petrol station, which isn't easy on a Sunday.'

Now he starts swearing – not at me, but at his wife, his car and France in general.

'Look,' I tell him hastily, 'I'll put it on my card, and you can pay me the cash.'

'Would you really do that?' he asks, open-mouthed. 'That's incredibly kind. Are you sure?'

But it's not incredibly kind. '*C'est normal*,' as they say in France, where the kindness of strangers no longer takes me by surprise.

# 41

## HIGH FLIGHT

The following afternoon is so dazzling that I return to the aeroclub. I can't resist it. I want to see how high I can fly.

On the radio, I tell the nice lady at Limoges air-traffic control that I want to begin a climb to eight or nine thousand feet. France itself may be staunchly metric, but the sky above it is still measured in imperial plates of meat.

'*Huit mille ou neuf mille pieds?*' she exclaims. '*Et pourquoi?*'

Even though most private pilots rarely fly above 3,500 feet, I wasn't expecting an inquisition. I feel as if the princess in the *boulangerie* has demanded that I justify my choice of baguette.

'To test *le moteur. Et pour l'expérience.*'

There's a silence, while *Madame* has a word with her boss.

'All right, Golf-Zulu-Alpha,' she grumbles. 'But call me when you pass 6,500 feet. I'll need to transfer you to Bordeaux Control.'

And so I start climbing in big circles over St Juste; up,

up into the blue serene. I can feel myself pressing forward in my straps to urge the Luscombe onwards and upwards. This is going to take a while. Ten minutes later, *Madame* is on the blower again.

'*Golf-Zulu-Alpha, vous êtes à 6,500 pieds?*'

'*Négatif*,' I reply, conscious that she is casting aspersions upon my manhood. '*Je suis à 5,900 pieds. Golf-Zulu-Alpha.*' I feel like Scotty in the engine room of the *Enterprise*, with Captain Kirk demanding more power. 'Och, I'm giving it all I've got, Captain, but . . .'

*Madame* sighs and reminds me to call her back at 6,500 feet.

Finally I reach the required altitude, am transferred to the controller at Bordeaux, and tell him that I wish to climb as high as possible. He takes a deep breath.

So here I am, flying in circles above rural France, waiting for a man on the ground a hundred miles away to tell me what I am allowed to do next. Finally he tells me that he can clear me to 10,500 feet, but no higher. This suits me just fine, for I am not carrying oxygen, and it's getting pretty nippy, too. Icarus would have succumbed to hypothermia long before his wings melted.

Up we go, higher and higher. Two miles above the earth is not high compared with a migrating eagle or a passenger jet. But, alone in my little yellow plane, it still feels like the most remote place I have ever been. At La Folie, marooned on my distant hillside, I always know that Gilles and Josette are less than a mile away. Here, shivering through the glittering blue of this boundless welkin, gazing down on the ice cliffs of the clouds, I sense an awesome new solitude, as the grey lakes and ointment-pink villages shrink beneath me, and the unfiltered light becomes ever more brilliant.

Problems become distant, too: the health of animals,

renovation of houses, absence of pianos and my ongoing struggle to integrate myself into Jolibois life. All are far away from this ice kingdom, where everything is so clean and bright and serene that it makes me wish I never had to come back down.

'Did you go far?' mutters old Marcel, his cigarillo beating time on his bottom lip as I climb out of the Luscombe. Marcel has walked away from more plane crashes than anyone else I know, but he cannot fly any more, for his lungs are shot. And he is angry all the time.

'Only about three kilometres,' I reply.

'Only three kilometres?' he growls. 'But you were gone for almost an hour. Where were you?'

I point straight up above my head. 'Up there. It felt like I was in another world.' And then I brace myself for the sneer and the sarcasm.

But Marcel does not sneer. And from the way his eyes seem to mist over as he rolls his cigarillo between his grey lips and does his best to smile, I know that he has been there, too.

With animals, it's the comings and goings that get you. The births, the copulations, the deaths. Once they're grown up and healthy and comfortably installed in their *pré* or *poulailler*, they mostly just do their sheepish, henful thing, until a surfeit of males leads to yobbish behaviour and unplanned pregnancies. After that, it's the new arrivals that create the headaches, while the departures – planned or unplanned – do something similar to the heart.

Melissa, bless her, has been so knocked sideways by her sister Mildred's death that she has begun sitting broodily on a clutch of eggs. Unconscious as this may be, I cannot help rejoicing to see her labouring to bring new life to La Folie. Among my friends from school, it was often the ones whose parents had died the youngest who most looked forward to having children of their own.

But Melissa's chick-generation project is playing havoc with egg production. No sooner has she spread herself in one of the nesting boxes, like a battleship in a dry dock, than the lovely Martha decides that she has maternal longings, too. With both nesting boxes occupied, everyone else is having to lay their eggs wherever they can find a hiding place. Unfortunately they're rather good at this. I haven't found a single egg for days.

The two broodies only leave their nests for one sniff of freedom daily. Martha is a marathon runner in a comedy chicken suit, snatching a few gulps of water before waving to the crowd and settling back into her rhythm on the nest. Melissa is more like a house-bound mum nipping out for a guilty fag and a cream cake while the children are at school.

Out she totters on her stiff pins, feathers fluffed out in her best don't-you-know-who-I-am fashion. She looks like a fat snowball. The idea seems to be to go mental for five minutes, whilst eating and drinking as much as chickenly possible, taking a frenetic dust bath, and shrieking at the other girls about her sore bum and how motherhood isn't all it's cracked up to be. This is accomplished with much charging back and forth, and giddy bows to all four compass points, like a tiddly dowager duchess who's lost a contact lens at a hen party.

My chicken book tells me to check which eggs are fertile by candling them – holding them in front of a light source and peering at what's inside. A special lamp is recommended, rather than relying on old-fashioned candle power. But when I rattle down to Gamm Vert to buy my chick gear, forty-two euros seems an awful lot to pay for a flimsy 1950s ray-gun made out of rubber and aluminium, even for a self-confessed Useful Gadget junkie like me. So I settle for a big bag of chick crumbs and a mini-feeder, lining them up at the till as proudly as an expectant mum buying romper-suits at Mothercare. The cashier beams at me. I think she's impressed.

Still attracted by the idea of any other Useful Gadgets I can buy for the chicks, and in need of a product with which to treat the sheep against fly-strike, I head off to Alliance Pastorale, the farmers' wholesale store.

'What's this, Yvette?' I ask the smiley blonde lady behind the till, as I hold up a board with canvas straps attached. 'It looks jolly useful.'

'With only four ewes, Michael, I'm not sure you need it,' she giggles, explaining that it's a dye-covered raddle for attaching to a ram's chest, so that you can tell when all the ewes in a flock have been tupped. 'Ah, but you English are so funny,' she adds.

Marie-Claude, my strict cleaning lady, of whom I grow fonder by the week, is not so sure.

'You can immediately spot an English person in a shop,' she tells me, in between whacking cobwebs, 'because they're the ones who don't say *bonjour*.'

'And because we're the ones who shout all the time,' I remind her, remembering our last conversation on the subject.

She smiles. '*Oui, les Anglais sont sans-gêne.*'

'*Sans-gêne?*'

'The English are thoughtless. They're the ones who barge into you in the *supermarché* and don't say sorry. Or walk straight in front of you without so much as an *excusez-moi.*'

'But are we really as bad as all that?' I ask. 'I know there are too many of us here in France, and that we shake hands too little, and attempt to kiss too much. I know we dress shabbily, and have a reputation as hooligans who drink too much. But there is goodness, too, in the English. You may even find we're not all that different from the French.'

I must be looking pained, for Marie-Claude relents. 'Well, at least *les Anglais* are better than the Germans,' she says kindly.

'The Germans?'

'Oh, yes.' She nods. 'They're even more *sans-gêne*.'

And so, desperate to be a good ambassador for Blighty, I spend a week saying '*Bonjour*' to everyone I pass. I also make sure to give my fellow shoppers an especially wide berth in the *supermarché*, and then surprise them from afar with a '*Pardon, Monsieur*' or an '*Excusez-moi, Madame*,' in case they haven't noticed me behind the frozen *escargots*.

When Tuesday comes around, I report my progress to Marie-Claude.

'*Non*,' she tuts, wagging her finger. 'You mustn't say *bonjour* to everyone you pass in the street. That's not correct. You should only say *bonjour* to the ones you know.'

Rrrrrrright. Even though I have lived in France for almost a year, there is still so much to learn; so much, for all my eagerness, that I have yet to grasp. The trouble is that many people in Jolibois by now look vaguely familiar to me. And I can't be sure which ones I sort-of know, and which ones I sort-of-don't. I've always been hopeless with faces. At Sainsbury's in Vauxhall, I once waved at someone I was sure was an old friend, and it was only when she politely waved back, with a bemused smile, that I realized it was Joanna Lumley.

'Fair enough. But what about when I go into a shop?' I ask Marie-Claude.

'Then you must say *bonjour* to everyone as you enter.'

'Aha! Even if I don't know them?'

She nods.

'Even in the *supermarché*?'

'Except in the *supermarché*,' snorts Marie-Claude, who thinks this is the silliest suggestion she ever heard.

And then there is the shaking-hands problem. I'm all right when I wander into a café and dutifully shake hands with all the old boys. This is easy enough, because there are only a few of them, and they tend to be heavily sedated. It's when a lot of people are circulating that my Facial Recognition Deficit Disorder begins to haunt me. Shaking hands with everyone in a room is appreciated. But only once. Attempting to shake hands with the same person twice tends to be greeted, I find, with Mr Bumble-style *froideur*.

Arriving at the tennis club *assemblée générale* – when we will have a chance to vote on changing the rules regarding voting – I'm relieved to spot Claude, the electrician with the strong forehand. No problems in recognizing *him*. But he rejects my outstretched hand.

'I already saw you earlier,' he explains.

'Ah.' I bite my lip. 'But that was this morning.'

'Yes, and one should only shake hands once a day.'

A vast chasm opens up before me, as the implications of this sink in. I shall have to start carrying a digital camera and a telephone directory. Or perhaps I might buy that ram raddle from Alliance Pastorale after all. I can't wait to ask smiley Yvette if she thinks it would work on humans.

# 42

## JULY: FAIR PLAY

Over the past few weeks, I have been teaching English to a young French student called Sara, whose grandparents live in a nearby village. This week we translated a section of T. S. Eliot's *Four Quartets*:

> *What we call the beginning is often the end.*
> *And to make an end is to make a beginning.*

The longer I am here, the more these lines make sense to me.

Having begun my time in France with a lily-livered townie's knowledge of farm animals, the best moment so far has been the birth of my lambs, despite being swiftly followed by the slow death of Emil. And now comes the second most thrilling event: the imminent birth of the chicks, hard on the heels of the death of poor old Mildred. I now see that all those questions from Cruella De Vil the estate agent, about how many outbuildings *Monsieur* wants, were not entirely academic. I thought outbuildings were for deluded people to convert into unlettable *gîtes*.

Yet my pigsty has proved a worthy *poulailler* for the chickens. And with chicks ahoy, I'm jolly glad to have the barn, too, as a safe haven for Martha, Melissa and their unborn dynasty.

Others may go in for lavish barn conversions with gothic double-glazing and *faux*-medieval chandeliers, but my old barn has already proved its worth as a swallow sanctuary, wood store and infirmary for sick sheep.

With the help of Carrie, an ex-girlfriend who is over from New York for a few days, I've rigged up a makeshift chick run, using two stone carvings left behind by Zumbach to prop up the heavy wooden worktops I bought for the kitchen of the *maison des amis*, in the days when I thought the plastering might be finished before the Beijing Olympics. At least now they'll have chicken *in* them, if not *on* them. That's if any of the eggs are fertile: I've done my best to candle them with a torch, an oil lamp and a household candle, and can't see a damn thing through any of the shells.

I like it when old friends like Carrie come to stay at La Folie: city people who yearn for the countryside. Pretty and petite, Carrie jets around the world for UNESCO, has a brain the size of a planet, and has won every argument I have ever refused to have with her. In London, we would have our frantic catch-up chat to the soundtrack of a noisy restaurant before hugging goodbye and promising to see each other more often. Here at La Folie, there's no television, no radio, no nothing. There's just Titus, punctuating the silence with his piercing *cocorico*, and now the pleasure of sharing the birth of my first ever real-live chick with someone who will appreciate its magic.

My main worry is that the eggs aren't all going to hatch at the same time. This is my own fault. Ignoring the advice in *Starting with Chickens*, I failed to separate Martha and Melissa from the sisterhood as soon as they became broody, thinking that this was only necessary if punch-ups broke out. But the real reason for separating them becomes clear during one of their comfort breaks.

With both mums AWOL at once, I take the opportunity to change the hay in the nesting boxes. *Mon Dieu.* While Martha's nest still contains just five eggs, Melissa's hides a vast stockpile of twenty-seven, over which she has heroically been managing to spread herself. The other girls have clearly been adding new ammo to her arsenal on a daily basis. I perform a hasty cabinet reshuffle, make it sixteen apiece, and hope they don't notice.

I now have absolutely no idea how many chicks to expect, nor when. But with two mums and thirty-two eggs between them, it could be mayhem. I'm secretly hoping for two complete rugby XVs, plus a referee and someone to bring on the oranges at half time.

Next day, I know something's wrong as soon I open the barn door. An epic pong defiles the air. And Melissa's nesting box is full of green slime. At once sour and sweet and rotten and ghastly, this noxious odour vaguely reminds me of something I once ate in South Korea, or the strange whiff I experienced when I got hit on the head by a cricket ball at school. I never want to smell it again.

An egg has exploded. Suddenly that ray-gun from Gamm Vert begins to seem like excellent value. I don't want any more eggs to self-detonate. What if Melissa and Martha are sitting on thirty-one UXBs, each of them powerful enough to stink out half of Jolibois?

But a shriek distracts me from my thoughts. It's Serge's wife, Jacquie, who has come to help me paint all the windows and shutters the wrong shade of lavender; lurid eye-shadow on the face of an old woman. Between finger and thumb she holds up a freshly shed snakeskin she has found just outside the kitchen window.

'You should cut that thing down,' warns Jacquie, waving the snake husk fiercely at the dense creeper that runs from the flower beds straight up to my bedroom window, 'or *les serpents* will be up it, and into your room.'

Thus perturbed, I'm relieved when Gilles drops in for a chat after milking. 'There aren't any snakes around here, are there, Gilles?' I ask as casually as possible, having introduced him to Carrie and asked after Josette.

'*Si!*' he retorts. 'There are vipers whose bite can kill you. But they won't usually attack you unless you step on them.'

'And if I do?'

'Get to the doctor fast.'

'Don't I have to kill the snake first, to show the doctor what bit me?'

'That helps.' Gilles hesitates. 'But in your case, I suggest you get straight in the car and drive.'

'Ah.'

'Don't worry,' he chuckles, relenting. 'Your chickens will kill any snakes they find.'

'*Mes poules?*' I watch Gilles carefully, to see if he's pulling my leg. But no, he's deadly serious, launching into a terrifying mime of a chicken grabbing a snake and peck-ing it to pieces. Or else he is pretending to be a furious toddler trying to escape from a play-pen. Either way, it's scary. And though I don't want to count my chickens before they hatch, I'm beginning to think that the more the merrier.

I am wondering, too, how Martha would feel about sleeping in my bedroom. She could perch on the towel-rail for snake duty and story time. Well, why not? The Tower has its ravens. Manlius had his geese. Why shouldn't I have a chicken?

The main problem is that the cat would feel deeply miffed. Oh, and the hypothetical *copine* who has yet to wander into my life is unlikely to be thrilled to discover that I am most comfortable sleeping with *une poule*. Particularly if I am forced to explain to her that it's either that, *chérie*, or a bunch of snakes.

Sound the alarums, sennets, tuckets, and what you will. Most days, when I go into the barn, the only sound is a disgruntled clucking from Martha and the shrill trilling of the swallows. But today there's another sound bouncing off the walls, like the bleeping of the time bomb just before 007 disarms it.

I peer into the straw-lined nesting boxes.

Melissa blinks back at me. And there, poking out from under her wing, are two new faces, each a winsome ball of fluff with a beak like the tip of a golf-tee and two grains of caviar for eyes.

'What's all the yelling about?' asks Carrie, hurrying in.

'I wasn't yel—'

'Oh . . . my . . . God,' she murmurs, her hushed voice rising a major-seventh with each word. She is so desperate to pick up the chicks and cuddle them to death that I have to make her swear not to touch them. One of them is pure black, and Carrie insists that I name it after her.

Next day, Melissa has three more cuddly toys under her wing. She looks deeply smug, while Martha waits, alone and confused, for the glory of motherhood.

But by the time seven chicks have hatched, the two mums have clearly decided to make a go of it together. While Melissa snoozes with just a single chick stashed below decks, Martha sails out – proud as you like – with the other six munchkins in tow. So not only have I now witnessed the birth of my first chicks; I've seen my first ever French lesbian chicken adoption, too. We're nothing if not progressive, here in Jolibois.

There is more and different glory to come. I have absolutely no idea how this happened. Indeed, I fully expect a *gendarme* with an outsize moustache to come and tell me it was all *une grande blague* and that I'd better give the thing back sharpish.

No, Monsieur Étang the plumber has not come to build the bathroom upstairs, and Monsieur Laveille has not come to lay the floor in the summer sitting-room. Douglas the giant still hasn't finished the rendering, because his wife Jill has reasonably insisted that he construct a roof for his own house first. No, the fact is that I have just been presented with a vast and glittering trophy at the tennis tournament in Peyrat de Rocher.

Miles away, in the real world, England's drubbings in every sporting contest on the planet have not escaped me. It was quite clear that something had to be done. And I'm happy to say that I have done it. Yes, Wright has stiffened the old sinews and brought home the international silverware. The Englishman can now look the Frenchman squarely in the eye once again. Rule Britannia. Taran-tara. God save the king.

And I didn't *just* win a trophy, either. Alongside my golden cup (which I dare not leave in the sun, lest it melt), I have also been presented with two biros, a spooky glass ornament painted with woodland creatures, a game of Spillikins, a pack of cards and a craft knife. I bet you don't get Spillikins when you win Wimbledon.

So spectacular is my trophy that Claude the tennis-playing electrician goes quite pale when I show it to him in the kitchen of the *maison des amis*. I was hoping he'd find it funny, but he doesn't.

'*You* won ... *that*?' he says, slowly laying down his screwdriver to stare at my prize. This makes me uneasy. For a second, he looks like Gollum gazing at the Ring. And then he remembers himself just enough to gasp: 'But *how*?'

'*C'est une bonne question, Claude* ...'

Over the past few weeks, I have been desperately entering local tennis tournaments in the hope of finding someone horribly hung-over whom I can out-lob to get a classification, and thereby drag myself out of the *non-classé* (untouchables) bin. Everyone in France is classified according to his ability or, in my case, lack of it.

Fortunately, I meet a chap called Hubert in the first round at Peyrat de Rocher. Hubert is a cheery teddy bear in mirrored shades and a Hawaiian shirt, who prepares for our match by smoking several Gauloises, and can't stop telling me how terrible he feels. I don't think this is mere gamesmanship. His voice sounds like he has been gargling bicycle cogs.

'Didn't you sleep well last night?' I ask, attempting not to sound too pleased.

'No, I was with my friend, Jack Daniels,' he rasps, staggering on to court and making a few optimistic, Oliver-Reedy swishes in the air with his racquet.

And so follows a masterclass in French obscenities. Hubert isn't a very good tennis player, but his swearing is world class, and a small crowd gathers to listen to him play. I don't need to be able to understand the words to know that I am in the presence of greatness.

At the end, there is some polite applause. Not for my victory, I think, but for the breadth and depth of Hubert's vernacular.

My pyrrhic victory over Hubert is swiftly followed by an England-style collapse against *un joueur classé* in the second round: the silver-quiffed charmer who runs the hunting-and-fishing shop in Jolibois, and whose fifty-a-day smoking habit doesn't seem to have any negative impact on his tennis, at least not when faced with a challenger of my negligible abilities.

Nevertheless, beating Hubert has somehow qualified me for the tournament's *non-classé* final, where I am up against a strapping young SNCF railway worker called Christophe. Here again, I allow myself to dream briefly of glory, when it emerges that Christophe has only had two hours' sleep since coming off the night shift. Even so, he soon manages to make me feel like a diesel shunter beside his hurtling TGV. Serves and volleys whizz past me like a flashing landscape, and it's all over so fast that we arrive at our destination almost before I've had time to find my seat. But at least I win the odd point – I have come a long way since my whitewash at the hands of Norman Handley in his Dunlop Green Flash – and it is enough to have been present on the journey: my name is writ large in the annals of international sporting glory, and the finalists' cup is mine.

News of my unlikely triumph travels fast, so that everyone seems to know about it by the start of the next tournament on the calendar: the Jolibois Open. Sipping a drink with a few of the other players before my first match, I find it hard to believe that this is the same clubhouse where, all those months ago, I gazed out at the deserted clay courts with their advertising hoardings – Babolat, Banque de France, Roland Garros – and where Amélie Mauresmo is still about to clout a fizzing backhand, frozen in time and space on the wall. The trapped bird I saw, fluttering at a high window, has long since flown.

'You English, you come and buy all our houses, and now you steal our cups, too,' laughs a burly, handsome man with tousled black hair and piercing blue eyes, slapping me on the back hard enough to make me spill the glass of orange juice that I'm holding. Though we have never been formally introduced, I know exactly who this is. Everyone in Jolibois does. Le Grand Mermoz is the bullish fellow who runs the higgledy-piggledy hardware store opposite the cemetery, an Aladdin's cave of Useful Gadgets staffed by a workforce of such eccentric charm and helpfulness that it is easy to imagine them as the cast of an unusually heart-warming sit-com. 'But we like *les Anglais*,' he adds with unforced joviality. 'You are all *très fair-play*.'

'*Oui, nous sommes très fair-play*,' I reply, '*et vous êtes très généreux*.'

I hop from foot to foot as I wait for my first-round opponent to arrive. But he never appears, and Jean-Michel, the hawkish club president, declares a walk-over.

'*Tu vois, Michael?*' he says, cheerily putting his arm round me. 'Now that you have won a cup, everyone is scared of you.'

For a second, I almost catch myself believing him. And when Le Grand Mermoz tells me about next week's sports club *pétanque* tournament, I sign up on the spot.

Admittedly, I've never in my life played *pétanque*. But, thanks to the bowls gene that runs in the family, I am quietly confident of bringing home another trophy for the nation. In the 1970s my parents had a set of carpet *boules* from Habitat, and it can't be all that different. The game – tiddlywinks played with cannonballs – looks easy enough. Buying the equipment is, I am about to discover, another matter.

*

'*Vous êtes pointeur ou tireur?*' asks the daunting lady in Jolibois Sports when I make my request. Perhaps she thinks I've come in for a job interview. Statuesque, fiftysomething, and with a lacquered ash-blond hairdo that would do Princess Anne proud, *Madame* looks as though she should really be selling Chanel gowns in Paris, not shin-pads in Jolibois.

'*Er, je ne suis pas sûr . . .*'

'Well, do you point or do you shoot?' she repeats, folding her arms.

'That depends . . .' I mumble. They never ask you this down at the Megabowl in Streatham. There, the man behind the till just says 'Showsoys?' to which the correct response is 'Forty-two, please,' and to start untying one's laces.

*Madame* looks at me pityingly as I wring my hands and scan the shop's brown carpet-tiles for inspiration.

'I shoot,' I guess at last, looking her firmly in the eye.

'Most beginners,' she sighs, 'prefer to start by learning to point.'

'I point,' I say, correcting myself.

But *Madame* is not listening. Real *pétanque* players, she explains, specialize either in landing their *boules* close to the jack – *le cochonnet* – or else in smashing their opponents' balls out of the way. Hence pointing or shooting. I think I know which one *Madame* would be. But where do my own special gifts lie? I feel like I'm trying to buy a dress for a woman I've never met. Suppose I'm an all-rounder? *Madame* doesn't seem to think this is very likely.

And so, twenty-five minutes and sixty euros later, I emerge from the shop clutching a clacking trio of championship *boules*. I am a committed *pointeur*, and let no man say otherwise.

At the town stadium, while others warm up for the tournament with a massed Pastis session under a canvas awning, I hide behind a lorry for a spot of furtive pointing on the gravel. And then I almost land one on the soft top of Le Grand Mermoz's flashy convertible, and decide to rely on hidden potential. At least my *boules* don't look quite so shiny and virginal now. No one will ever guess I'm a *débutant*.

The tournament doesn't go quite according to plan. I was right about *pétanque* being an easy game. The problem is that all the other players – perhaps seventy of them – find it even easier than I do. And though I manage to notch up a couple of jammy victories in my four matches – thanks to being paired with *super-bons tireurs* – it is not to be England's day. I have to watch as someone else collects the trophy: my trophy. That enormous statue of a *pétanqueur* would have gone very nicely on the high oak ledge of the summer sitting-room at La Folie.

I'm glad I came, nonetheless. There is much laughter over the fact that *un seul Anglais* has been foolhardy enough to enter the tournament, and at least by letting the French win I have helped preserve the *entente cordiale*.

'What's everyone eating?' I ask one of my playing partners afterwards, seeing people tucking into something that looks meaty and irresistible, served on a procession of paper plates emerging from behind the bar.

'*Couilles de mouton*,' says Christophe. His smile is not entirely encouraging, as if he were enjoying a private joke. 'You should try.' Before I can stop him, he's ordered me a plateful.

'Is this what I think it is?' I ask, suddenly not hungry after all.

'*Oui*,' chuckles Christophe. '*Bon appétit*.'

'*Ah, formidable*,' I hear myself say, when what I really

mean is 'Eeuuwgghhh.' And then I am grimly tucking into my plateful of fried sheep's testicles, doing my best to swallow them without tasting them too much, and thinking how unfortunate it is that here in rural France it's so much easier to buy balls than *boules*.

Out in the barn, I'm pretty sure that the last few eggs will not hatch, now that both Martha and Melissa are busy teaching their chicks to peck, cluck and do the Charleston. Frankly, I'm relieved. From what I can tell from the size of the tiny combs on the chicks' heads, I have a nasty feeling that the fluffy brood includes just three trainee hens and four cockerels-in-waiting.

There may be trouble ahead. I happen to know that keeping even two cockerels is a recipe for disaster. It's also a recipe for *coq au vin*, although I don't like to think in those terms.

When it comes to animals, you can't have too many women. Girls are just plain better. They lay their eggs in the hay each morning. They produce their hop-skippety lambs in the spring. They are always gentle and sweet-natured. It's the chaps who cause all the mayhem, and – when I think of Charlie and the boys – the heartache. Those *couilles de mouton* have a lot to answer for.

This is chauvinistic of me, of course. But I speak as one who has just staggered half a mile across three fields and two barbed-wire fences – the second of which now sports a significant fragment of my trousers – with a sweaty black ram in my arms. Fed up with being butted and baited by Ramekin and even the tiny Camillo, Gaston went AWOL over the weekend, treating himself to two full days of Bunburyism in a ewe-filled field so distant that I didn't even think to search it at first.

My heart went out to Doris, Ella and Daphne as they

stood abandoned in their field, gazing at each other with 'so what do we do now?' wretchedness. Some of the light appeared to have gone out of their lives. If I walked near them, they began to follow me in a kind of daze, rather like those desperate rock groupies who, if they fail to pull the lead singer, will latch on to the bass guitarist instead. And when I finally brought Gaston back, they gathered round the old boy, nuzzling and nibbling at him, re-establishing the old intimacies of the flock.

Only Ella, his constant companion, stood apart. The deep mahogany of her wool is now beginning to go grey. I suppose she has seen it all before. And from her wounded stance, I cannot help thinking that, each time, it becomes a little harder to forgive.

Still slightly out of breath from my exertions with Gaston, I peer at the remaining eggs in the barn, and listen. I'm sure I heard something. There it is again. I can just detect a muffled cheep, and see something poking through a hole in one of the speckled shells.

My chicken book is very clear on this subject: don't help any chicks to break out of their shells, because they're unlikely to survive even if you do. But what if the eggs have become too hard and dry to crack? It can't hurt to help just a tiny bit, can it?

Once I've pulled away one piece of shell, the cheeping intensifies. And then I shudder as a thin line of blood trickles from the egg. The chick's delicate skin is coming away with the shell. I try to push the fragment back into place, but it's too late.

The torn chick looks like ET. In a panic, I pick up Martha, and lay her beside her stricken baby. But Martha isn't having any of it. Seeing the blood, she pecks viciously at the helpless chick, which shrivels like a crisp packet on a fire.

So I snatch away ET and take him outside into the light. I can see that his own light is fading fast. *What we call the beginning is often the end.* Bleeding and contorted, he looks like a day-old swallow that has fallen from its nest. I lay the twitching body on a rock in the shade, and find another stone, shaped like the head of a sledgehammer. And then it's done, and I feel like I've turned into someone else.

# 43

## AUGUST: ENEMY AIRCRAFT IN SIGHT

One day I shall rebuild the old well at the top of the hill behind the house. Right now, it looks like something out of the final scene of *Planet of the Apes*. All that's left is a pile of rubble surrounded by some unusually lush greenery: an oasis amid the scorched scrub of La Folie.

High summer has hit town, bringing with it a disconcerting invasion of tourists: big-bummed bumblebees in fur coats and thigh-high boots; lizards sipping fly-daiquiris as they soak up the rays; ants on a cheap package tour; tattooed wasps gunning mopeds; stoned crickets strumming guitars; hornets in hairnets; and so on.

I tend to think of the local creepy-crawlies as people, because they're less scary that way. Rural France may not be the Colombian rainforest or the Malaysian jungle, but there's no doubt that you get a bigger and better class of beastie here than you do in East Dulwich.

Bees and wasps and hornets have always given me the willies, though I have never in my life been stung. Even I find this hard to believe. But as a child, I saw my little brother, Nicholas, savaged between the toes by a bee, and was quite sure I would die of pain if the same thing happened to me. From the way Nick yelled and squealed and hollered, it was obvious that this was the worst thing that could befall a six-year-old; worse even than missing *Crackerjack* or discovering a slow puncture in your Space Hopper.

I haven't become much braver as an adult. I will don a pair of gardening gloves just to put one of the cat's lizard lunches outside the door. I have been known to shout at mosquitoes in the dark. And if I'm having lunch outside, I have Very Bad Thoughts about people who flap ineffectually at wasps with their napkins. I just know that the enraged beastie will soon be turning his gun button from SAFE to FIRE, at the very moment when he's got me in the cross-hairs of his gyroscopic sight.

Even ladybirds unnerve me, ever since Great-Aunt Beryl's husband, Jock, got one stuck in his ear. The thing buzzed and buzzed against his ear drum, until he managed to kill it with a cotton-bud. And then it went septic. And Great-Aunt Beryl was awfully cross.

The trouble with all this, of course, is that I am a bloke, and blokes are not allowed to be frightened of insects. Our job is to catch them and put them out the door, and to announce that it's quite safe to come out of the larder now, *chérie*.

In the cool stillness of the kitchen, I assemble my usual lunch. A slab of *pâté forestier* and a lump of glistening goat's cheese, a tomato the colour of Titus's comb, a loaf of *pain aux céréales* from Céline's *boulangerie*, and a glass of cheap Gamay. Melissa, Martha and their chicks – already looking like gangly adolescents – come clucking to the open back door in a hop-skippety frenzy when they hear me hacking into the loaf, and the shorn Rastafarians start up a cacophonic bleating in sympathy. Ah, the peace and stillness of the French countryside. I carry my plate and wine glass out on to the sun-dazzled terrace, my bare feet almost sizzling on the hot gravel.

'They won't sting you if you leave them alone,' I tell myself, resisting the urge to scarper as two wasps buzz around me like a pair of Me-109s pestering a Lancaster. And then, utterly without provocation, one of the blighters stings me on the forearm.

'What the . . . !' I exclaim. And then: 'Rrrrrghhhh!' And finally: 'Gosh.'

This poetic little monologue charts my three-stage response to the assault. First: righteous indignation. Next: panic, because I'm worried about the mounting pain and lingering death from anaphylactic shock that are even now winging their way towards me. And finally: embarrassed relief, as it emerges that being stung by a wasp is not half as bad as I expected.

The sting feels like lemon juice in a cut, or the first mouthful of a cheap vindaloo, or as if I've just been flicked hard with the end of a furled, damp towel. It's hot, it throbs, and it is decidedly bearable. I can't imagine how I could have spent thirty years fearing this.

By next morning, any trace of discomfort has vanished. I am just about to don my boxer shorts when I hear a low-frequency buzzing, and something heavy drops out of my undies on to the bedroom floor. It makes such a thud that I think I must have dropped my watch. And then I see a hornet – a hornet, I swear – roughly the size of a Renault Clio, crawling under the bed. *Sacrebleu*. That was a close one, vicar. Two stings in two days, after a lifetime of being spared, simply wouldn't be cricket. And I know from the size of that wee beastie that the pain he could inflict would be exponentially worse than yesterday's baptism of fire: a Grand Slam after a Tallboy; the cane, rather than the slipper.

I resolve to shake out all my clothes in future, before putting them on. Yet even the wisest resolutions are soon forgotten and the next night I am nonchalantly pulling up my pyjama bottoms when I hear that same ominous buzz. I freeze.

It's coming from inside my PJs. And in a most unsporting spot, too.

Time stops. I have a nasty feeling that I know exactly what is going to happen in 0.2 seconds' time, and that this is going to hurt – like when le Pug Rouge and I were spinning uncontrollably across the *route nationale* last year, a moment before hitting the ditch. Tonight's emergency is less likely to be life-threatening . . . but that doesn't include the possible impact on my prospects of fatherhood.

I am the dangling climber watching the rope fray; the surfer surprised by the dorsal fin. And then the buzzing stops. The doodlebug is about to strike.

'Phhhgghh!' I yell, clutching my goolies, hopping around, desperately trying to rip off my jim-jams. I feel like Hercules struggling to fling off his poisoned cloak – except that he was a heroic demigod in the throes of death, whereas I am an Englishman stung in the organ loft by an insect the size of a suppository.

The hornet falls to the floor, and I respond to his assault with disproportionate force, grimly registering the crunch of thorax and abdomen as I despatch him to hornet heaven with my slippered heel.

A subsequent examination will reveal that the late hornet has missed Targets A and B, and merely made my inner thigh feel as if the fairies are having a bonfire there. So perhaps I over-reacted. But when someone's jabbing you with what feels like an acid-tipped red-hot needle wired up to a 24-volt car battery, it's not always easy to pinpoint where they've hit you.

Next morning, the cat brings me a large green lizard, and lays it beside the bed, presumably to cheer me up. An hour later, wounded by my sniffy response to her first gift, she raises the stakes. Her next love offering is a baby viper, still very much alive.

Granted, this snake is not much thicker than a bootlace with a knot in one end. But some bootlaces can be deadly. And the way the serpent blinks and flicks out its forked tongue at me is unmistakably snaky.

'That's *very* good, Eva,' I tell the cat, partly because I'm impressed, and partly because I don't wish to spur her into going back for Momma. This week is proving to be character-building for both of us. Catching a snake is not something the cat ever achieved in East Dulwich. And as I eye the serpent from what I hope is a safe distance, it dawns on me that I'm not scared of wasps or hornets any more.

Leaving me with her catch, the cat saunters back out through the cat-flap. I notice that she has adopted a Gallic swagger, presumably to reflect her elevated status as a scourge of rodents and reptiles. And then there is a frightful shrieking, as four young cockerels rocket past her with Titus on their tails.

If hornets and snakes are an occasional pain, the local mosquitoes are a constant irritation. One unexpected corollary of living alone is that there is no one with whom to share the mosquitoes. With a full household, they could have a Happy Meal each, and feel sated. As a child in Colombia, I was almost never bitten, because the mozzies preferred my mum and my sister. The two of them complained bitterly as they became lunch, and the rest of us – unbitten – naturally felt that they were both being big girls' blouses, because we didn't know what we were missing.

But with only me to gorge themselves upon, I am a daily buffet for the buzzing nasties; a human pin-cushion; a gold-star blood donor. I have counted thirteen bites on my left ankle, and fourteen on the right. Most are so close together that they are beginning to agglomerate into a single red welt of irritation. But at least the bites on my ankles take my mind off the ones on my knees, behind my knees, in the small of my back and – worst of all – the one just under my watch.

Marie-Claude arrives to do the cleaning, tapping on the back door so quietly that I assume she's one of the chickens.

'*Oh-là-là, il fait chaud, oui* . . . What the hell is that doing there?' she demands, with a grimace that would not disgrace the Gorgon Medusa.

'Oh, it's just a young snake that the cat brought in,' I murmur.

'But why is it on the kitchen table?'

I don't have an answer to this. The truth is that I'm fascinated by this snake. I've only ever seen them in reptile houses, before now. And I like watching the way it slowly straightens itself as it grows in confidence, and then coils up again when I come too close.

'I'm seeing if it will recover.'

'What are you going to do with it?'

'I suppose I'll put it outside again.'

Donning my thickest pair of chainsaw gauntlets and a pair of wellies, I trap the little snake in a tupperware box, and carry him outside. After the cool of the kitchen, the heat hits me like the blast of hot air they blow at you when you walk into Debenhams on a cold day. My sunglasses are no longer dark enough for this sun. I really need to buy myself an arc-welding mask.

Holding the box out in front of me, I wander round to the back of the house, and on up through the wild jungle of that part of the hillside that I have not yet fenced for the sheep. The weeds and grasses are almost waist high in places as I make my way to the old well in the furthest corner of the field, and gently tip the baby snake out – coiled up like a mini-pretzel – on to the grey earth.

A few feet away, I notice a length of thick rope lying coiled on the stones. Funny: I don't remember that being there before – but it should come in handy when I get round to repairing the shaft. It will be good to do some grubby masonry work myself at last, instead of always leaving it to others.

Bending down, I am about to pick the rope up when it smoothly uncoils itself and disappears into a hole in the earth.

## 44

## BLESSINGS

I had expected the long summer evenings to prove easier than the icy darkness of winter at La Folie. But somehow the lovelier this place becomes, the lonelier it gets, just as the more content I feel, the more I find myself craving a special someone with whom to share that contentment.

Night after night, the cat and I sit outside on the terrace, gazing at the long shadows across the valley. I sip a glass of Sauvignon from a five-litre box that should last me a fortnight but probably won't, and wonder if she remembers London.

All those cranky neighbourhood cats she used to flirt with; the stream of human visitors to the house in East Dulwich; the sounds of revving engines and police sirens and hip-hop. It all seems so far away from here, where the only sounds are the whirring of a billion crickets, the shrieking of the owls and – every so often – the drowsy hum of a *bourdon* buzzing home from the wisteria.

I had no idea, when I bought La Folie, how many hours we would both spend in this one spot, absorbing this one view, noticing the way it waxes and wanes with the changing seasons. Views lend perspective: thoughts shift, when the eyes can relax into the far distance.

Having a cat helps, too. *Chat boulanger*, I learn, is what the French call it when a cat sits on your lap and kneads you, making you flinch as the claws dig into your skin, but also persuading you to accept the pain as the necessary price for this most perfect sign of pleasure. I can feel alone and tired and worried about the sheep, and this happy cat makes everything all right.

Gilles and Josette come to supper and we eat some vaguely Mexican tacos I've produced from a kit. I hoped these might amuse Gilles, and am not disappointed.

'C'est *quoi*?' he demands, wrinkling his nose as if he'd just found an eel in the bath.

'Tacos,' I reply. '*Ils sont mexicains.*'

'*Ah, nous sommes très international, ce soir,*' he says, taking a huge bite. His eyes widen in surprise. '*Et c'est bon.*'

'*Gourmand,*' whispers Josette affectionately. Though I have given her a cushion for her back, her stiff movements betray her constant pain. I have never heard her utter a single word of complaint.

'Is it still bad?' I ask.

'Yes, it hurts,' she admits now, not looking up. 'But I'm used to it.'

Gilles pushes his food around his plate with his fork, saying nothing.

'It's very kind of you to invite us,' he says at last. '*Comme ça on se sent moins seul.*'

Alone? You feel alone? You, who have been married for more than thirty years, who have farmed in this region for ever, whose cosy house is set in a cheery little hamlet of other dwellings? I look at my friend, touched by his admission, and my heart goes out to him. One does not have to live all by oneself in a foreign country to feel alone.

Next morning, having left the chickens to guard La Folie, and the cat to guard the chickens, I am flying the Luscombe over a sunlit landscape, en route to Sarlat in the Dordogne. It lifts my spirits to be here, high in this crystal sky. I have been spending too much time merely pottering in the airspace near St Juste, zooming high over the top of La Folie for a look at the Rastafarians from a different angle, and occasionally rocking my wings over Gilles's farm. I was hoping that Peter Viola and I might make some flights together in our two machines, double-barrelling through the sky in a loose formation. But Peter has had to return to England for a while – 'various secret projects, old boy' – and although I have taken some of the other aeroclub pilots for flights in the Luscombe, it's not the same as gazing down at the fields and seeing the shadows of two planes side by side, or tail-chasing each other through the tops of the shining clouds. Last night Gilles said he would come flying with me '*bientôt*', but I think he wants me to fly a bit more without crashing before he puts his life in the hands of an Englishman.

I've chosen Sarlat because it's there, and because my flight-guide says the aerodrome has its own restaurant. In England, pilots will fly miles across the country for a hundred-pound cup of tea. In the USA, it's a hundred-dollar hamburger. Here in France, where both food and flying are relatively cheap, one hopes for rather more for rather less. A month's hangarage for my plane at St Juste costs roughly the same as dinner for two at Pizza Express in Dulwich Village. Whereas for the money I was paying to house my Luscombe at Rochester, I could take thirty people out to lunch at the Café Limousin in Jolibois.

The countryside en route to Sarlat makes me shake my head in wonder. Fields and lakes stretch themselves out before me as if someone had printed a life-size map of France on to khaki velvet. Gazing down from four thousand feet, I have an inkling of how northern Europe must have looked before human beings came along and began to spoil it.

And then I tap the altimeter, and check that I have it set for the correct sea-level pressure. For the ground rises over the Dordogne, making everything look closer than I'd expect. The houses are different, too. The walls appear sandier than in the Limousin; the stone redder, as though the sun had burned the skin of a grey old man. And then the land falls away, and my four thousand feet above sea level suddenly feels high after all, as if I had snorkled over the edge of a reef and into deep water.

A few minutes later, and the earth's surface rises again. I can see Sarlat aerodrome, perched on its plateau like a cake on the edge of a table.

'*Sarlat, Golf-Zulu-Alpha est un Luscombe en provenance de St Juste, à destination de vos installations. Je suis à cinq minutes au nord; je rappellerai vertical du terrain à mille-cinq-cents pieds fox-echo, Sarlat.*'

I land – whoopsadaisy, let's hope nobody saw that one – and head hungrily for the restaurant. A deep-fried hippo would go down a treat. But the place is deserted.

'*Bonjour, Monsieur,*' chirrups a voice behind me.

'Have you already stopped serving lunch?' I ask, turning to face a fiftysomething man with round specs and a smile that makes his whole face crinkle like a cobweb.

'About two years ago,' he sighs. 'The restaurant is gone.'

My lower lip must have started to tremble, because the

man adds quietly, 'But you're welcome to share *our* lunch, *Monsieur*, if you would like.'

'Well, I . . . I . . .'

'It's not much,' he adds, extending an arm towards a chart-table where two children have begun laying out cutlery, 'but there should be enough.'

I'm so busy feeling touched and blessed and unworthy that I almost forget to say yes. I can't remember the last time I spontaneously invited a foreign stranger to lunch, because I know I never have.

I start stammering about wanting to pay, but my host – Daniel – saves me from my own ungraciousness.

'What make is that *joli petit avion, Monsieur*?' he asks, pointing at the little aeroplane glinting in the winter sun.

'Luscombe Silvaire. From the USA. 1946.'

'So will you give us your beautiful plane, if we give you lunch?'

'It's a deal,' I laugh.

And the airport staff share their lunch with me. A home-made quiche, served by the children. A few tomatoes. Some hastily divided steaks and a grilled *magret de canard*, cooked by the lantern-jawed Chief Flying Instructor. A floppy lettuce. A ripe Camembert. *Tarte aux pommes*. Coffee prepared by the white-haired airport manager. It is so perfect, I feel like I've just wandered into one of those black-and-white films you long for on a rainy Sunday afternoon. I must learn to be more spontaneous.

Over coffee, I ask them about the town down in the valley.

'We hardly ever go there,' says Daniel sadly, 'because it's too expensive for us now. A Coke in town will cost you four euros.' I know why this is – it's the curse of *les Anglais* – though they are too polite to say so.

After lunch, I want to offer Daniel a flight in the Luscombe. But that won't leave me enough fuel to get back to St Juste. And if I refuel, I risk being late to play the organ for Mass.

I refuel. And up we roar, into the clear blue sky. At five hundred feet, I ask Daniel if he'd like to take control. That cobweb again. And he gives me a panoramic tour of his valley.

'What's the agriculture here?' I ask him, gazing down at the fields beneath us.

'There's nothing here now except tourism,' he replies, glancing at the instruments. 'Everything is English.' He doesn't sound bitter; merely wistful.

We land, and I keep the engine running while Daniel climbs out, thanking me profusely, his grey hair flying in the prop-blast.

'It is I who must thank you,' I yell, 'for giving my aeroplane back to me.'

He grins. 'Think of it as an extended loan,' he shouts. 'That way, you must come back.'

As I take off into the sunset once more, the deep voice of the airport manager crackles over the r/t: '*Merci pour la visite, Zulu-Alpha.* Hope we see you again.'

'Thanks, Sarlat,' I reply, almost with a lump in my throat. For I feel as if I am leaving an old friend.

My route home takes me over Lascaux, with its celebrated cave-paintings. I peer down at that unspectacular hill, and try to imagine a hairy little man creating beauty beneath it, by the light of an animal-grease lamp, seventeen thousand years ago.

The cave is locked up now. Too many people wanted to see it, and their breath was poisoning the paintings. So the French have buried a concrete facsimile two hundred yards away, to give visitors a similar experience without destroying the real thing. Sometimes I wish they could find a way of doing the same thing for the whole country, before it is too late.

# 45

## SEPTEMBER: THE STYMPHALIAN BIRDS

For months, ever since Gilles told me I must mow the field behind the house, I have been on the hunt for *une tondeuse autoportée d'occasion* – a second-hand ride-on mower – powerful enough to cope with the wonky terrain at La Folie. But tracking down the right gadget is easier said than done. Much as I love browsing collections of manly power-tools, I soon lose count of the number of times I have stood in the chatty melee that passes for a queue *chez* Roland, purveyor of chainsaws, brushcutters and other weapons of mass destruction to the *paysans* of Jolibois.

Roland is a lovely man, who looks more like a toy-maker, twinkling behind wire-rimmed specs, than a chainsaw-mender. Like almost every man over fifty in the region, he sports an impressive moustache, which he care-fully strokes when he wants to emphasize a point.

'You say your land is on a slope,' he says on one of my visits, clenching his fist and offering it to me in what looks like an impromptu game of scissors-paper-stone. The first time the man in the Renault garage did this to me, I got all confused and tried to bump knuckles with him. But now I know that I'm simply required to shake Roland's wrist, because his hands are oily. 'So just how steep is it?'

I stretch out my fingers and indicate the gradient with my forearm. '*Nee-hai-yaaaa!*' is what I don't say to Roland, though I am tempted. He doesn't look like a Bruce Lee fan.

'That's steep all right,' he murmurs, stroking his moustache. 'All I have is a machine that isn't powerful enough. But it may help until something suitable comes in.'

'You mean I can hire it?'

'No. I'll lend it to you.'

'But I feel I should pay you something.'

Roland waves away my objections. 'I'll get someone to deliver it,' he says. 'You live at La Folie? Is tomorrow OK?'

He doesn't ask me for a deposit, or even my phone number. We simply shake wrists and smile, and know that all will be well. I suppose that people must – once upon a time – have known that all would be well in England, too, in the days when we used to trust one another.

Next morning, a man who faintly reminds me of Buddy Holly in a green boiler-suit comes and mows several strips of my jungle for me whilst demonstrating how to use Roland's machine. 'As long as you stay in first gear, it should do the job,' says Buddy, pushing his glasses up his nose and shaking his quiff at me.

And so I begin. It's a long afternoon beneath the baking sun, and frankly, it's all a bit much for Roland's machine.

I'm on the penultimate strip when the beast begins to emit a series of haunting groans. After a final death-rattle, I am left sitting on a horrible silence.

Gilles is waiting for me and an *apéritif* as, dripping

with sweat, I haul the dead machine back to the barn.

'*Salut, Gilles,*' I pant, wiping my grimy hand on my shorts before shaking his. Gilles and I don't do wrists.

'What have you done?' he asks.

'I think I've broken Roland's *appareil.*'

'Not that. *Ça!*' Gilles is gesticulating at the field I've just mown.

'I mowed the field, just like you told me to.'

'But it's too hot for that now. The short grass will dry out and die. We've had no rain for weeks; none is forecast for a while to come. You should have left it well alone, so that the sheep could graze at the base of the long stems.'

I think about this for a moment. I consider setting fire to the mower. I even consider setting fire to Gilles. But in the end I say the only thing that makes any sense to me right now.

'Come on, Gilles. It's six o'clock. Let's have a drink.'

Next day, cap in hand, I go and tell Roland that I think I've broken his *autoportée.*

'*Ah, c'est pas grave,*' he says. 'Not to worry.'

'But I must pay for the repairs.'

'No, it's not your fault. The thing wasn't powerful enough. Hopefully something else will come in soon.'

Lovely man, Roland.

After lunch, there is an unexpected eclipse of the sun. Douglas the giant has come to call. Like me, he keeps a few chickens. But he has no cockerel. And he must have heard through the grapevine – from Fred the Viking, I presume – about my surfeit of roosters.

While we're standing there, admiring my quartet of young varmints – each still no bigger than a pigeon, and all doing their best to stay out of Titus's way – I tell Douglas about the mower, and my high estimation of Roland.

'Ah, now, well, you *say* that,' says Douglas. 'But I went

in there to look for a mower with Jill. And it was . . .'
Douglas removes his prayer-cap and scratches his head.
'. . . it was, cor, dear.'

'So what happened?'

'Well, we were interested in this mower, right?'

'Right.'

'And I suppose I must have just touched it with my
foot.' Douglas peers down into the far distance at his feet,
each of which is roughly the size of Luxembourg. 'I mean,
it wasn't as if I kicked it, or anything. I used my toe to
point something out to Jill. And I dunno, maybe I . . .' He
purses his lips.

'Anyway, suddenly the old boy's rushing over, isn't he?'
continues Douglas, 'and pointing at his machine, and
wagging his finger at how I've made this tiny little crack
in the plastic.'

Remembering the scene, Douglas raises his hands and
recalls what he attempted to say in his Estuary French.

'I said "*Non*, mate, *non, non, non je ne sais pas. Je n'ai
pas kické ton lawnmoweur. Vous avez le wrong idée.*" But
this bloke, Roland, was having none of it. Because then
his wife comes racing over, too, doesn't she?' Douglas's
face reddens at the memory. 'And she's backing him up.
They're both having a right go at me. But I can't seem to
get it through to them that it wasn't me. I mean, I know
I've got big Bronskis and everything, right, but I couldn't
have broken it just like that.

'So anyway, I'm about to walk out, because they're trying it on, and Jill grabs my arm, and then she starts having
a go at me, too. "Douglas," she says. "Douglas, just *listen*
for a second. They're not blaming you. They're saying they
know about the crack, and they're sorry. And the machine
therefore has seventy euros off. So what do you think?"

'I think I feel a right twerp.'

*

It's still light when I return to La Folie from this week's French class, and the chickens are pecking at the last few grains of corn in their feed-tray before turning in. Weary with subjunctives and conditionals, I pour myself a glass of cold Muscat from the fridge, and wander out on to the terrace. The cat comes and rubs herself against my legs, tail held high as a Rajah's parasol, and then jumps on to the table as she waits for me to sit and make a place for her on my lap. Today is the first birthday of my new life in France.

As the two of us gaze out over the trees in the valley, I try to remember how this view looked to me, exactly a year ago.

Did I see it more clearly then, when it was new to me? Or do I see it better now; now that the misty glow of romanticism has been wiped away like the condensation from a steamed-up bathroom mirror?

The inside of the house was once an organic whole to me, but now I am newly aware of it as a tangle of constituent parts. The pointed stonework. The insulated roof. The rendered walls. There is no piano to transform the summer sitting-room into a music room, for the floor remains stacked up, in bundles of broad oak, in one corner. And the scaffolding, gathering dust even now, lends the room the air of a building site, or the stage set for a post-industrial production of *Macbeth*.

A gaggle of young cockerels squawks past the terrace, running for their lives, pursued by Titus: four Stukas chased by a Blenheim. I don't like to think about it, but their days are numbered; all except whichever one I spare for Douglas. Behind me, the Rastafarians start up their evening bleating, hungry for their granulated *luzerne*. The grass has still not recovered from the incinerating blasts of summer, and my ill-timed mowing has only made things worse. Their desperate foghorns always make me feel a pang, especially Doris's. But yet more heart-rending is the fragile piping of the lambs, Camillo and Claudette, who still sound like children even though they are almost as big as their mums.

Smiling to myself, I gaze across at the trees, and at the shining whiteness of the clouds that decorate the beckoning sky. Perfect flying weather. If anything, I think this sky looks more beautiful to me now than it did a year ago.

Tomorrow will be a flying day. I have invited Sandrine, the younger daughter of Yves-Pascal and Ariane, to come for *un petit tour d'avion* in the Luscombe. Still in her early twenties, Sandrine is far too young and cool to be interested in a square thirtysomething like me. But it's fun to be in the orbit of her sparkle. And I can't help wanting to impress.

'*C'est ça?*' gulps Sandrine, fluttering her long eyelashes in horror at my fifty-nine-year-old two-seater dream machine. We are standing in the opalescent light of hangar three at St Juste, surrounded by dusty flying machines in varying states of airworthiness.

'*Oui, c'est magnifique, non?*' From her silence, I think she was expecting a LearJet.

'And why is nobody else flying, on such a wonderful day?' she asks.

Good question. I appear to have joined a flying club where no one actually flies. Among the regulars, there's Roger, who always wanted to fly, and Roland, who is building a kit-plane that looks as if it will never fly. Then there's Alain, with his kit-plane he no longer dares fly, Patrice with his plans-built plane that is too expensive to fly, Monsieur Rémy, with his detailed notes about the planes he used to fly, and wily old Marcel, with his tales of the planes he attempted to fly and invariably crashed. These chaps may not fly themselves, but they do like to gather at the aeroclub to lament the fact that no one flies any more.

With my head buried inside the Luscombe's cowling, I recognize the sound of Marcel's shuffling gait on the gravel of the hangar floor. Please, let the old fox not be in one of his moods.

'*Salut*, Marcel,' I say as cheerfully as I can manage. 'May I introduce my friend Sandrine?'

Hands deep in his pockets, grey hair slicked back, Marcel nods. A cigarillo twitches on his bottom lip.

'What are you looking in there for?' he growls at me.

'Ah, you know, checking the hoses are all properly connected, plugs all tight . . .'

'*Bof!*' Marcel rolls his eyes and pulls a face like a burnt omelette. 'You don't know anything about engines.'

'I know enough to feel confident about this one.'

'*Bof!*' He smirks at Sandrine. 'With the compressions on those cylinders, it's amazing that thing ever gets off the ground.'

'*Merci*, Marcel.' I glance at my young passenger, who has never flown in a small plane before. She manages a brave smile.

'The tyres look a bit flat,' snorts Marcel. 'What are you doing *now*?'

'I'm topping up the oil.'

'Have you got a leak?'

I resist the urge to pour several glugs of multigrade into his trouser pocket.

'Marcel, what's the problem? Why are you being like this, suddenly, today?'

The old man shrugs, and kicks the gravel. I can't help thinking about what Gilles told me recently: that rams rarely fight unless there are ewes in the same field, and cockerels will also happily co-exist until you mix them up with some shapely hens.

'Look, let's go flying together, one day,' I say, after a pause.

Marcel shrugs. 'It's not a bad aeroplane,' he mutters to Sandrine, and kicks at a piece of gravel on the hangar floor.

After we have pushed the Luscombe out on to the shimmering apron, I show Sandrine how to climb up into the tiny cockpit's right-hand seat.

'Put your right foot on the step, and grab the strut inside the windshield with your right hand. Now swing your left leg into the footwell, watching out for the control column on your side. *Et voilà: Bob est ton oncle.*'

While Marcel smirks and smokes in the shade of the hangar, I bake on the apron, running through the start-up procedure I have followed so many times before. Brakes on. Wheels chocked. Throttle set. Contact. With rivulets of sweat already dripping down my temples, I stand in front of the plane and give the prop a mighty swing. Nothing. Then another swing, and another, and – having waited until I am properly red in the face, and Marcel is beaming with misanthropic glee – the wheezy old Continental splutters into life.

And then we're taking off, and Sandrine gives a little squeal when the sun-browned earth falls away, with the engine roaring at full-tilt, and the Luscombe's nose pointing at outer space. As we surge high into the cold, clear air, the houses shrink beneath us until they're small enough to use in a game of Monopoly.

'Is he a friend of yours?' asks Sandrine, her voice crackling in my headset.

'Who? Marcel? Did he frighten you?'

'No,' she says firmly.

I smile at the sweetness of this young woman's trust. And I do not make the mistake of assuming that Marcel's mood today was because he is French and I am English. No, Marcel and his ilk exist everywhere: people who are only really happy when they are downright miserable. One day I should introduce him to Nigel.

Nor do I make the mistake of attempting to flirt with Sandrine. Well, maybe I flirt just a little, but only in what you'd call an avuncular way. Far safer to be a reliable old friend than an embarrassing suitor.

When we reach a thousand feet and turn downwind, I glance back at the aerodrome. On the apron, a tiny, stooped figure stands in front of the empty hangar. And it dawns on me that that could be me one day, if I do not learn to live my life bravely and generously: a tired, embittered old man, alone in France, muttering at the young as they spread their wings and fly.

A week later, on another furnace-hot day, I feel a different sort of dread as I drive down to Gilles's house. For today we are killing chickens. Or rather, Gilles is killing chickens, and I am there to learn. As a meat-eater, I feel I should know what it is to take an animal's life. The idea appals and frightens me, but only because I'm a hypocrite. I'll eat meat that has been shinily shrink-wrapped at the supermarket, without giving a second thought to the animal from which it came. So why am I so repelled by the prospect of having to kill one myself?

Up at La Folie, I have four young cockerels besides Titus, and – sentiment aside – that's at least three too many to keep. Even sooty Carrie has turned out to be a boy, and is therefore now called Harry, his black down exploding day by day into a burnished golden plumage.

Not only are the young chaps fighting amongst

themselves, but they're already beginning to display Oedipal longings for their mums. And Titus has no interest in playing Laius at the crossroads. On the contrary, he chases them down without remorse, immune to their screams of terror as he beetles after them, head lowered, beak cocked, savagely determined to show them what for. Catching one, he rips out a beakful of feathers from the back of its neck. Or, if he's in a particularly beastly mood, he goes for the coxcomb. And from the squeals that follow, this hurts considerably more than being stung in the goolies by a hornet.

'*Tu es prêt?*' asks Gilles, as I climb out of the Espace and we shake hands. Last night he stopped by La Folie to let me know that today was the day, and I was amazed – and strangely relieved – to hear him say that he finds it difficult to kill a chicken.

'*Prêt à tuer,*' I reply grimly. Josette appears from the kitchen, and we kiss each other lightly on both cheeks. She is walking almost normally now. And then there's an almighty flurry of flapping and shrieking and Gilles is dragging the first of three white cockerels out of its cage by the feet. So soon? I was hoping to have a bit more time to collect my thoughts.

I had expected the killing to be fast and brutal – just grab the head, twist and *crkkkk* – give or take the odd post-mortal tremor. But that is the English way.

Instead of wringing the bird's neck, Gilles hangs it up by the feet with a length of blue baling-twine attached to a low beam. The cockerel seems improbably calm, its white wings hanging from its body like an opened fan, its head pointed vertically downward like a spear. I can feel myself gritting my teeth, and I have pulled my shirt up over my mouth.

Then Gilles is pulling the next bird out of its cage, and

I wonder if it has any idea what is to come. It looks so big, so alive. I avoid catching its eye. Again, the blue twine is tightened around the long grey feet, and the heavy white body is left to hang beside the first like an unfurled umbrella. I don't know how much they recognize, upside down.

And then the third bird is making its final struggle for freedom, and my heart leaps as it almost evades Gilles, forcing one leg free of his grasp, and drawing blood from the back of his hand with its spur. I'm praying for it to escape, and hope that it doesn't. But Gilles has done this hundreds of times before, and the third cockerel is soon dangling from its blue twine beside its comrades.

Now there's not much time left, and my mouth is dry as a bell jangles in the distance and I can hear a train rumbling towards the level-crossing.

Gilles picks up a small knife, the sort you'd use for chopping a carrot, its blade worn thin from years of sharpening.

'*Qu'est-ce que tu f—?*' I begin to ask.

'*Et voilà,*' he says quietly, as he draws the knife out of the neck of the first chicken, and a ribbon of scarlet hangs down to the ground.

There is no struggle. Unflinching, the second chicken appears unaware of the life blood seeping away beside it. I watch Gilles take the bird's head gently in his left hand, and hear the rasp of blade on bone as he presses the knife through its neck with the other. It looks like he's opening an oyster. Another ribbon of blood. Another life ending. I'm never going to be able to do this.

And then the first chicken begins to flap violently, trying to raise itself, fighting against the suffocating blood in its throat. Other chickens in the farmyard approach, heads cocked, unmoved. Gilles steps backwards. I bite the inside of my cheek, watch blood on white feathers through narrowed eyes. Already, I've seen too much.

A third red ribbon connects the last bird to the earth.

Now the second victim is flapping violently. With a burst of frenetic flapping it manages to fly upwards for a second, but collapses again, exhausted at the end of its rope. The first is almost still. A series of spasms, each one weaker than the last. The third, too, begins to struggle upwards for breath, and for a moment – in a frantic froth of blood and feathers – all three birds make a last great effort for survival. And then they simply hang there, twisting lifeless on their blue strings. The other chickens peck at the fallen red ribbons before they melt into the earth.

It is finished.

Except that it isn't finished because now we have to pluck the dead birds. Josette emerges in rubber gloves. Gilles cuts each bird down, and dunks it unceremoniously in a blue bucket of steaming water. There is a bad smell, like a wet dog with a festering sore.

'This makes the plucking easy,' says Gilles. Then he hangs them up again, and each of us begins to rip the feathers off a bird.

Gilles is right. It is easy. The feathers come away from the skin just like pulling fluff off Velcro. There's a faint ripping sound, but this new smell is not as bad as I feared.

'These as well?' I ask nervously, indicating the big wing plumes, the flying feathers.

'*Oui, bien sûr*,' says Gilles.

The thick quills don't come out as easily as the down, and they leave behind ugly black puncture marks. How could something so alive suddenly be so dead?

Next comes the blow-torch – '*il faut les flamber*' – to scorch any hairs, roots and pimples that remain after the plucking. Gilles gently wields the flame as though he were spraying paint on to a model aeroplane, and – as frazzle replaces gloop - I'm happy to see the chickens looking a little bit less like murdered living creatures, and a little more like something inanimate you might barbecue.

As a child, I remember seeing my father gutting a salmon he'd caught when we were on holiday in Scotland. The sight of all those gleaming, squishy, fetid nasties squelching and bursting between his fingers was as much as I could bear. I would have imagined that gutting a chicken would be even worse. But my senses are so numb, after what I've just witnessed, that I could probably remove the adenoids of the Prince of Wales without so much as a blink.

'Why can't men bring themselves to gut chickens?' Josette asks Gilles teasingly.

'Killing them, that's our job,' says Gilles with a cough. '*N'est-ce pas, Michael?*'

# 46

## OCTOBER: THE CHIMAERA

Serge's wife, Jacquie, was right to warn me about snakes. Hot and grimy from an afternoon spent splitting logs with the axe, I've only come into the dark bathroom to splash some water on my face. And there is this grey-green *thing*, furled around the taps on the basin like a mooring rope. A foot and a half long, thick as a bicycle pump. Right between the *Savon de Marseille* and my shaving cream. A viper.

> *A snake came to my water-trough*
> *On a hot, hot day, and I in pyjamas for the heat,*
> *To drink there.*

Slowly, I back away. Then freeze, as a forked tongue flickers from the dragon head, and the coiled rope begins to unwind. Please let him not disappear into that hole under the bath, or I swear I shall never wash again.

I don't know what to do, short of going to fetch Martha and Mary, and leaving them to tear the creature apart.

You'd think I could just coax him back out through the window. But each time I approach, he slides a little further towards the hole under the bath. In an ideal world, I would phone International Rescue and wait for Scott and Virgil to arrive in Thunderbirds 1 and 2. But this is rural France, so I phone my old school friend, Survival-Kit Toby. Now Toby is an animal-lover, but he also happens to have trained with the Gurkhas in Borneo, and has eaten all sorts of snakes in his time.

'Are you sure it's a viper,' he asks, 'and not some poor little grass snake?'

'I'm sure he's a viper. He's got a knowing glint in his eye. Should I try and coax him outside?'

'Not if you don't know what you're doing. No, you've got to kill him.'

'Right. *What?*'

'Bash him over the head with a big stick. A cricket bat would be ideal.'

'I've got to kill a snake?'

'Bludgeon the bastard. Don't hold back.'

'Toby, I'm not sure that . . .'

'Look, even vipers have their place in God's Great Scheme and all that, but not in your bathroom.'

'Right.'

'And Michael, don't be fooled if he acts stunned. Be ready to hit him again.'

'Right.'

I've done some beastly things to my fellow creatures in my time – I used to work as a theatre critic, after all – but I've never had to kill a snake in cold blood. There wasn't much of a call for this kind of thing in East Dulwich. And watching Gilles kill his chickens the other day doesn't seem to have helped – any more than does the knowledge that I must, before long, do the same with four of my own. Nevertheless, I can feel my upper lip stiffening as I don my wellies and my chainsaw gloves.

Distant snare drums rattle. Far trumpets swell. Clutching a great big stick that I have found in the barn, I tiptoe back to the bathroom.

The snake hasn't moved. But my Wilkinson Sword Activ Gel is in the way, so I have to run and fetch the barbecue tongs to shift the canister. I don't think Sigourney Weaver ever had to do this in *Alien*.

I watch the snake: placid, handsome and doing nothing to aggress me, save for the unfortunate fact that he or she is *here*, now, and constitutes a threat. If not to me, then to the next guest – a child, perhaps – who enters the bathroom.

After taking careful aim, I shut my eyes as I drive the snake's skull against the wall with the stick; hold it pinioned there. I can feel the wood tremble as the body begins to flail and spasm like a hooked salmon.

Teeth clenched, I strike again. I want it to be over soon. Only this time I miss, and the snake slithers into the basin. Again, again. I don't mind if I shatter the porcelain, just so long as it's dead.

At last the snake hangs limp from the basin, its stretched, gleaming skin now as matt and wrinkled as a baby that has aged eighty years in a day. I feel roughly the same myself.

Three minutes later, the beast starts putting itself back together. Oh God, Oh Montreal: I've taken on the Terminator. The taut glossiness returns. So does the flailing and the coiling, stronger and faster than ever.

Panicking, I strike it some more.

This time the poor creature really is dead. When I lift it by the tail, it flops like a lank entrail, or a chicken on a length of blue twine. I feel fear and pity, but no catharsis. I leave it in a bucket on the step.

Ten minutes later, I pick up the snake once more. Necessary as it may have been, I feel ashamed at what I have done. And birch me with hawthorn if it doesn't suddenly begin to coil and twist itself upwards yet again, drawing back its head as if about to strike me with those mangled jaws. Spooked, I drop it and run.

Next day, the pretty *pharmacienne* refuses to come out from behind the homeopathy display until I promise her that the snake in my tupperware box is dead.

'I want to confirm it's a viper,' I explain, 'and buy an antidote.'

'*Oui, c'est une vipère.*' She grimaces, peering into the box. 'There are a lot this year. And the antidote is chickens.'

'*Excusez-moi?*'

'Chickens kill snakes.' Well, yes, I know. But I have thirteen chickens (some of whom may be about to receive a last-minute stay of execution). And this blighter still managed to find his way into my thunderbox.

'Can't I have a serum, too?' I ask. 'I live alone, out of town, and may need to inject myself.'

'There used to be a serum,' says *Madame*. 'But more people were dying from the injection than from the snake.'

'*Ah, bon.*'

'Better to stay as still as possible, and call the fire brigade,' she says. She also sells me a red vacuum pump that looks like a water-pistol, for extracting venom, and tells me I can buy snake repellent from the *droguerie* in the Rue du Coq.

'*Ah, bon.*'

Later that night, I spend a few minutes with Titus and the girls in the *poulailler*. It feels the safest place to be right now.

'Now look, everybody,' I begin. The girls squawk to attention on their perches. 'You have a job to do out there, and I'm worried you're not doing it.'

Silence. Thirteen pairs of eyes glint at me, wondering what I'm on about this time.

'All right, boys and girls,' I sigh. 'At ease.'

Shutting the chicken-house door behind me, I can hear my protectors clucking indignantly at one another within. I presume they're totting up all the vipers they saved me from today. The ones I never saw.

So I go to the *droguerie*, where an old lady – tiny, bird-like and pretty – in the queue behind me asks me why on earth I want to repel snakes.

'You should be stroking them, or hanging them around your neck, *Monsieur*,' she says.

'Well, yes. But only if they're dead.'

The *droguiste* confirms that many people have been asking for snake repellent this year.

'Last week there was a lady who found a viper in her kitchen-utensil drawer. It slithered out and hid behind the kitchen units. And she made her husband dismantle the entire kitchen to find it.'

'Ah, well. At least it's rare to hear of anyone being bitten,' I say, waiting for them to nod sagely and agree with me.

'I know of two, personally,' says the old lady. 'A four-year-old boy, who died. And an older child, paralysed.' She sounds quite cheerful about this.

Oh, good. 'I think I'll take two pots of that stuff, please,' I tell the man behind the counter.

Still no rain. Every morning this week, the cat and I have been woken by a deep fog-horn just outside the bedroom window. It's the bleating of a sheep, but pitched more like a bass-baritone than one of my tenor Rastafarians. And sure enough, whenever I go to the window to investigate, there are two or three fat white ewes munching in the parched flower beds: more escapees from over the hill.

Today, when I chase them down the drive, I come face to face with a muscular lad with big shoulders and a face lined with concern, who is on his way up. I recognize him as Young Boulesteix. I've heard that he took over his father's farm a few months ago. I'm not sure if he has also inherited his father's Anglophobia.

'Sorry,' he says, shaking my hand. 'No matter what I do, they keep escaping.'

'*Ce n'est pas grave*,' I reply.

'I've lost ten,' he continues, correcting me. 'Are the others up there, too?' He points up the drive to La Folie, searching my face for signs of hidden sheep. Boulesteix is that rare thing: a young man starting out as a sheep-rearer in rural France, when others are stopping in their droves. Last summer, he was a cheery, strapping lad, tucking up the sleeves of his T-shirt to show off his muscles. Right now, he looks like an old man.

'I'll have a good look,' I tell him. 'Give you a call if I do.'

Later, I drop round to Gilles's house for *un apéro*. In silence, we watch the weather forecast on his big black television, which looks as incongruous in his ancient kitchen as a Dalek in a cowshed. Further unbroken sunshine is forecast for the next few days.

'*C'est grave*,' he mutters. 'Usually there'd be grass for the sheep until November, and they've had none since July. If this carries on, even the trees are going to start dying.'

It's true. For weeks, the leaves of the tall acacias in front of La Folie have been fox-marked with brown and gold.

Some of the fruit trees have gone further still, and look as if they're getting ready for winter, not autumn. The splashing river at the bottom of the hill fell silent months ago. The Rastafarians stand bemused in their field, their black shapes standing out against the frazzled grass like distant wildebeest on the plains of Africa. They gaze at the desert that surrounds them, and then they peer at me. What have we done to offend you?

I give them a granulated feed morning and night, so they will not starve. But they seem as bored and irritable as teenagers. It's bad enough having to eat hay in winter – Ouessants despise hay – but when the summer lushness turns to dust, a sheep's life is bleak indeed.

Though I am not a proper farmer myself, I am close enough to the parched landscape to feel the farmers' anguish, and the misery of their beasts.

In the afternoon, I receive another visitation from Young Boulesteix's ewes. I'm almost tempted to let them stay for a snack, but instead I shoo them off down the drive. Boulesteix is down there once again, this time with his mother beside him, though she looks far less smiley than usual.

'We're so sorry, *Monsieur*,' she says, wringing her hands. '*C'est la sécheresse*. All the grass is scorched. They've nothing to eat. That's why they keep running away.'

'I've given them hay,' adds her son. 'But that doesn't seem to be helping. And we'll run out of hay, too, before the end of winter.'

I know they really need to be giving the sheep a granulated feed, to fatten the young lambs and strengthen the expectant mums. But this is an expensive business. Gilles says he's been getting through almost a tonne of feed a week.

I walk back up to La Folie, feeling helpless. A few minutes later I hear Boulesteix shouting at his sheep. Only he's not shouting. He's screaming at them, with an edge of despair in his voice that frightens me.

Let it rain, and soon.

## 47

## NOVEMBER: GATHERING DARKNESS

The colours grow warmer as the days at last grow cooler. Autumn blows over the hill behind La Folie. The last remaining splashes of green become golden; the yellows darken to red. The traffic lights are changing once more.

As a child, autumn was my favourite season. Now that I am a grown-up, thirty-eight years closer to the end of my life, it is spring that calls out to me.

Back then, I cherished the rich Victorian hues of the leaves as they turned, warming my retinas, spreading their crackling carpet upon the pavement. The sharp outlines of the trees and the houses; of the Surrey church-tower where I rang the bells with the only local people I ever knew, and felt I was touching history as we hauled on our ropes and rang changes from another world.

There is still beauty in these colours. But, like the butterflies flitting out their last hours, it will all be over so soon.

The rains come at last.

It is not a deluge. It is not enough.

But it's a start. I can't remember when I was last so pleased to see mud.

I never saw the coming of winter like this before. I never saw winter as death. In London, I was merely aware of the weather turning cold and wet, the trees shedding their leaves, the long nights drawing in. It didn't occur to me that in the shortening of the days lay the falling of the leaves.

I know that every day further from my birth brings me a day closer to my own death. I wonder if I will notice it creeping up upon me, in slow motion. Or will I be spinning in a car across a dual carriageway, thinking about the approaching juggernaut, or spinning in a Tiger Moth towards the earth, with a windscreen full of trees?

Nature withers slowly on the bough. And we humans, we animals, can be so swiftly snuffed out.

Last night, I went to put three of my four young cockerels into the concrete rabbit hutches behind the chicken house. I have asked around locally, and no one can offer them a good home, except Douglas, who confirms that he is prepared to take one to squire his four bald-necked hens.

In the darkness, I pulled the lads from their perches alongside their brothers and sisters, father, mothers and aunts. I know it is foolish to anthropomorphize a creature with a brain the size of a broad bean, but chickens are special creatures, with a curiosity that always touches my heart. They just can't resist something new; an open car door, an upturned rock. And they like to chat, too.

Separated from the rest, incarcerated in the rabbit hutches left behind by a previous owner of La Folie, their shrieks of outrage echoed out across the moonlit fields as I ate a late supper. So I turned up my CD of Ashkenazy playing Chopin just a little louder, and tried not to think of death camps. And I felt sick in my stomach, knowing what I knew. To each of them I gave a final meal of a little grain and some water.

'Not too much grain,' Gilles warned me, 'or you have a frightful mess – and a bad smell – when you gut them.'

Harry is my favourite, but there is another – The Blue Max – who is the biggest and strongest and most impressive. If Douglas wants to breed from his future cockerel, then I owe it to him to give him the best I have.

## 48

## DECEMBER: THE BLUE TREES

My search for a dishy French *copine* has come to nothing. My ill-judged attempts to chat up the vampish *coquine* in the tourist office are behind me. The white-wellied Botticelli who used to work behind the fish counter at Carrefour has moved on. And I never did go dancing with the lovely Marianne from the bank, after she turned out to be happily married.

Zumbach was right: I have about as much chance of finding the woman of my dreams while I am living here in Jolibois, as little Gaston has of finding one of Young Boulesteix's fat ewes – the ones he has been ogling from afar for days – munching hay in his field.

I have therefore decided to stop looking. I'm happy, after all. And I take it that the universe will, in its wisdom, provide. Eventually. Trouble is, it's tricky to explain this to the locals. In East Dulwich, I grew used to my female friends attempting to match-make for me, but the men in Jolibois are far, far worse.

'You need to get married, Michael,' says Luc the *pâtissier*, over dinner at his house. Luc is not being funny or clever. He is just attempting to set me right, as he might straighten a picture on the wall. Something must be done, if social symmetry is to be maintained.

'But Luc, it's better to remain single than to spend a life-time with the wrong woman,' I protest. I'm looking for a soul-mate, not a cell-mate. He glances at Céline, his wife of thirty-seven years, and smiles sympathetically at me, as if I had just told him my plan for extracting sunbeams out of cucumbers.

Then there is Hubert, the gravel-voiced Jack-Daniels-gargler who taught me the gamut of French profanities on a tennis court last year. Despite my protestations that I'm not desperate to conjugate, Hubert tells me that I really should check out Véronique, one of the check-out girls at Champion.

'Ah, Michael, she is *very* available,' he whispered. From the way Véronique has begun to tousle her hair and smile coquettishly at me as she passes my bananas through her laser beam, I have an uncomfortable feeling that Hubert has told her the very same thing about me.

Isabelle, up at the big house, is doing her best to help, too. Over the past few weeks she has twice invited me to dinner, ostensibly because her children want to see me, but I think more because she rather hopes I may rescue her beautiful niece, Éliane, from her singledom. This may sound arrogant, but the way Éliane and I have twice been left by ourselves in the vast *salon*, while the others whisper and titter in the kitchen, cannot simply be so that we can admire the etchings.

I feel a bit like one of those giant pandas that used to get ferried into London Zoo every few years, in the hope that Sing-Sing might finally mate. Éliane and I chat away about London and Paris, and – lovely though she is – there is little enough chemistry between us that the prospects of our getting down to any physics or biology together remain entirely outside the curriculum.

Jérôme, down from Paris, invites me to lunch, and I explain my predicament.

'You do know the French look with suspicion on men who live alone, don't you?' he warns, chuckling to himself as he pours me a glass of wine. 'I should know.'

'But I have chickens and sheep, too,' I protest.

From the glance he throws back at me, I fear that this will not be enough. And then – too late – I remember the nine horses and the nine bicycles.

'And you, Jérôme,' I continue, changing the subject. 'What is *your* news?'

'Some wonderful news,' he says, his eyes sparkling. 'The grandchildren are coming.'

'*Ah, Jérôme, c'est formidable*,' I reply, thrilled for my friend. 'And how many of them will come?'

'All of them. All nine,' he says, leaning back in his chair and basking in pleasure at the thought.

And so we talk and talk, and I am struck by how lucky Jérôme's children and grandchildren are, to have this wonderful man devoted to creating a haven for them; a haven where, I sense, he is already dreaming of how their grandchildren, and their grandchildren's grandchildren, will be able to come and play. It feels a relief to be able to share his happiness, and not to dwell on my own wistful solitude.

Later, back at La Folie, the cat comes and rubs herself against my legs, wanting her supper. Martha and Margot tap angrily on the cat-flap with their beaks, demanding the same service. But as I wander out to feed the sheep, only six of the Rastafarians come charging down the field to greet me. For blow me down if old Gaston isn't nuzzling up to the haunches of a beautiful white ewe almost twice the size of him, who has somehow snuck over the fence to join the adoring Othello. I've no idea how they managed this. But I can't help laughing. And feeling strangely encouraged, too.

'Don't you get scared,' asks Marie-Claude, my scary cleaning lady, when Tuesday comes around again, 'living up here on your own?'

'No,' I laugh, and wonder if I'm lying. 'There aren't too many drug-crazed robbers armed with bazookas here in Jolibois.'

'Ooh, I'm not sure about that,' she says reassuringly.

'Ah.'

'I suppose it makes a difference that you're a man,' she huffs. I puff out my chest and resist the urge to grunt, '*Moi, Tarzan. Vous, Marie-Claude.*'

'*Et ce n'est pas monotone,*' she asks, 'with nobody to talk to?'

'I talk to the chickens.'

Marie-Claude laughs nervously. I think she thinks the funny Englishman is joking.

At La Folie, despite the departure of Georges *la fouine* from my bedroom ceiling, I sometimes have such vivid dreams of an old couple living at the other end of the house – which, in my nightmares, they are dismantling stone by stone – that I begin to wonder if the renovations haven't disturbed a few ghosts.

'It's quite obvious what this is about,' says the Eminent Psychiatrist, when I make the mistake of sharing my dream on the phone. 'You're lonely, Michael. So your unconscious is inventing imaginary companions.'

'But it's not as if we're sitting down to dinner or playing poker together,' I protest.

'Even so . . .'

The truth is that I have now made more friends among the locals than I ever expected, mostly thanks to the tennis club. People such as Le Grand Mermoz, the beery-cheery force of nature who runs the local hardware store and plays tennis as if he were fighting the Crusades. Blaise, the gruffly gentle PE teacher who roars around Jolibois on his Harley-Davidson, and his wife, the Proustian Madeleine, a sparkling firework of a woman, whose beaming face always seems to be illuminated from within. Seurel, ostensibly a guard on the trains to Paris and Lyon and beyond, but a thoughtful philosopher, too, who always picks up what I am trying to say long before anyone else catches on. Maxim the welterweight boxer, who is really an economics teacher, and whose twanging Toulouse accent is as much of a challenge to me as his sliced backhand. Claude the electrician, who sometimes stays for lunch after working on the wiring in the summer sitting-room.

Yet I do retain a niggling sense of separateness, as I struggle to forge those intimate connections that go beyond words. And I am still not dreaming in French. So I'm thrilled when Claude invites me to dinner at his house, with several of the others from the tennis club. Here I also meet Katya, Claude's husky-voiced wife; Jeanne, the spirited consort of Le Grand Mermoz; and Kiki, a twice-divorced heavy smoker who strikes me as falling into the 'dangerously attractive' category. Especially since one of her ex-husbands, I am told, is a *gendarme*.

'I used to be such a nice person,' laments Jeanne, to much laughter, 'until I met my husband.' And then the laughter dies, because we realize that she is being serious.

'What do you say to that, Mermoz?' asks Blaise, elbowing his friend in the ribs.

Undaunted, and smiling bravely, Mermoz looks around

the table, his piercing blue eyes travelling from face to face.

'What I say is this,' he says. 'Why don't we all go skiing together for the weekend in February?'

'*Formidable! Impeccable! Nickel!*' comes the response from every side except Jeanne's, who smiles wearily at her husband's latest inspiration.

'And if you play your cards right with Kiki, Michael,' continues Mermoz, in a mischievous stage-whisper, 'your luck could be in.'

I blush, and cravenly do my best to avoid eye contact with Kiki for the rest of the evening.

Jolibois is fluffing up its feathers for Christmas once more. In the manner of a sweet old lady who always wears the same string of pearls to Midnight Mass, the familiar ropes of naked bulbs have been strung across the Rue du Coq. I'll bet people gazed up at those very lights in 1955. The trees outside the church are slung with twinkling lamps, too, much like the ones outside the Dorchester on Park Lane.

Well, almost. There's a naivety about the Jolibois version that I find irresistible, especially when combined with the clumsy Christmas-tree offcuts that have been tied to the railings up and down the road. It looks as if Pike and Godfrey have attempted to camouflage them, under the supervision of Corporal Jones. ('You can't be too careful, Captain Mainwaring.')

Inside the church, Fabrice the organist has once again decorated the crib. This is always a treat, because Fabrice is trained in both plumbing and electrics, so we have green and orange lights to illuminate the baby Jesus, and real water gushing over a mill wheel beside the three kings. I like to think this is where the shepherds wash their socks by night. And if people sing loud enough, they might even drown out the buzzing of the Bethlehem waterworks.

'What do you think of the blue trees, Michael?' asks Le Grand Mermoz's wife, Jeanne, over dinner at their house. With her jaunty yellow jumper and bobbed hair, she looks younger and somehow less weary than she did at Claude's the other night.

'*Les arbres sont bleus?*' I ask, glancing out of the window into the darkness.

'Not *those* trees. The ones at the top of the Rue du Coq.'

Now I come to think about it, I *did* notice two glowing blue cones there yesterday. In place of last year's noble firs, these illuminated spikes looked sleek and threatening, and it never occurred to me that they were trees. You certainly wouldn't expect an elf in a jingly hat to step out from behind them. You'd expect Ann Robinson.

'*Ils sont pas mal,*' I offer.

'*Ils sont moches!*' snorts Jeanne with an amused sneer. 'And what do they lead to? A deserted old street with a few branches stapled to the railings. *C'est fou!*'

To be honest, I just like the fact that someone has gone to so much trouble to decorate the town. But Jeanne is right. One of the reassuring things about living deep in the countryside is that what you see tends to be what you get. Metaphor is a city construction; nature plays it straight. Trees are made of wood, not fibreglass. Cows are made of beef, not concrete. This is what I love about the story of Letellier, a grizzled Normandy farmer who, at Christmas each year, leads several of his cows into troubled urban estates, so that children can touch them. 'The cow represents the earth,' says Letellier in an article in *Le Populaire*. 'I want to restore hope in people who feel they have no roots.'

In one Paris suburb, an old woman from Algeria came

out to stroke Letellier's cows, because they reminded her of the ones she had reared in her own country. She said she had been living in France for seven years. And this was the first time she had ever set foot outside her apartment.

Back at La Folie, I sit at the kitchen table, not quite ready for bed. Trees and farm animals are time-machines: at once quiveringly real, yet timeless and universal, too. And as human beings, we appear to have a weakness for those rare and beautiful moments of simplicity when we feel ourselves connected to the past, sharing precisely the same experience – or witnessing the very same view – that someone else must have seen or felt, decades or even centuries ago.

I have felt it when flying a Tiger Moth high over the fields of Kent, or playing the pipe organ in Strasbourg that Mozart once played. Here at La Folie, I feel it when I watch the sleet soaking into the feathers of my chickens, as they peck for grain in the doorway of the ancient barn. The sheep trotting after me as I bring them another bundle of hay. The shadows rustling as I trudge down the old footpath through the woods at night, swinging my oil lamp and telling myself that I am not afraid.

At the weekend, when I fly to England to join my parents and brothers for Christmas, I will feel it when we find hidden in the Christmas pudding, yet again, the very same old sixpences and silver threepenny bits that my great-great-grandmother used to hide. And I feel it now, as I sit at Zumbach's old kitchen table and gaze out at the dark shapes of my flock silhouetted against the frosty hillside, just as they might have been, on such a night as this, two thousand years ago.

# 49

## JANUARY: COLD COMFORT FARM

Christmas has come and gone, and still the weather grows colder, dashing my hopes that my second winter alone at La Folie will be easier than the first. This is good; I wouldn't have it any other way. But when the Rastafarians gallop down the hill to greet me each morning, I notice with a pang that they have turned from black to white overnight. The winter sitting-room is heading in the opposite direction, as the stove-belched soot blackens the whitewashed walls. The summer sitting-room, meanwhile, reminds me of a giant fridge with a dusty, cement floor. Even when it is finished, it will be uninhabitable when there's an 'r' in the month.

Outside the back door, Titus and the girls rage at me, as if I am personally responsible for making the ground so chilly underclaw. It wasn't half as cold as this last year. I feel for Silent Mary in particular, who currently looks a bit like a pheasant that has just been sucked through a jet engine.

Mary is the gentlest, steadiest chicken a chap could wish for. She is one of those shrinking souls you don't even notice when you walk into a room, and who – while everyone else is partying – quietly goes and does all the washing-up. I think she must have been born without a voice, because she never, ever clucks. Instead, she suffers in silence, whether it's children trying to pick her up or Titus flattening her with his ardour. She is also the only chicken I've ever seen who can do the Charleston.

But Mary has not been right for a long time. She waddles around with her stomach dragging on the ground, as if her crop were full of lead shot. She smells funny, too. I believe I once read about an ailment called Sour Crop, and treating it with Epsom Salts. Yet I can't be sure. I ask around, and none of the local farmers is quite sure either. As a last resort, I take Mary to the vet.

Gilles hates it when I take any of my sheep to the vet, because he says it's too expensive, and the vet only really knows about poodles and guinea-pigs. But the vet saved old Gaston when he had pneumonia last year, so I have faith in him. Obviously, if I tell Gilles I'm taking a *chicken* to the vet, he'll never speak to me again.

The vet examines Mary. 'Nope, definitely not a poodle,' I can see him thinking. 'And probably not a guinea-pig, either.' He ascribes her problem to an 'untreatable internal lesion' which, he says, doesn't seem too serious. Thus reassured, I ignore the problem and assume it will just go away. But the freezing weather continues, and – as far as I can tell – the problem doesn't go away.

'*Brrr . . . Ça caille*,' says Céline from the *boulangerie*, as she and I arrive at the church for the Saturday-evening Mass, she wearing seventeen overcoats, I weighed down with a foot-high stack of organ music and a spare pair of shoes.

'You can say that again,' I reply, taking a wild guess at her drift as we peck each other on both cheeks.

'You're not planning to play *all* that music, are you?' she asks nervously.

'No, but I can never make up my mind beforehand.'

'Is that why you have two pairs of shoes, too?'

'Ah, the shoes are for the organ. These . . .' (I gaze down at my clumpy Timberlands, each encased in a thick Cornish pasty of mud) '. . . are not much good for the pedals.'

Raphaël le Prêtre arrives, and we all shake hands.

'*Brrr, ça caille,*' I tell him.

Raphaël bursts out laughing.

'What's so funny?' I ask, feeling like Eliza Doolittle. 'Did I get it wrong?'

'*Non, non,*' he says. 'It just sounds funny, coming from *un Anglais.*' As I stomp up the stairs to the organ, I make a mental note to use my new phrase as often as possible.

At least the plummeting temperatures make me feel better about having installed such expensive roof insulation in the *maison des amis*. Serge the mason has covered the bare tiles between the gnarled oak beams with a combination of thick Rockwool and high-tech foil-cum-foam, which I'm sure will do a splendid job of conserving the warmth that I have not yet worked out how to create. Indeed, in a masterpiece of energy efficiency, my current scheme for this part of the house doesn't involve any heating at all.

'Have you noticed that it's warmer outside than it is in here?' asks Claude, the tennis-playing electrician, blowing on his hands. I take this as a generous compliment to my insulation. It's so cold that I have even considered buying a second-hand tennis umpire's chair, so that I can sit closer to the ceiling.

My heating problem extends to the other end of the

house, too; the one that is technically habitable. It's only a small glitch, but both the kitchen and winter sitting-room generally fill with smoke within an hour of my lighting the wood-burning stove. I even consider driving to St Juste to borrow the carbon-monoxide detector from my plane, since I never look at it in mid-air. After all, I'd hate to poison the cat. And so – tired of sitting at my desk with tears streaming down my face – I decide that reparations are in order.

After giving the chimney a jolly good sweep with a set of old poles and *un hérisson* that I've found at the back of the barn, I make one of my regular trips to Le Grand Mermoz's hardware shop. Snow falls lightly from a pewter sky as I drive down to Jolibois. What's required today is some expensive glass-fibre jointing-cord to replace all the manky old rope on which sit the stove's heavy iron plates.

Once I've laboriously glued the new cord into place, I glue my fingers together, and then glue myself to the kitchen taps.

Some time later, I am free to fire up the stove.

The result of my fix is immediate and impressive. The beast now blows out twice as much smoke as before. After a day of this, the cat's nostrils have gone black and, when I catch sight of myself in the bathroom mirror, I look like Yosemite Sam after he's just been blown up by Bugs Bunny.

On balance, I think I may have overdone the glue. So it's back to Mermoz's shop for some thicker jointing-cord. '*Re-bonjour!*' says the sit-com lady on the till, who must think I'm stalking her.

Back at La Folie, the snow is now falling thick and fast. The phone rings, and it's Ralph the artist on the line, calling from his centrally heated townhouse in Jolibois.

'Are you all right up there, darling?' he asks. 'We've been worried about you.'

'Yes, thank you, sir,' I yell. 'All's well here at Ice Station La Folie.'

'You're not getting too cold, are you?' he says. 'I mean, you know, just phone us. You can come and stay if you want.'

This is a tempting offer ('Say yes! Say yes!' implores the cat, wild-eyed, clawing at my trousers), because Olga the spy is a wonderful cook, and I like the idea of sharing house-room with Ralph's paintings. But I haven't forgotten that I've come to France to toughen myself up. So I'm not about to start complaining about being stuck out here on my tod in a little bit of a blizzard. Especially since Nicholas gave me a splendid furry hat for Christmas, with ear-flaps that may be worn in either the up or down position.

No matter that the temperature in my bedroom barely climbs above freezing, nor that the house is about as draught-free as an international draughts convention. I get an atavistic thrill from staggering back from the barn with another armful of logs, thinking of all the French *paysans* over the centuries who have done this before me, all muttering the same expletive as they have slipped in the same mud. The only really painful aspect of the cold is watching the misery of the chickens outside, and Mary in particular, who has timed her annual moult for the worst possible time of year.

The cat opens one green eye as I barge through the door with my logs, my face glistening with sleet. 'About time, too,' she gestures with an imperious blink, as cats over the centuries must have done, in this very room, before her.

Whatever the cat may think, I know that facing up to the cold is part of the pleasure of living in my ramshackle old house. If many have lived this life before me, others, I fervently hope, will follow. For I feel as if I am in touch with some secret source of goodness here, and I have no wish to keep it all to myself.

As I stand at the back door, I lay my cheek on the cold glass, and gaze out at the snow. It's so beautiful that my first emotion is a kind of wistful longing, a craving to share this scene, these next fifteen seconds, with someone else. And then I look again, look a little longer, trying not to label what I see as beautiful.

I look out at the gnarled old trees, and the pile of discarded stones I know so well, and the snow blowing in all directions. These are my familiars now, these trees, these stones, these snowflakes. We have been through something together, though we have never spoken, and never will.

I trudge out to the sheep with another armful of frozen hay, my fingers throbbing as I pluck fat chunks of ice out of their water trough. The stove finally fixed, I shove another log on to the fire, and think about how lucky I am. Winter is here, and we're keeping the home fires burning at Ice Station La Folie. Let it snow, let it snow, let it snow.

## 50

## THE BEGINNING OF THE END

After the snow comes the rain. It has been lashing down for a night and a day, and – once again – most of it appears to have flowed under the back door into the kitchen. The good news is that the kitchen has a stone floor. The bad news is that so much water has entered via this route that it has flowed right on through the kitchen, politely turned ninety degrees to negotiate the steps into the winter sitting-room, and trickled on out under the front door.

I am not exaggerating. I have never seen the film *A River Runs Through It*, and now I don't want to. La Folie is the first house I've ever lived in where you can play Pooh Sticks while reading the newspaper.

The cat clatters in through the cat-flap, skips a few paces through our new water feature, and freezes. She glares at me with unfeigned disgust before shaking her dripping paws, one by one, into a blur. I can see why dancers call this move an *entrechat*.

By early evening, the rain has cleared and the temperature plummets. The sky is glitter spilled on to black velvet as I trudge out to put the chickens to bed. I don't remember the nights ever being this dark in East Dulwich, where the stars were never more than a handful of dim pinpricks in the sodium gloom.

The Egg Squad are still jockeying for position on their perches when I enter the chicken house with my oil lamp. Everyone wants to be in the middle of the top row, where it's warmest. Except Titus, bless him, who is still on sentry duty by the door. I collect four eggs from the nesting boxes, murmur my congratulations and gently close the door of the chicken house behind me.

Next morning, I am planning to head down the autoroute to Limoges, to buy a heater. The radio thermometer says it's minus-five degrees outside. Yet as I gaze out of the window, I can see that it is raining. Not hail, not sleet, not snow, but *rain*.

I now do something very foolish, as anyone who has ever experienced freezing rain will immediately recognize. I step out of the front door to investigate. A second later – *whumpf whumpf whumpf* – both feet have slid out from under me and I am bum-skating down the three ice-slicked steps like a canoeist shooting rapids.

The cat, hearing the fall of man, rockets out of the barn and gallops up the steps to the cat-flap. *Big* mistake, as anyone who has ever experienced freezing rain – me, for instance – will immediately recognize. Clawing for traction like Scooby Doo, she skids backwards off the second step and ends up in the flower bed. This just makes me roar with laughter. Not sharing the joke, the cat casts me a look of such bitter hatred that I fall silent and curse my puerile sense of humour.

At the second attempt, the cat slithers up the steps on her belly, commando-style, and inveigles herself through the cat-flap, leaving me wishing I could do the same. But every ice-slicked surface is so slippery that the simple process of re-entering my own home has turned into something out of *Jeux Sans Frontières*. I can already hear the commentator crying with annoying laughter. I think it's safe to say that Great Britain will not be playing their joker on this one.

Next day, the local paper reports that 114 people broke their wrists in Haute-Vienne following the freezing rain, and that the autoroute to Limoges became such a skating rink that it had to be shut for several hours. So the cat and I got off lightly. And I now understand what all those Brits mean when they say they have come to France for the weather.

I am also beginning to understand that my renovations will not be finished before Doomsday. I can take my time about painting the doors in the summer sitting-room, because Laveille, the joiner, won't be here to lay the oak floor until 2008. Then there's Monsieur Duruflé, the tiler, who complains that he's already completely *débordé*, and as for poor Monsieur Étang, the yellow-anoraked plumber – always in demand, despite being named after a lake – I can't bring myself to spook him by phoning him again.

Accepting such delays takes no Zen mastery on my part. I like living in my small submarine and I wouldn't know what to do with all this space if the rest of La Folie were ever finished.

And then the phone rings, and it's Monsieur Laveille. Now I've always had a good feeling about Laveille, because he is the only man in Jolibois whom I've seen wearing shorts in December. Either his charges are so reasonable that he cannot afford a proper pair of trousers, or else he is a fiendishly hard worker whose legs often overheat.

Contrast this with Duruflé, the tiler, whose picture-book lawn is crowded with tiny windmills and superior-looking gnomes. You wouldn't think gnomes could make a chap look flush, but these ones do.

'I'll be there in a fortnight,' says Laveille.

'*Impeccable*,' I reply, steadying myself.

After months of waiting, I am caught with *les culottes en bas*. Before the floor can be laid, there are all those doors and the huge French windows to paint in the summer sitting-room. Another coat of emulsion required on the west wall, thirty feet up. Myriad fiddly timbers to varnish. A scaffolding tower to dismantle. And the stair-case next door can't be built until the floor it stands on has been tiled.

I phone Gnome Central.

'Is there any chance, *Madame*,' I ask, 'that your husband could tile the floor before the seventh? It's rather important.'

'Ah, would that be when Monsieur Laveille is coming?' asks *Madame*, who is linked to the Jolibois grapevine via broadband. '*Pas de problème*. We'll do the tiling next week.' It's amazing what a specific date and a little urgency will do. I should learn from my animals: the order in which I feed them is in direct proportion to the anguish they express.

Making a mental note to be more of a cat and less of a sheep in my next life, I phone Serge to ask if he'd be willing to remove the scaffolding before the seventh.

'*Pas de problème*,' he says. 'I'll be there on Wednesday.'

Electrified with action, I shin up the tower and start splashing paint on to the west wall, imagining how marvellous it will be when my piano arrives. I crouch where the piano will go, and examine the view. I bellow some tuneless Wagner – the arrival of the Gods in

Valhalla – safe in the knowledge that no one can hear me.

And then Titus fires up outside, reminding me that I shall always have not just an audience, but competition, too.

Next thing I know, I'm lying in bed with the cat on my head and a lorry rumbling outside. Egad, it's Wednesday, I've overslept, and that must be Serge. Bleary-eyed, I pull Zumbach's old flasher-mac over my jim-jams, slide into my chilled clogs, and clump downstairs to unbolt the door.

'*Salut*, Serge,' I croak, shaking his hand and trying to sound as if I've been up for hours.

'*Salut*, Michael,' he replies, grinning. 'What have you been painting?'

'Myself mostly, but I think a bit went on the wall. *Et vous, ça va?*' I ask.

'*Ah, oui. Comme toujours.*' Serge is about as likely to complain as a block of granite. He scratches his head, and looks up at the scaffolding.

'How long ago did we put this up?' he asks.

'Almost exactly a year.'

He laughs. 'As long as that? And now you see: everything is finished in the end.'

'But that's just it, Serge,' I reply, as I head off towards the chicken house, where the girls – ready to start their day – are squawking to be fed before the sheep. 'I still feel as if I've only just begun.'

# 51

## FEBRUARY: THE ERYMANTHIAN BOAR

This can't be right. There must be some mistake. The looming stack of oak in the summer sitting-room has been conjured into a flawless floor. Bernard and Benoît, the little-and-large double-act sent by Laveille (now in long trousers, I'm happy to see), have married timber to stone as seamlessly as syrup poured into a flan case.

It's a minor detail, but they have also imported a load of mud from the quagmire outside, and stencilled it all over the unsealed wood in bootprints little and large.

'Oh, don't worry about that,' says Benoît, waving at the footwork on their handiwork; palimpsests on an ancient manuscript. 'It'll soon come off when the floor is sanded.'

'*Ah, d'accord*,' I gulp. While I may not be man enough to do my own plumbing, extract my own teeth or, indeed, lay my own floor, the five-hundred-euro charge for sanding by a third party that Laveille has included in his quote has made me feel unusually tough and resourceful. I know I can rent an *appareil* from Castorama in Limoges for a tenth of that – one of those self-propelling sanders you walk behind – and do it myself. I might even graduate to a yellow belt in DIY in the process.

And then I listen to Bernard. Now Bernard is a man who, by his own admission, never sands floors himself. But he suggests an even cheaper solution to my *petit problème* of how to prepare forty square metres of boot-marked French oak for *finition* with varnish or wax.

Reader, learn from my folly. If a charming and expert *menuisier* in green overalls should ever come and lay an oak floor in your house, be sure to have your shipmates stop their ears with wax and chain you to the mast before he can lull you to perdition with his siren song. Bernard murmurs that I could save myself fifty euros and a trip to Limoges by using that little Black and Decker sander he's spotted in the *cellier*.

This sander resembles a small household iron. When you plug it in, it is fair to say that the lights of La Folie do not dim. No, the piddling thing simply whirrs and buzzes like a moth in a jar. Its surface area is two thousand times smaller than the floor which I propose to sand with it.

Luckily, I have seen *Zulu*, and am not afraid.

The prospect of this small exploit gives me a goofy pleasure. I'm looking forward to the task. My warped, dilettantish brain still associates repetitive physical labour – the more tedious and gruelling the better – with heroic self-improvement. And after three hours, I have almost erased the bootprints from a tenth of the floor.

'It's not too late to give up and go to Castorama,' says a voice in my head.

'Man or mouse, Wrighty?' comes a familiar reply. So I compromise and, in my English tea-break, visit Mermoz's store for some Useful Gadgets instead: coarser sanding sheets for the piddle-whirrer, a dust-mask and a pair of knobbly black knee-pads. These are expensive, but might encourage me to weed the *potager* in the summer.

Le Grand Mermoz happens to be behind the till today, and beams with bonhomie as he pumps my hand in a meaty handshake.

'Looking forward to the skiing?' he asks.

'*Tout à fait*. Can't wait.'

'Kiki will be there, remember,' he says, winking at me. I groan, and laugh.

Knee-pads and dust-mask strapped on, I don a thick pair of gardening gloves and the furry helmet – flaps down – that Nicholas gave me for Christmas. Then the cat races in from her latest sortie, glimpses me and freezes: broadside, ears flat, back arched, fur electrified, tail stiff as a broom.

'I – am – your – *father*, Luke,' I rasp.

The cat shoots straight back out through the cat-flap, presumably sensing that the force is stronger in me than in her just now.

With my new equipment, I tear through another couple of square metres in less than half an hour. And then I glance behind me. *Sacrebleu*. The floor I've sanded resembles the runway at Limoges airport, covered in black skid marks from underpaid 737 pilots anxious about overshooting. *Out, damned spot*. These blasted knee-pads. I drop *les pantalons*, strap the pads to my bare legs, pull my trousers back up, and go back to square one.

Morning, noon and night, I sand. I sand in my dreams, until I have left the Zulus behind and I feel like I'm rowing across the Atlantic in a coracle.

Halfway across the ocean, it's still not too late to bail out and go to Castorama. But I've started so I'll finish. And as I sand ever onwards, I make little resolutions as to how I am going to live my life differently in future; become a better man. I will never sand another plank, type another ampersand, touch another sandwich, go flying with Sandrine, nor shop at Marks and Spencer ever again. Oh, and I will never *ever* let anyone walk on this floor.

Land ahoy. Lacking any red flares to ignite, I cheer myself to the finish by picturing a sexy, black and curvaceous form reflected in my gleaming *parquet*, and wonder what to play when the grand piano finally arrives. I always imagined it would be Chopin, the 3rd Ballade. And then I recall the composer's affair with a French lady novelist I cannot bring myself to name.

Later, Bernard returns to pick up a tool he has left behind.

'Nice job,' he says, bending down to stroke the floor with the palm of his hand. Then he strokes his chin, as if to compare the two. 'I assume you'll be going over it with a fine-grade paper next, will you?'

Next morning, sore of back and aching of limb, I am riffling through piles of paper, looking for the quote I was given a year ago for moving a piano to France, when my attention is caught by something moving on the hillside above La Folie. In the distance, a sheepdog is rounding up Young Boulesteix's sheep. I didn't know Boulesteix had a dog. But I can see that this hound is doing a splendid job, marshalling the flock over hill and dale. Then a beaten-up Citroën drives up to La Folie, and Young Boulesteix himself jumps out.

'Your ram is terrorizing my sheep,' he gasps. 'There are eighty pregnant ewes up there. If he carries on like that, they'll all miscarry. You've got to stop him.'

I take another look at the small black creature chasing a swirl of white across the far hillside, my mind whirling with a nightmare flashback to a car journey in Scotland,

and a yellow-spittled farmer roaring at my parents for allowing their wee duggie to terrorize his sheep. *Nom de Dieu*. Boulesteix is right. That's not a dog. It's Gaston.

'*Pas de problème*,' I reply. 'I'm on my way.'

The truth is that I rate my chances of catching Gaston single-handed, on an open hillside, about as highly as I'd rate my chances of catching a direct flight from Jolibois to Wooloomooloo. Ouessants are not like other sheep. They are wild and fast and crafty. Last time I attempted to round up my eight Rastafarians to give them an injection, it took me a fortnight.

Creaking in every joint, I don my running shoes – wellies just don't have the acceleration – grab my shepherd's crook, and head outside. The air is so cold that I can taste it. I'm not sure what exactly the crook – one of my less useful Useful Gadgets – is for. But bringing it feels the right thing to do under the circumstances, just as you're supposed to bring towels and plenty of hot water when a woman goes into labour in a cowboy film.

The chase begins. In the lead: eighty fat French ewes, their plump thighs frotting together like a scrum of yummy mummies racing for the Pimms tent at a Berkshire point-to-point. Hard on their heels: one black ram, about the size of a prep-school tuck box, with aristocratic horns and a Benny Hill twinkle in his eye. Bringing up the rear: one breathless, stiff-limbed English townie, waving a shepherd's crook.

Gaston has my sympathies. The old boy has the gentlest nature imaginable and almost none of his own teeth. Each day he has to suffer the butting and barging of Ramekin and Camillo as – even now, when Doris, Daphne, Ella and Claudette cannot possibly still be on heat – they attempt to muscle in on his harem. I may have promised myself never again to take my sheep to market, but I need to do something with my priapic lads.

It can't be easy for poor Gaston. And now, after a lifetime of servicing petite black ladies, the sight of a coach-party of Rubenesque white Sabines, just on the other side of his fence, udders swinging voluptuously in the breeze, must have been more than he could resist.

But each of these girls is twice the size of him. I don't know how to break it to Gaston that, even if he does get lucky, he's going to need something to stand on.

For those who have never chased an amorous Ouessant ram all over a steep French hillside, I can recommend it as a very high-impact form of aerobics. With his jinking side-steps and explosive acceleration, Gaston would make a world-class scrum-half. I would get a stitch just bringing on the oranges at half-time.

A pattern develops in the match. We give each other a long, hard stare. I sprint; Gaston sprints. I lunge; he jinks. I fall over. And we both give each other another long, hard stare. (Repeat until exhausted.) It's just like my Christmas point-to-point with Doris in the snow, only without the slush.

And there's another difference, too. Panting and wheezing, I begin to gain on Gaston. My wayward Casanova is running out of steam. The sprint becomes a canter; the canter becomes a trot. The toy mechanism has almost wound down. I make one last lunge, grab him by the fleece.

'Come on, old fellow,' I say, hauling him into my arms like an overgrown toddler. 'That's enough fun for one day.'

Gaston is back in his field now, pacing with lust, still pining for big women. Doris comes up and gives him a hopeful sniff – what's wrong with us then, eh? – but

Gaston turns away. He's probably dreaming, even now, about buying himself a red sports car and a pair of embarrassing shades.

It has been quite a game, if only it were a game. A few days later, I drop in on Gilles to tell him about my adventure, and to ask if he'll be willing to feed the cat and the chickens, and to keep an eye on the sheep, when I go skiing for the weekend with Mermoz and my friends from the tennis club.

'You weren't at the funeral, then?' he asks.

'What funeral?'

'A young farmer, only thirty-one, committed suicide the other day after his ewes miscarried. Terrible business. That's the second young *éleveur* in eighteen months. He left a wife and two young children.'

'Not . . . not Young Boulesteix?'

'No, not Young Boulesteix,' says Gilles, gazing out of the window. 'Somebody else.'

# 52

## HANNIBAL

I am just back from Gilles's house when a navy-blue Renault 4 rattles up the drive to La Folie. The driver – a hunched frown with bushy eyebrows – looks alarmed to see me, and mutters something to the bleached-blond perm in the passenger seat beside him.

'We're lost,' he growls at me in French, pushing open his window, and not bothering to latch it up.

'Well, where are you trying to get to?' I ask.

'We were looking for La Folie.'

'This is La Folie.'

'Yes, I know. A lady who used to live here, before the war, told us about the place. She's seventy-nine now.'

I consider this for a moment. 'So you're not really lost at all, are you?'

'Ah . . . er . . . *non, Monsieur,*' he chuckles, shrinking in his seat.

'But look,' I say, 'why don't you bring this lady you mention back with you, for a visit?'

'Are you sure, *Monsieur?*' he says, wide-eyed. 'She did tell us she would love to see the old place again.'

Off they drive again, in a cloud of black exhaust, and I don't give my unexpected guests another thought. How can I, when Mermoz's skiing weekend has come round at last?

A day later, I am standing on the side of a mountain in the Massif Central with four couples, three young children and Kiki, who is still on the run from her ex-husband(s).

With three bedrooms between thirteen of us, there is, naturally, great excitement amongst the others as to whether Kiki – the closest Jolibois comes to having a *femme fatale* – and I will end up sharing more than just a chair-lift together. But I am too busy concentrating on bending ze knees and planting ze poles to contemplate any off-piste après-ski.

Mermoz is our leader. He is the biggest and strongest and loudest and funniest, and everyone loves him, except his wife Josette, occasionally, because he cannot stop being big and strong and loud and funny, even at home. And he always has to win at everything.

Mermoz has thoughtfully put Kiki and me in the same room as smiley Maxim the boxer, his wife Marie, and their two-year-old called Nicolas, who has the ability to beam with pleasure and be violently sick, both at the same time. '*J'ai vomi*,' he chirrups after dinner, indicating the beautiful new pattern he has made on his jumper.

'Bagsy not sleep anywhere near *that*,' I think to myself. In the event, Marie, Kiki and I sleep in the three single beds up on the mezzanine, while Nicolas and his dad take the two beds downstairs. The dormitory atmosphere transports me back to my school days.

'I hope you don't snore, Michael,' says Kiki, as we all start shyly getting ready to turn in.

It's not the snoring I'm worried about. It's the sleep-talking. I tend to have rather a lot to say once the shutters come down.

Next morning, I wake with the dread suspicion that I have had a chatty night. And Kiki can't wait to tell everyone all about it.

'Michael does snore! *And* he talks in his sleep!' she announces at breakfast, with what I really think is unnecessary relish. 'And what's amazing is that he does it *en anglais*!' She's so impressed that you'd think I'd been doing my times tables in Japanese. But of course, to her, I must sound as if I've been dubbed.

'I heard you, too,' chuckles Maxim. 'But I couldn't work out what you were saying.'

'Look, tonight I'll try really hard, and see if I can sleep-talk in French,' I promise.

It's a glorious day, and I feel my heart fluttering with a happiness that verges on exultation as I swish down pistes and paths through the mountains with my friends, the edges of my skis carving tramlines through the hissing snow, the sun making the entire landscape gleam with dazzling glitter.

I imagined the Massif Central would be much like the Cairngorms, with a few icy runs and a lot of rocks. But not a bit of it. The pistes are well groomed, the lifts are fast, and there's plenty of snow. And here am I, always the very worst at sports, on holiday with the sporting crowd of Jolibois: with Blaise the gruffly genial PE teacher, and his sparkling wife, the Proustian Madeleine; with Maxim and Claude and Mermoz and the rest.

Then Kiki takes a tumble. She's crashed a few times already, always with a theatrical scream. But this time I see her knee twist as she goes down. And she doesn't scream; she groans.

'Looks like you've damaged a ligament,' murmurs Jeanne, who works as a nurse, kneeling beside her. Kiki can barely stand. And she says she isn't insured. So a ride down the mountain in a blood-wagon doesn't bear thinking about. Mermoz will surely carry her.

Seeing what the group does next is like watching a well-drilled mountain-rescue team giving a public-service demonstration. Snow is applied to the injured knee. Instructions are issued. Histrionics are calmed. Before long, Maxim is carrying Kiki's boots and Claude has her skis. Blaise and the Proustian Madeleine direct the traffic around us. I'm about to pick up Kiki's poles, but Mermoz is standing in front of me.

'You're the strongest here, and the best skier, Michael,' he says, not looking at me. 'Do you think you can carry her? I'd do it myself, but I'm worried about my back.'

For a second, I do not answer. I must have misunderstood. It is as if I were standing on the touch-line of a windy football pitch, and one of the team captains had picked me first. There must be some mistake. Am I not Michael, who was always the weakest and weediest, who never won a point against Norman Handley?

But I do not give Mermoz a chance to change his mind.

In seconds I have Kiki on my back, and am making cautious snowplough turns back down the mountain, via a route carefully scouted by Blaise, who carries our poles in one hand. The others ski down on either side of us, like an escort of police outriders, offering support, cheering us on. Kiki is sobbing too much for me to feel any frisson of intimacy.

We're almost down when a rescue dude in mirrored shades roars up on a snowmobile.

'That's not your husband, is it?' I mutter.

'No!' giggles a tearful Kiki, just behind my ear.

'I heard a woman was injured,' says the rescue dude hopefully.

'*Ce n'est pas grave*,' I reply, praying he won't make her dismount and pay him three hundred euros for the privilege of being strapped to a sledge and towed backwards for the last hundred yards.

And then we're down, and everyone is slapping me on the back, and Kiki won't stop telling anyone who will listen what a hero I have been. I beg her to stop, because this is not heroism, this is nothing. And I discover that there is no pleasure at all in being hailed a hero when one is not.

That night, I lie awake in bed, thinking about heroes.

I used to think that heroes were the doers of great deeds: battle-winners, dragon-slayers, strivers after far-off goals. Either that, or men of courage and endurance, pushing themselves to unfeasible limits, grinding out achievements through sweat and grit alone. But now it dawns on me that true heroism is very much simpler – and very much more human – than that.

A hero, a true hero, is that man, woman or child who willingly and consciously accepts unnecessary suffering for the sake of others.

By this reckoning, I must know more heroes than I once thought. When I used to walk outside in East Dulwich, to gaze at the night sky, the brightest stars were sometimes visible in the sodium gloom. But at La Folie, free of the city's luminous pollution, more and more stars appear – dim glimmers from thousands of light years away – the longer I gaze.

The stonemason who works ten hours a day, six days a week, to feed his family.

The farmer who labours without cease in the fields, and then will sweat to help a foreigner build a fence.

The wife who endures constant pain without complaint, so that lambing will not be interrupted.

The hungry mother who, day after day, year after year, puts her children first.

The gawky child, bullied at school, who says nothing of her agony to her parents, for fear that it might upset them.

The lady in the supermarket, who has worked behind the same till for the past eighteen years, and still greets every complaint with a smile.

The season-ticketed commuter who dreamed of something more, but who grinds forty years of his life away on a job that bores him to death, for the sake of his wife and kids.

And so on. And so on.

I do not know what binds these people together in my heart. But as I lie here in bed, gazing out at the moonlight on the mountains, I do know that something about the way they live their lives makes me want to live my own life better.

An hour or two later, I am sleep-talking again. But it's not about heroism. No, I'm issuing an urgent warning to the others in the group about why they mustn't throw snowballs at the wall. I don't know why. And somehow it dawns on me, in my sleep, that they won't be able to understand me, because I'm speaking English. So I repeat my instructions about not throwing *boules de neige*, loud and clear. In French.

Fortunately, the mental effort that this demands wakes me up. And with a sinking heart, I realize what I've just been saying. Oh, brother.

I listen. The room is so silent that I just *know* everyone is wide awake, holding their breath in the darkness, desperately trying to suppress their giggles.

In the morning, I shall have to face another merciless

ribbing. But for now, I allow myself a moment of secret jubilation. I may not quite be dreaming in French yet. But I'm on my way.

# 53

## MARCH: THE PIANO

Tootle the bugles and hoist the flag, for a day that I had begun to fear would never dawn is almost here. My piano is on its way to France.

I suppose that really it should appear through a break in the clouds, like Heracles come to redeem Philoctetes, or be lowered into the summer sitting-room from a golden thread held aloft by a formation of ten thousand un-usually restrained swallows. But I am having to rely on a removal firm.

I will not shame the British company who are finally transporting my piano to France by naming them. But Bolton's of Hampshire know who they are.

I have chosen Bolton's because they make regular trips to France with the chattels of the English Diaspora, and because they assure me they have moved many grand pianos, and know exactly what they are doing. I should imagine that the Jumblies said roughly the same thing just before they set sail.

One of the highlights of the Bolton's experience is the ineffable Ray, whose unique approach to customer service appears to be that the customer is there to provide a service.

'Shall I give you a credit-card number, or would you prefer a cheque?' I ask, a week before D-Day.

'Nah,' huffs Surly Rod. 'Cash on delivery only.'

'But I'm in France,' I explain. 'I don't keep a big stash of sterling under the bed.'

'Then we'll take euros, at the NatWest tourist rate.'

'Isn't there some other way I can pay?' I wonder.

'Well, I suppose you *could* make a bank transfer,' mutters Ray. So I do.

Four days later, conscious that the piano should already be rumbling through France, I phone Rod again. 'Any idea when the piano will arrive?' I enquire cheerily.

'Soon as we get the money,' he rasps.

'But I made the transfer on Thursday.'

'I don't care,' he snarls. '*We* haven't received it. And I'm not delivering a piano to France until it's paid for.'

'What happens if the transfer doesn't complete in time?'

'We'll take the piano back to England.'

This is a classic hostage/ransom scenario, and I spend the next couple of days expecting to receive a severed middle-C in the post. To keep my spirits up, I ask Monsieur Duruflé, the chirpy tiler who is putting the finishing touches to the floor of the *maison des amis*, if he'd be willing to haul the piano – should it ever arrive – up the drive on his truck. Attempting the ascent with a removal lorry would, I suspect, be like trying to ride a walrus up a spiral staircase. And I am still emotionally scarred from that nasty business with the man who came to empty the *fosse septique*.

'*Pas de problème*,' replies Duruflé, beaming at the prospect of being able to be even more helpful than usual.

The fact that he has a slight squint only adds to the innocent delight of his smile.

The cold has been squeezing La Folie in its vice for as long as I can remember. Some mornings, I have been struggling to break the ice on the water trough for the sheep, even with an iron bar. At least Gaston's ardour has finally cooled. But Silent Mary is looking weaker than ever, and the rest of the Egg Squad have been in a puffed-up sulk since December. Last week, after I returned from the skiing, I was snowed in for four days, the Espace beached like a whale on the steep right-hander at the bottom of the drive.

Thanks to the cold, I've even abandoned my decision to resist lighting the stove until the temperature indoors became unbearable. It was when the cat came downstairs with a quarterstaff over her shoulder and all her belongings tied up in a knotted handkerchief that I realized it was time to stop kidding myself that I was becoming tough.

To be fair, however, being snowed in was almost fun. There was no repeat of the freezing-rain fiasco. And we're not talking about Napoleon's retreat from Moscow, what with Céline's *boulangerie* being only half an hour's trudge away. No, having the Espace marooned in a snowdrift gave me a chance to feel thoroughly medieval as I staggered into town with my oil lamp to play the organ for Mass, secretly hoping to bump into somebody en route because I was feeling so picturesque.

Today is Tuesday, and the ice and snow have finally melted, so Marie-Claude has come to sort me out. Marie-Claude is a card. When I ask her to clean the new tiles in the unheated *maison des amis*, she insists on taking a thermometer with her, to test the brutal conditions under which I am making her work.

Just after she has vanished with her mop, there is a frantic commotion outside. It sounds as if all the girls are shrieking at once. *Mon Dieu*, I hope that's not another fox. I dash for the back door and out into the slush. And stop, spellbound, my eyes widening with awe.

The sky is full of birds, and they're not chickens. Arranged in a giant V-formation that stretches far out across the valley, they are mournfully *kroo-kroo*-ing their calls like an airborne massed band. Zumbach told me I could expect a lot of swallows at La Folie. He didn't tell me about the cranes.

There must be a thousand birds up there, lined up in interconnecting chevrons, fluting to each other as they beat time with their seven-foot wings. The formation is almost half a mile wide, its two great arms divided and sub-divided like the boughs and branches and twigs and shoots of some vast flying tree. Squinting into the sunlight, I follow the last of the rippling branches, only to see that this, too, is connected to yet another huge formation beyond.

I don't know why, but seeing these creatures flying in such numbers, single-mindedly supporting each other on their epic voyage, and hearing their heart-rending calls, makes me . . . well, I'm embarrassed to say that it makes me want to cry. I can't explain this. What is so moving about a sky full of birds that I should feel myself melting within?

I am no twitcher. My parents have reached the age where they gasp and grab the binoculars every time anything feathered flutters into their garden. I have not. Bird-watching is really not my thing. The only birds I can confidently identify are as follows: robin; magpie; pigeon; sparrow; chicken; parrot.

But cranes . . . cranes or their ilk were alive when

dinosaurs roamed the Earth. You rarely see them in Britain, because they tend to migrate from Spain to Scandinavia via a narrow corridor that cuts through the heart of France. And what I am just now discovering, as I stand and watch in awe, is that La Folie is located slap-bang in the middle of their international flight path. I immediately decide that cranes are one of my favourite things, along with tennis, Spitfires, chickens, Chopin and the *crème brûlée* they serve at the Toquenelle in St Juste.

Behind me, Marie-Claude appears with her mop.

'You know what this means?' she says. 'When *les grues* arrive, it marks the beginning of spring.'

And then she waves the thermometer at me, to show what an ordeal she's had.

'I should lodge a complaint,' she declares with a brave smile.

'But you hardly look blue at all,' I reassure her. And we both stand and gaze, open-mouthed, at the sky.

Marie-Claude is just warning me that I shouldn't keep tomatoes in the fridge, and that cabbages should be wrapped in foil, when the phone rings.

'Mr Wright?' English voice, Estuary accent. 'Just to let you know that we're in Poitiers with your piano. We should be there in a couple of hours.'

'Incredible. I'll meet you at the bottom of the drive.'

I have known that piano since I was twelve years old. I have waited months to bring it to Ice Station La Folie, conscious that in Jolibois I have not once heard the sound of music floating out of an open window, if you discount the days when Ralph the artist is torturing his saxophone. And now there are only hours to go. It crosses my mind to hug Marie-Claude, but she is drying the carving knife, so I think better of it.

Again, the phone rings. They're there, at the bottom of the drive. I run to find Duruflé, and he drives me down in his beaten-up white truck.

The two Frowns who descend from the Bolton's lorry do not say hello. Duruflé, twinkling with the pleasure of tiling a damp room in sub-zero conditions, shuffles forward to shake hands, and then shuffles back again, embarrassed.

'A handshake with my friend wouldn't go amiss,' I murmur to one of them.

'You what, mate?' he sneers. 'Oh, yeah, right. Just as long as he doesn't start any of that kissing malarky.'

And then we are rumbling up the drive on the back of good Monsieur Duruflé's truck: three Englishmen and a grand piano. That sounds like it might be the start of a joke, and – as I shall discover – in some ways it is.

But for now, all's right with the world. The sun glitters through the trees, and the piano doesn't topple over as we ride the Cresta Run in reverse. With my old friend looming between us like the dorsal fin of a mighty whale, I am Ishmael. I am Fitzcarraldo. I am twelve years old.

Even the two Frowns can't help grinning at the Laurel-and-Hardiness of it all. I give a thumbs-up to Duruflé each time his smile illuminates the rear-view mirror. On our right, Titus and the Girls stand stock still beneath the lone pine, heads cocked sideways, keeping an eye on the huge black beast coming up the drive. I can't wait to introduce Martha to Chopin.

And then we're at the top, and it's time for the Englishmen to take over.

'*Merci mille fois*,' I say to Duruflé, shaking his hand.

'Seen that, Del?' says one of the Frowns.

'Wossat?' asks the other.

'We're never gonna get it up them stairs.' He jerks a

sulky shoulder at the three stairs I told Bolton's about weeks ago.

'But I said there would be stairs,' I murmur. 'And look: there are only three of them.'

'Nah,' he continues, sitting down. 'Nobody never told us, mate.'

'Would it help if I went and fetched a plank?' asks Duruflé in French, beaming with helpfulness.

His teenage son, who has been working on the tiling next door, comes out to help. And so we lower the piano from the back of the truck, and slowly haul it up the stairs. As far as I can see, Duruflé – at least twenty years older than the rest of us – takes most of the weight.

'We'll drag it,' says one of the Frowns, when the piano is resting in the doorway.

'I'd rather you didn't,' I respond hastily. 'That floor is rather special to me. What about using the piano trolley?'

'Chuck us one of those blankets, then, Andy,' he says, the muscles in his jaw bulging as he clenches his teeth. The piano trolley remains untouched on the back of the van.

And so they drag the piano across the floor, while the unseen shard of broken glass that is embedded in the blanket etches a long, curving scratch mark in my carefully sanded oak, like a bright vapour trail cutting the sky.

Duruflé looks long and hard at this scratch and, after giving me a smile of rueful sympathy, goes back to finishing his perfect tiling. The Frowns hastily re-attach the piano's legs and the pedals, and one of them suggests, without enthusiasm: 'Play us a tune then, mate.'

I don't feel like playing anything, not just now. I pictured myself alone when I struck the first notes. I even start to try to explain, and then stop myself. Go on. Play something.

So with trembling fingers, I gently sound a chord:

C major, both hands, the intervals widely spaced. And the sound is gorgeous in the towering room's churchlike acoustic; like warm butterscotch sauce drizzled over a perfect scoop of my dad's homemade ice cream. And then another sustained chord: E-minor seventh, first inversion. And a third: A-minor seventh, first inversion. *I can't help falling in love with you.* But Houston, we have a problem. We have a big problem.

'It's not right,' I say.

'What's not right?' asks First Frown.

'The dampers. They're not touching the strings. Can't you hear how it all blurs into one?'

'It sounds all right to me,' he grunts.

So follows an hour in which the three of us lie underneath the piano, attaching and detaching the pedals, examining the brass connecting rods, puzzling over what could be wrong. The rods just seem too long. And these two of my fellow countrymen just seem too ... too English, with their so-called expertise and their boorish ways. I catch myself wishing I'd asked a French removal firm to pick up the piano from East Dulwich.

'It must have been like that all along, mate,' says Second Frown eventually, 'and you just didn't notice.'

'There's got to be a simple explanation,' I reply, ignoring this.

'Well, you'll be having it tuned, right?' says First Frown. 'So when the tuner comes, he can just saw a bit off one of the rods, and then they'll fit.'

'I can't believe you just said that,' I reply.

'Well, all right. So maybe you don't want to wait,' he continues. 'But I bet that cross-eyed bloke next door's got an angle-grinder. We could do it now.'

'No,' I say. 'Leave it now. Have another cup of tea. I'll sort it out later.'

In the end, I manage a temporary bodge, inserting a piece of cardboard between the pedal-frame and the piano to make room for the over-long rods. I make yet another cup of tea for the Frowns and leave them grumbling at each other in the winter sitting-room. Finally, alone with my piano for a few moments, I play the opening of the Schubert A-major sonata, A664, that was on my parents' scratchy Ashkenazy LP that I heard so often as a child, dreaming of rippling out its lyrical themes for myself one day.

*Clack, clack, clack* goes the sustain pedal each time I press it. *Clack, clack, clack*. I feel as if I have waited months to meet a long-lost friend, only to discover that they are not the person I thought they were.

The Frowns do not say goodbye. Good Monsieur Duruflé gives them a lift down the drive in the cab of his truck, while his son shivers on the exposed flat-bed behind them.

Heavily depleted on the euphoria front, I head off for tennis coaching at the Jolibois *gymnase*. Running around and being yelled at by Grégory, the brilliant young coach, does me a power of good, and – with endorphins buzzing around my brain – I drive back to La Folie with renewed purpose.

What do I have to feel down about? I'm no worse off than I was yesterday.

I sit under the piano with my torch and have another look at the problem that stumped three of us for an hour. After approximately seven seconds, I spot a small dowel that is out of place. I wobble it with my finger, and it clatters out of the bottom of the piano.

Bingo.

Then I play Christmas puzzles with the dowel for a while, trying to work out how to get it back into position.

I unscrew something here. Tighten something there. Ah. *There*.

Holding my breath, I sit at the keyboard and start to play.

Chopin, the 3rd Ballade.

And I know, as my fingers stroke the keys, that I shall not feel alone again.

# 54

## SILENT MARY

Every day now begins and ends in the summer sitting-room, rattling out Chopin and Schubert and 'Someone To Watch Over Me' at my beloved keyboard. The cat joins me, sitting under the piano to pick up the vibrations, especially from Chopin, who is her favourite composer. But outside in the field behind La Folie, other and more resonant melodies are making themselves heard.

Black, fragile and hop-skippety cute, the first of this year's lambs has just been born. Fortunately, Ouessants are hardy creatures, and tend to handle the messy bit of lambing themselves. So from last year to this, I have never yet had to don the rubber gloves and a faraway look to help.

Gilles and Josette come up to check on my new arrival, and find me so triumphant about the lamb that they must think it was me, rather than Daphne, who has given birth. Cooing at the tiny creature, Josette tells me about the simultaneous arrival of their first grandchild. I want to explain that I'm hoping to become a grandfather, too, if my dear little Claudette becomes a mother this spring.

'They would have to have it slap-bang in the middle of lambing, wouldn't they?' growls Gilles. He doesn't think they'll be able to go to the christening in Châteaudun.

'But *I* can look after the lambing for you, Gilles,' I tell him, with all the confidence of one who has read *Sheep for Beginners* from cover to cover.

Gilles throws me a glance of raw pity, although I can't for the life of me think why. 'And I can do *les vaches*, too,' I add, even though I haven't read *Cows for Beginners* yet.

'*On va voir*,' he says, looking pale.

In the end, despite my lobbying, Jean-Jacques, a picturesque neighbour with a face like a kindly potato, is given the cow job. Old Boulesteix is placed on lambing watch. And I am left to look after the rest of Gilles's sheep.

Now I know sheep are rather good at looking after themselves, but I still feel touched by the trust this implies. There is a world of difference between playing Marie-Antoinette with my seven – sorry, eight – little Ouessants behind La Folie, and taking responsibility for someone else's livelihood, if only for a weekend. I am to feed, water and generally oversee six hundred-odd ewes, rams and lambs in fifteen different fields and barns, some of them several miles away. *Pas de problème.*

As I accompany Gilles on his rounds, I'm reminded of that thrilling moment in learning to fly, when my instructor, Sinking Anand, finally decided I was ready to go solo, climbed out of the plane and left me to screw up all by myself.

Unfortunately, counting sheep turns out to be harder than landing an aeroplane.

'There should be forty-five ewes,' declares Gilles, in the first field.

'*J'ai quarante-quatre*,' I reply, after some time. 'Someone must have kidnapped one.'

'Count again. Do it in twos.'

'Ah, that's better. Now there are forty-eight.' I make a third stab – '*vingt-six . . . vingt-huit . . . trente . . .*' – but Gilles has already moved on.

'If you don't get it right first time, *tu es foutu*,' he explains, waving his sawn-off finger at me. No wonder this game is a hit with insomniacs.

Clambering over the barbed-wire fence towards the jeering mob of sheep in the next field, I manage to spill my feed-bucket in the wet grass. Gilles looks away, as – brown-kneed – I do my best to scoop up the mess.

'I'll distract them while you fill up the first three troughs,' he says. 'Then, when they run to you, I'll fill the other three troughs. Do it fast, or they may knock you over.'

Over the next couple of hours, we clamber over innumerable barbed-wire fences and deliver umpteen buckets of feed to countless uncountable sheep in various fields and dilapidated barns. Then we come upon a ram, collapsed in the grass, who looks to me to be very dead.

'*Non, il n'est pas mort,*' says Gilles, slapping the creature around the chops. 'But I'll have to bring the tractor, to take him to the vet.' I bless the poor ram for choosing to have his seizure today, and not in two days' time.

In the evening I return for another training session. 'I hope you're not going to worry too much,' I tell Gilles, as we sip our *apéros* after work.

'*Ah, non,*' he laughs, swigging his Salers with the air of a cowboy about to have a bullet removed from his chest. 'I have total confidence in you, Michael.' Well, that makes one of us, at least. 'Incidentally,' he adds, 'have you heard about the *train à vapeur*?'

'No? A steam train, coming down the line here?'

'In a couple of weeks' time, from Limoges. It's a one-off.'

'I shan't miss it.'

Back at La Folie, I wander outside to take a last look at my own little flock. I need to practise this counting lark. '*Deux . . . quatre . . . six . . .*' Strange. I could swear I had eight this morning. And now there are nine.

'Oh, well *done*, Doris,' I whisper into the gathering dusk.

Next morning, I am quietly admiring Doris's new lamb suckling from its mother when, behind me, I hear a lawn-mower straining up the drive. Of course; I almost forgot the couple with the navy-blue Renault 4. And now they have returned with their lady-friend, who used to live here in the 1930s.

'*Bonjour, Monsieur,*' says the bushy-eyebrowed frown at the wheel. This time he is smiling. 'Do you remember us?'

'Of course,' I reply. 'And you're welcome.' I open the back door of the car for the elegant woman who is sitting behind the driver and his blonde companion. '*Madame . . .*'

Antoinette turns out to be a wonderful lady: a trim octogenarian in a floral-print dress, with clear blue eyes and neatly coiffed auburn hair, who unfolds herself from the back of the little Renault with the aplomb of a duchess. Then she shakes my hand, and looks about her, turning a full circle like a ballerina on a musical box. Monsieur Bushy Eyebrows stands edgily behind her with his hands outstretched, as if he might have to catch her at any moment.

'I remember,' she whispers, pressing both hands to her mouth as she glimpses the view across the valley. 'But the trees are so big now, aren't they?' Then she turns and looks up at the house; slowly shakes her head. 'Oh, thank you, *Monsieur*, thank you for letting me come and see it all again.'

I shrug, embarrassed. And we all stand in silence for a while.

'I'm sorry, *Monsieur*,' says the man. 'We should not have presumed . . .'

'May I ask you, *Madame* . . . ?' I interrupt, turning to Antoinette. 'What was your life here like?'

'Our life was very hard,' she replies simply, staring at the field behind the house, as if she has spotted her father there, still ploughing behind a pair of cows. 'But I was so happy.' She wrings her hands, and I don't know what to say. The man looks as if he wants her to climb back into the Renault 4.

'Don't you want to see inside the house?' I ask.

'Are you sure?' She looks terrified and excited as I lead her up the steps into the winter sitting-room. The others follow.

'The fireplace hasn't changed,' she gasps, pointing a trembling finger at the hearth. 'But there are so many windows. I can't believe it.'

'These weren't here before?'

'Oh no, we only had one window in these two rooms. When you are working outside all day, you don't need to look out of the window when you come home.'

'It must have been very dark,' I observe clumsily.

'That was where my sister and I slept,' she continues, pointing at the kitchen. 'And this was the room where we all lived and ate.' She gazes, open-mouthed, at the walls of the winter sitting-room, hardly able to believe that this was the place, the very place, where her six-year-old self once dreamed about the future, in 1933.

'I suppose the only water was from the tap behind the house, that runs off the well at the top of the hill?'

'No, there was no tap.' She looks confused. 'My sister and I were sent up the hill every day, to fetch the water in buckets. And it's not a well. It's a spring.'

'*Une source?*' I ask, incredulous. Zumbach assured me, when I bought the house, that the rubble at the top of the hill marked an old well, and not to drink the water, which might be polluted by the sheep. I've only ever used it for watering the *potager*. But to have a fresh-water spring: that would be something else.

Together, we walk through into the soaring space of the summer sitting-room, with its polished oak floor and grand piano.

'This is where the cows lived,' she giggles, covering her mouth with both hands in a mixture of shock and amusement. 'I can't believe it. They were right *here*.' She waves her arms at the piano, as if hoping to transform it into a heifer. 'And they were happy, too.'

'Come along now,' says the man with bushy eyebrows gently, his eyelashes glistening. 'It's time we took you home, *Maman*.'

The vet said Silent Mary's problem was not serious. But it still hasn't gone away. The poor girl is close to collapse, and she hasn't done her Charleston for months. After re-reading all my chicken books for the umpteenth time, I bring her into the kitchen, feed her on parsley and Weetabix, and drive down to the pharmacy.

'*Sel d'Epsom?*' I ask, having looked up Epsom Salts in my French dictionary. The pharmacist looks at me blankly, as if I'd just asked him for Eccles cake or Dorset knob. 'I think it's magnesium sulphate,' I add.

His face flickers and he opens his mouth to speak. Then

he disappears into a back-room. When he reappears, he is clutching a dusty, leatherbound volume which looks like a manual for turning base metals into gold. I certainly hope it's not the Epsom telephone directory. He runs his finger down the pages as if he were searching for a dead person: Monsieur Sel, I presume.

Then he whistles and jabs his finger at the page. SEL D'EPSOM = SULFATE DE MAGNÉSIUM. 'It is a good day when one learns something new,' he declares, beaming at me.

So I put Epsom Salts in the girls' drinking water, and in three days Mary has made a wonderful recovery. The change is so marked that I wonder if I shouldn't retrain as a vet. I feel so relieved that I make myself an omelette to celebrate, and then head down to the church to practise the organ.

I have just finished blasting out Karg-Elert's *Nun Danket* chorale prelude on the farty reeds when I hear footsteps stomping up the oak staircase to the tribune. Funny. I could have sworn the dark church, lit only by a few votive candles, was empty. Probably Fabrice, or perhaps Raphaël le Prêtre. But a face I half recognize – a bald head, like a snowman, with currants for eyes – pokes itself round the corner and squints at me for a moment, dazzled by the bright lights of the console, before breaking into a mournful smile. The man's cheeks are wet.

'So beautifool . . .' he rasps in a hoarse whisper, reaching out a trembling hand to shake mine. 'Making me sad.'

'I hope I didn't disturb . . .'

'No, no, your music is beautifool, thank you very much.' He wipes his eyes, nods an apology, before turning to stomp back into the shadows. 'Desert rats. Am thanking you, Mister. God save the kings.'

'God save the kings, Édouard,' I reply softly.

By the end of the week, Silent Mary begins to slide again. I put her back on the *Sel d'Epsom*, but the signs are not good.

She lies in the barn, eyes closed, neck outstretched, panting for breath. Her food and water sit beside her, untouched. I spend much of Saturday in the barn with her, hoping for some flicker of improvement.

At last, there comes a kind of miracle. As I watch, Mary suddenly rears up, spreads her wings wide and high as a heraldic crest, and begins to beat them. Blow me down if the old girl isn't trying to fly. I feel like cheering.

Next, a violent shudder passes through her body, as if she were being electrocuted. Then she collapses like a burst balloon in the straw. A clear soup trickles out of her beak. Ladies and gentlemen, Mary has left the building. All that remains is a rumpled costume left behind after a fancy-dress ball.

So I blow my nose and bury Mary beside Emil, beneath the trees beside the *potager*. And there, I give myself the fright of my life. For as I lay the body in its tiny grave, it emits a faint squawk.

I jump back in alarm, and emit my own squawk, beginning with 'f'.

Still alive? No, very dead. But the gas squeezed from Mary's frail carcass has made her cluck. It is a shock that I shall not forget in a hurry, any more than I shall ever forget Mary, the gentlest, steadiest chicken a chap could wish for, who did have a voice after all.

# 55

# A CELEBRATION

Silent Mary's death has quite knocked the wind out of me and, right now, I can't think of anything I feel less like doing than socializing. Nevertheless, tonight I have to cook the dreaded *repas anglais* for my friends from the tennis club. Claude the electrician has been to La Folie before. But for Mermoz and Jeanne, Blaise and the Proustian Madeleine, for Kiki the *femme fatale*, Maxim the welterweight economist and the rest, it will be their first visit to outer darkness. Though these hardy souls somehow survived my snoring and my sleep-talking when we went skiing together, Mermoz is convinced that my cooking is going to finish them off.

Hard on the heels of Mary's death comes the most joyous consolation. Claudette, one of my two Ouessant lambs born last year, produces a gorgeous lamb of her own. This is my first 'second generation' birth at La Folie; the first time an animal born under my care has itself given birth. So we are a grandfather at last.

It's amazing to see this tiny creature bouncing around the field after only twenty-four hours on the planet; an arched body on four splayed limbs, like something you might have knocked up in carpentry at school. A lamb so black that he looks like his own silhouette. I shan't name him, for I learned my lesson after Emil's death last year.

So let this be Nemo. I can easily stand and let the hours go by, just watching this fragile thundercloud taking his first steps in the world. But I mustn't, for I have to cook.

'If we eat your English food, there will be no one left to represent Jolibois in the leagues this summer,' Mermoz warned me last week, making me wonder if word of my green egg hash with black shrapnel has somehow got out. Since Mermoz also has acute cat-phobia, he is being very brave in coming to La Folie at all.

For starters, we're having Delia's salmon fishcakes, followed by chicken korma (I know, I know) with rice, nan, poppadoms, mango chutney, etc. Then cheddar and un-French biscuits, ferried hither by a charming Portuguese anaesthetist from the little tennis club by the railway line in Dulwich, on one of his trips to the Algarve. For the skiers' dinner, I was going to do ice cream with Mars Bar sauce, too, but the Proustian Madeleine has offered to bring *dessert* (pronounced with a hissed 's', not a 'z', she corrects me, or else people might think I was serving a few buckets of sand and a cactus).

Frankly I'm grateful for all the help I can get, because whenever a recipe says 'Preparation time: twenty minutes', that's how long it takes me just to mentally prepare myself to roll up my sleeves. I can add another nought for the time it will actually take me to chop and mash and incinerate the thing. I bet it doesn't take Delia seven hours to make fishcakes.

Tonight is special to me, for the strands of my French life are coming together, and it is a baptism of sorts. For the very first time, we are going to eat in the newly finished summer sitting-room – and I may even have the chance to play the piano for everyone afterwards. I can't quite believe this. I'm still so used to thinking of the echoing void as a building-site that whenever I go in there now, it feels like I'm entering Narnia.

'*On va pendre la crémaillère*,' Mermoz's wife, Jeanne, tells me on the phone.

'*Oui, bien sûr*,' I reply, without a clue as to what she means. It's only when I look up the phrase in my dictionary that I realize she's describing a house-warming: we're going to suspend the fireplace hook.

It may be a house-warming, but it's a dress rehearsal, too. For next Saturday I am undertaking a more daunting *soirée*, in the shape of a dinner-cum-concert for the workers who did the renovation work in the summer sitting-room, with Gilles and Josette for moral support. Zumbach, the reclusive former owner of La Folie, has even promised to drive over from Limoges as the guest of honour. Since it was he who conceived and started work on the summer sitting-room, years ago, I want him to be here to see it finished.

Twenty minutes before the skiers arrive, I'm still trying to light the wood-burning stove, whip up a sauce to go with the fishcakes and muck out the chicken house when a silver car pulls up and a bearded ogre with a familiar smile climbs out. *Oh-là-là*. Please tell me that isn't who I think it is.

'*Bonsoir, Michael*,' growls Zumbach, shaking my hand as if he were ringing a firebell. 'I'm not too early, am I?'

'Er . . . about a week, Ludo,' I gulp, peeking at him from between my fingers.

His face changes colour. My cheeks are burning, too. I invite him to join the skiers for dinner anyway, but he won't hear of it. And he's not free for next week's dinner, either.

'There's only one thing I ask, Monsieur Wright.'

'Of course, Ludo. Anything.'

'May I walk around, just for a few minutes? I shan't get in your way. I'd just like to see the old place, see the wonders you have worked.'

'Oh, I'm not sure they're wonders . . .'

But Ludo has already walked into the summer sitting-room. I hear him gasp, and emit a little groan. When I follow him in there, he has slapped both hands to his mouth, and is turning a slow circle, gazing up at the roof.

I don't know what to say. But I want to give him a gift, and I want to mark this moment in some way. And so I slide on to the piano stool, and I launch into the Fantaisie-Impromptu of another Polish artist who made France his home.

Usually my fingers fumble over some of Chopin's fiddlier phrases, but today something magical happens. I can only say that the piece begins to play itself. I watch my hands flying over the notes, as what was once tricky and technically challenging seems to be flowing from my fingertips like water from an underground chasm. I feel a sense of vertigo, fearing that if I look down I shall fall. I don't want to think about it too much. So I simply lose myself in the music, and let it fly up to the rafters. In the lyrical middle section, the trills that I usually fluff glitter like sapphires, and the music ripples to its conclusion with minimal interference from me.

I turn, expecting to see Ludo's face illuminated with shared pleasure. But he has gone.

Alarmed, I slip out of the huge French doors into the chill spring air. No sign of him. I check the barn, the workshop; even the chicken house. Nothing. I wander around to the sheep field, to see if he is there. Not there either.

And then, at last, I see a grizzled, heavily built figure slumped on the corner of the stone pool where the goldfish live. He is not looking at the fish. Zumbach is gazing out across the valley, to where the last rays of the sun are falling on the little chapel at St Sauveur. There are tears in his eyes.

'Ludo . . .' I begin. But Zumbach shakes his head. So I sit down beside him, and we both sit there together for some minutes, gazing out at the same view that we both know so well, just as the six-year-old Antoinette and every former owner of this ramshackle house must have come to know it, too. But I can only guess at what Ludo is seeing, for he has the air of a man who is looking not with his eyes, but with his heart.

It was self-indulgent of me to play the Chopin. He once told me that Chopin's music was too sad for him. I should have known it would be too much for him here, today.

'*Oui*,' he murmurs at last, gesturing around him, at the house, at me, at himself, the setting sun, a solitary swallow that is carving arcs in the sky above us, and finally reaching out both arms as if he wanted to embrace all of it. The twinkle has returned, though his eyes are still wet with tears. He turns to me and nods, and as I look into his eyes he doesn't need to explain.

And then he shakes his head and tries to speak. He clears his throat and tries again, wiping his eyes with the back of one hand. '*C'est de la folie*,' he croaks, with a hoarse laugh.

'Come on, Ludo,' I say, hearing the tremor in my own voice. 'Let's go inside.'

But he waves his hand, and pulls away, stumbling down the rocky old drive that he has walked so many times before. I watch him disappear into the dappled shade of the great oaks, like a polar explorer vanishing into a blizzard, or Hector marching to face Achilles from the gates of Troy.

And then he marches back again. 'Forgot my car,' he growls.

A few minutes after Ludo's silver car has vanished in a cloud of dust, the skiers start to arrive.

'*Calme, calme!*' coos the Proustian Madeleine, sensing my edginess that everything should be just so. '*On va passer un bon petit moment, quoi qu'il arrive.*' The wives immediately set to work, washing the salad and polishing champagne glasses, while the men do their bit by wandering outside to view the sheep.

'How much did you pay for this place?' asks Kiki, still hobbling with a stick after her skiing accident. French directness about money never fails to take me by surprise. Fortunately Mermoz and Jeanne, in matching walking boots and anoraks, appear at this moment, so I can stop squirming. But Mermoz can't, for the cat – sensing a cat-hater – makes a special point of coming to greet him.

'*Putain!* Look at the size of that thing,' yells Mermoz, somewhat hurtfully, as he jumps for cover behind Jeanne. It's true that the cat *is* still a little on the starboard side of portly, but she's been on the diet food for months. 'Who did he eat for breakfast? You can still see the blood on his jaws.' Though Mermoz's joshing is brave enough, I can see the raw panic in his eyes, too. So I grab the cat, and shut it in my bedroom.

We move through into the summer sitting-room, and I

feel suddenly embarrassed, because everyone bursts into applause.

'This is really a chateau,' declares the Proustian Madeleine, making me feel glad that there are still some exposed lightbulbs dangling from dusty wires, and that I left the ancient cattle stalls in place when Douglas rendered the walls.

'I can take no credit,' I explain, beginning to tell them about Ludo, and how I have merely been finishing the work he began.

'We'll be able to play tennis in here next winter, if Kiki will let us,' chortles Mermoz, giving Kiki a hearty nudge in the ribs.

Dinner is served in silence, in the flickering light of a dozen candles and three naked wall-lamps. Eyebrows are raised. Nods are exchanged. An ambulance is not required.

'*C'est formidable*,' murmurs the Proustian Madeleine, after trying my chicken korma.

'*Super bon*,' concurs Claude the electrician, looking shocked. I have done my bit, for now, for Blighty. Mind you, despite the mildness of the sauce, its un-French spiciness does take some people by surprise.

'I can see why you need these things,' says the smiley (and habitually ice-cool) Maxim, fanning himself with a poppadom.

'Where's the bread basket?' asks Kiki, scanning the table.

'I'm so sorry. I don't have one,' I confess.

'No matter,' says Jeanne kindly. 'A board is just as good. Oh, *this* is nice.' She looks more closely at my cheeseboard, with its green floral tile, circa 1979, embossed in two flat slabs of linseeded plywood.

'Actually that's the cheeseboard,' I explain.

'Is it old?'

'It's something I made at school, a long time ago,' I call, over my shoulder, hurrying to fetch the breadboard.

'You see, Kiki,' laughs Mermoz, in a stage-whisper loud enough for me to hear from next door. 'He's a craftsman, too.'

'It's a lovely thing,' says his wife, swapping me the green cheeseboard for the breadboard. 'You must keep it for your children.'

'Actually I gave it to my parents, years ago. And they gave it back to me.'

But Jeanne isn't listening. She gasps when she sees the two baguettes, upside-down, on the board. Hurriedly she turns them over.

'You must never do that,' she warns. 'It's very bad luck.' And, in case I think she's being superstitious, she adds that her mother would never serve bread without scratching a cross on the bottom first.

'Tonight you really should be riding a horse and wearing one of those big feather hats, Michael,' declares Mermoz.

'*Chéri*,' sighs his wife, 'I think you're thinking of the wrong kind of Indians.'

After dinner, I cannot resist heading to the piano and singing the one French song I know: '*Clopin Clopant*', about a lovesick man with a limp, which is especially for the hobbling Kiki. The performance is greeted with such generous rapture that I know I should stop. But of course the skiers beg for another – they want to sing, too – so I dig out my trusty Abba songbook, because they say they know Abba. But 'knowing' a foreign language song is not the same as being able to sing along to it. So I just sing, horribly loud, on my own – which would be fine if I could actually sing. Instead, I am an ace practitioner of the art of tuneless yelling. I yell until the rafters are creaking, my voice is hoarse and the lightning is flashing in the sky outside. It's a relief when Claude the electrician comes to join me for the high bits in 'Money, Money, Money'.

'It's lucky that you don't have any neighbours,' says Kiki in the stunned silence that ensues.

'You certainly are . . . *unusual*, Michael,' adds the Proustian Madeleine.

'I think there's a storm coming,' says Maxim, gazing out through the French windows.

'Didn't we just hear it?' asks Mermoz.

Shortly after one a.m. we all kiss and shake hands, and they head off down the drive, into the night. Exhausted, I slide into bed, where the cat is curled up in a lifeless ball. She loves people, too, so it was tough on her to be deprived of so much company tonight.

Two hours later, the cat and I awake with a start; we both sit bolt upright in bed.

The rain is smashing on the roof tiles and thunder crackles overhead. But it is another sound that has woken us. Outside in the darkness, one of the sheep is emitting a throaty wail, like someone retching into a basin. The Rastafarians never bleat at night. And they never bleat like *that*.

I pull a coat over my pyjamas and head out into the storm with a searchlight, feeling the rain pummel my shoulders as I stagger up the hill. It may rain half as often in France as in England, but every raindrop is twice as wet.

I can see the sheep sheltering under the gutter at the back of the house, their eyes glowing green amid the glitter of the raindrops. And then I pick out the lone creature bawling her heart out: Claudette.

For a split second, a lightning flash illuminates the whole field, and I feel like I've wandered into a B-movie version of *Far from the Madding Crowd*. I pace across the hillside, raking the wet grass with the beam of my search-light, conscious that Claudette is thundering close behind. Perhaps Nemo, her firstborn, is caught in a fence. Perhaps he's alone; shivering, disoriented by the storm.

And then, in the sea of brilliant green, the torch's beam lights upon something very black and still. Something I've been searching for, and did not wish to find.

Nemo lies curled, eyes closed, soaking up the rain. Around his neck, a scarlet necklace. Beside him, his assailant has laid out his guts in the grass. *Habeas corpus.*

Claudette is making a furious din behind me, so I stand aside to let her look, shining my torch on her dead lamb. I need her to understand that he is gone. Last year, when I took the dying Emil from Doris, she screamed and hollered for two weeks, calling for her vanished lamb. I felt it was my fault. But the sight of this broken black puppet makes no more sense to Claudette than it does to me.

And so we just stand there, the two of us, as the torch-beam slowly dims. I, silent; she, screaming into the night. And in the end the light goes out, and we are both left alone in the dark.

Claudette now falls silent for three days, while Nemo's body lies in a box in the barn. I can't face dealing with it yet, not with the rain still bucketing down. From time to time I go in there to look at the perfection of him, fluffy as a black teddy bear, attempting to accept a reality that, even now, I somehow do not wish to believe. One of the things I wanted to learn from living alone, close to nature, was about birth and creation. It never occurred to me that mostly I would learn about death.

Gilles strokes his beard when I tell him about the lamb.

'I think it was a badger,' he says. 'A fox would have taken the whole thing, instead of just eating the entrails like that.'

Finally, next to Silent Mary's grave beneath the lone pine, I dig a deep hole. The chickens peck around me, searching for worms. With my boot, I begin to press down the earth on top of Nemo's body. And then I freeze. For at this precise moment, after days of silence, comes a new and eerie sound. From out of sight behind the house, it is Claudette, sending one last, desperate wail into the sky.

Slowly, I trudge back up to La Folie. Seeking comfort, the cat jumps on to my lap, and I stroke her cold fur until the purring starts. I can't help smiling as Martha appears on the window-sill in front of us, pecking at the glass. She reminds me that it's time I fed the sheep. So I wander up to their field, feel them nuzzling against my legs in search of an extra mouthful. Across the valley, the chapel of St Sauveur glows in the late-afternoon sun.

And here, now, at last, I have an idea for the first sentence of the book I have for so long lacked the courage and inspiration to begin.

It's not much of an opening, but it's a start:

*I am three years old, and I want to be Queen Victoria's train-driver.*

And then I lay down my pen, for in the distance I have heard the jubilant shriek of a steam-whistle. It is time.

I charge off down the drive like a six-year-old, almost blinded by the sunlight as I whip up clouds of dust with my clumpy shoes, racing to beat the train to the level-crossing. *Allez, allez!* Turn right up the road out of Jolibois, then sprint left down the track to Gilles's farm, where the railway line curves around his land like silver leaf on the rim of a plate.

Already I can see a plume of steam rising out of the trees in the distance. I can hear the *kiffa-kiffa-kiff-kiffa-kiff* of the pistons. And I can almost smell the coal-smoke belching from the funnel as I catch a glimpse of sunlight glinting on polished paintwork in the trees, and the great beast emerges from the shadows like a dragon from its cave.

Excitement electrifies my skin as I take in the iron monster's gleaming green beauty, feel the great clanking weight of it thumping into the soles of my feet. First comes the coolness as its daunting mass blots out the sun, and then the blast of damp heat as the steam belching between its wheels wraps me in sooty tendrils of pure bliss. Oiled pistons pump and hiss. Steel thunders on steel. Earth and air, fire and water, whammed into an elemental hymn.

And then I am cheering and waving like a child, and the passengers, hanging out of the windows like returning soldiers, are waving and laughing back at me.

*Kiffa-kiffa-kiff, kiffa-kiff* goes the train, and even though it's clanking as slowly as a steam tractor around the edge of Gilles's field, it's going far too fast for me.

If only it would stop.

For as the train begins to clank away from me, I'm sure I see a figure standing apart from the rest, on a wrought-iron observation platform at the very back of the final carriage.

A tiny woman in a black silk dress.

In one hand, she carries a lace handkerchief. In the other, she holds the hand of the small boy at her side: a bespectacled urchin in a flying-helmet, who gawps at me as if I were someone from another universe. Breaking into a grin, he gives me a shy wave, and proudly holds up the little brown hen under his arm.

I want to believe that they are saying hello. But I know, in my innermost heart, that we are finally saying goodbye.

# In memory of

Mildred

Emil

and Silent Mary